Teaching Naked Techniques

A Practical Guide to Designing Better Classes

**José Antonio Bowen
and C. Edward Watson**

JOSSEY-BASS™

A Wiley Brand

Copyright © 2017 by John Wiley & Sons, Inc. All rights reserved.

Published by Jossey-Bass
A Wiley Brand
One Montgomery Street, Suite 1000, San Francisco, CA 94104-4594—www.josseybass.com

No part of this publication may be reproduced, stored in a retrieval system, or transmitted in any form or by any means, electronic, mechanical, photocopying, recording, scanning, or otherwise, except as permitted under Section 107 or 108 of the 1976 United States Copyright Act, without either the prior written permission of the publisher, or authorization through payment of the appropriate per-copy fee to the Copyright Clearance Center, Inc., 222 Rosewood Drive, Danvers, MA 01923, 978-750-8400, fax 978-646-8600, or on the Web at www.copyright.com. Requests to the publisher for permission should be addressed to the Permissions Department, John Wiley & Sons, Inc., 111 River Street, Hoboken, NJ 07030, 201-748-6011, fax 201-748-6008, or online at www.wiley.com/go/permissions.

Permission is given for individual classroom teachers to reproduce the pages and illustrations for classroom use. Reproduction of these materials for an entire school system is strictly forbidden.

Limit of Liability/Disclaimer of Warranty: While the publisher and author have used their best efforts in preparing this book, they make no representations or warranties with respect to the accuracy or completeness of the contents of this book and specifically disclaim any implied warranties of merchantability or fitness for a particular purpose. No warranty may be created or extended by sales representatives or written sales materials. The advice and strategies contained herein may not be suitable for your situation. You should consult with a professional where appropriate. Neither the publisher nor author shall be liable for any loss of profit or any other commercial damages, including but not limited to special, incidental, consequential, or other damages. Readers should be aware that Internet Web sites offered as citations and/or sources for further information may have changed or disappeared between the time this was written and when it is read.

Jossey-Bass books and products are available through most bookstores. To contact Jossey-Bass directly call our Customer Care Department within the U.S. at 800-956-7739, outside the U.S. at 317-572-3986, or fax 317-572-4002.

Wiley publishes in a variety of print and electronic formats and by print-on-demand. Some material included with standard print versions of this book may not be included in e-books or in print-on-demand. If this book refers to media such as a CD or DVD that is not included in the version you purchased, you may download this material at http://booksupport.wiley.com. For more information about Wiley products, visit www.wiley.com.

Library of Congress Cataloging-in-Publication Data

Names: Bowen, José Antonio.
Title: Teaching naked techniques : a practical guide to designing better
    classes / José A. Bowen.
Description: New Jersey : Jossey-Bass, 2017. | Includes bibliographical
    references and index.
Identifiers: LCCN 2016041898 | ISBN 9781119136118 (paperback) | ISBN 9781119262633 (ePDF) |
    ISBN 9781119262640 (epub)
Subjects: LCSH: Curriculum planning. | Educational technology. | BISAC:
    EDUCATION / Higher.
Classification: LCC LB2806.15 .B66 2017 | DDC 371.102—dc23 LC record available at
    https://lccn.loc.gov/2016041898

Cover design: Wiley

Printed in the United States of America

FIRST EDITION

PB Printing   10 9 8 7 6 5 4 3 2 1

Contents

Acknowledgments

THIS BOOK HAS been a wonderful group effort. First, of course, this book includes the contributions of hundreds of faculty and thousands of students who have been in our classes and workshops and who kindly corrected our mistakes and missteps. In workshops across the country, faculty have generously shared tips, stories, and ideas. This book is dedicated to all of those teachers who seek to change the lives of their students.

In February 2015, we sent out a call to faculty and Center for Teaching and Learning directors at a wide variety of colleges and universities telling them of our idea for this book and asking if they would be willing to share their examples and applications of some of "teaching naked" ideas. We were overwhelmed with the varied, detailed, and specific demonstrations of great teaching that now fill the following pages. We limited most people to one or two examples so that we could acknowledge the greatest number of people. We also wanted to feature the widest variety of institutions (community, liberal arts, and technical colleges, along with research and regional universities), disciplines, and situations (residential, commuter, blended, and online).

Thank you to all of the faculty who contributed ideas and allowed us to weave your teaching ideas with ours. We are deeply grateful for your efforts and support. In the end, we have featured over 50 faculty whom we acknowledge as contributors of this book.

One special contributor and collaborator of this book was Erin Horan, educational psychology doctoral candidate extraordinaire and graduate assistant in the Center for Teaching and Learning at the University of Georgia. Erin helped us organize and then participated in the selection of the faculty contributions that are found in this book. She assisted our thinking in many ways throughout this process. We are grateful for her assistance, collaboration, and perspectives.

Thank you to the entire team at Wiley who also supported this complicated effort. David Brightman began the process and deserves much of the credit for convincing someone that teaching centers and faculty development staff would actually buy a book titled *Teaching Naked*. He passed the torch for this project to Marjorie S. McAnemy, who encouraged us until we ended up in the able hands of Alison Knowles and Connor O'Brien. Thanks to Connor, who read the entire draft and made important, thoughtful, and gracious suggestions. Thanks also to Aneesa Davenport, Shauna Robinson, and the rest of the support team at Wiley. We appreciate your help and support and know that your work is helping more faculty help more students every day.

Thank you to everyone who helped and encouraged us and to the many faculty and staff colleagues at our institutions who put up with us and the extra stress and work of having a book project percolating while we were doing our day jobs.

Thanks finally to our families and friends who have suffered and supported the most to create this work. We promise: we will stop talking about it now!

From J.A.B.: I thank Lillian Johnson in my office, who somehow managed to clear a few afternoons for writing, and especially my incredibly supportive wife, Kimberly, who spent many nights sitting with me in our office when we should have been doing something more relaxing. My daughter, Naomi, has offered many insights over the years, but of course, none of the stories included here are about her. The pets, Molly, Chloe, and Chelsea, were not really much help, but they provided much-needed moral support.

From C.E.W.: I thank those colleagues and students who talk with me daily about teaching and learning and have advanced my thinking over the years. The closest of these amazing friends include Carrie Bishop, Sherry Clouser, Peter Doolittle, Chase Hagood, Colleen Kuusinen, Kate McConnell, Edward "Earl" Schwartz, and Krista Terry. I also want to thank my "n of two" at home, Liam and Carter, who freely provide me with all of my best anecdotal teaching and learning stories to go along with what the research is telling us about how all of this works. My deepest gratitude resides with my wife, Joan. My richest discussions regarding teaching and learning happen with her, and her encouragement and support were foundational to the success of this book and, truly, all of my successes.

About the Authors

JOSÉ ANTONIO BOWEN is president of Goucher College. He has won teaching awards at Stanford, Georgetown, Miami, and Southern Methodist University, where he was dean of the Meadows School of the Arts for eight years. He was the founding director of the Centre for the History and Analysis of Recorded Music (C.H.A.R.M.) at the University of Southampton, England. He has written over 100 scholarly articles, edited the *Cambridge Companion to Conducting* (2003), and is an editor of the six-CD set *Jazz: The Smithsonian Anthology* (2011). He has worked as a musician with Stan Getz, Dave Brubeck, Hubert Laws, Liberace, and many others, and his symphony was nominated for the Pulitzer Prize in Music. His book *Teaching Naked: How Moving Technology out of Your College Classroom Will Improve Student Learning* (Jossey-Bass, 2012) won the Ness Award for Best Book on Higher Education from the Association of American Colleges and Universities, and Stanford honored him as a Distinguished Alumni Scholar in 2010. For more on his teaching, see his blog at teachingnaked.com or follow him on Twitter: @josebowen.

C. EDWARD WATSON is director of the Center for Teaching and Learning and a fellow in the Institute for Higher Education at the University of Georgia (UGA), where he leads university efforts associated with faculty development, teaching assistant development, student learning outcomes assessment, learning technologies, media and production services, classroom support and learning spaces, and the scholarship of teaching and learning. At UGA, he also teaches courses on college teaching. He is the founding executive editor of the *International Journal of ePortfolio* and the executive editor of the *International Journal of Teaching and Learning in Higher Education* and has published on teaching and learning in a number of journals, including *Educational Technology, EDUCAUSE Review,* the *Journal for*

Effective Teaching, and *To Improve the Academy,* among others. He is also on the board of directors for the Association for Authentic, Experiential, and Evidence-Based Learning and the International Society for Exploring Teaching and Learning. He has recently been quoted in the *New York Times, Campus Technology, EdSurge,* and *University Business Magazine* and on CNN and NPR regarding current teaching and learning issues and trends in higher education. For more, see eddiewatson.net or follow him on Twitter: @eddiewatson.

Contributors

Brenda Hardin Abbott is assistant professor of English and writing program coordinator at Bay Path University (Chapter 8).

Paul J. Antonellis Jr. is lecturer of management at Merrimack College (Chapter 3).

Janice Bergman-Carton is associate professor of art history at Southern Methodist University (Chapter 12).

Janine Bowen is professor of business management at Goucher College (Chapters 2 and 7).

Peter Scott Brown is associate professor of medieval art history at the University of North Florida (Chapters 1 and 6).

Jason Cherubini is assistant professor of business management at Goucher College (Chapter 5).

Marcia L. Cordts is lecturer of microbiology at the University of Iowa (Chapter 5).

Becky Ericson teaches astronomy for non-science majors George Mason University (Chapter 6).

Debra Ferdinand is an educational technologist at the School of Education at the University of the West Indies (Chapter 10).

Ann M. Fox is professor of English at Davidson College (Chapter 3).

Dara Friedman-Wheeler is associate professor of psychology at Goucher College (Chapter 3).

Oana Godeanu-Kenworthy is senior lecturer of global and intercultural studies (American studies) at Miami University (Chapters 1 and 6).

Rae Jean B. Goodman is professor of economics at the U.S. Naval Academy (Chapter 9).

Brooke Hessler is director of learning resources at California College of the Arts (Chapter 6).

Barbara Juncosa is instructor of biological, physical, and natural sciences at Citrus College (Chapter 8).

Jason Kaufman is associate professor of educational leadership at Minnesota State University, Mankato (Chapter 10).

Kendall Kennison is professor of music at Goucher College (Chapter 3).

Sarah Leupen is senior lecturer of biological sciences at the University of Maryland Baltimore County (Chapters 1 and 5).

Leslie Lewis is provost and professor of English at Goucher College (Chapter 12).

Sarah Lovern is associate professor of physiology at Concordia University Wisconsin (Chapters 5 and 8).

Regina Majestro is graduate student of psychology at Spalding University (Chapter 2).

Veronica McComb is assistant professor of history at Lenoir-Rhyne University (Chapter 9).

Sarah McCorkle is instructional technology specialist at Wake Forest University (Chapter 10).

Gretchen Kreahling McKay is professor and department chair of art and art history at McDaniel College (Chapters 2 and 7).

Tawnya Means is director of the Teaching and Learning Center at the University of Florida (Chapter 1).

Alice Miller is technology coordinator for the Welch Center for Graduate and Professional Studies at Goucher College (Chapter 10).

Mary Miller is professor of biology at Baton Rouge Community College (Chapter 9).

Andrew Mills is professor of religion and philosophy at Otterbein University (Chapter 4).

Mathew Mitchell is co-director of the Center for Teaching Excellence and professor in the Learning and Instruction Department in the School of Education at University of San Francisco (Chapter 9).

Katherine Moore is professor of psychology at Arcadia University (Chapter 7).

Paul Morgan is graduate student of psychology at Spalding University (Chapter 2).

Chris Mortensen is assistant professor of animal sciences at the University of Florida (Chapter 1).

Shelby Newport is department chair, associate professor of theater and dance, and resident costume designer at the University of Michigan-Flint (Chapter 10).

Pamela A. Patton is director of the Index of Christian Art in the Department of Art and Archaeology at Princeton University (Chapter 12).

Richard Pennington is associate professor of chemistry at Georgia Gwinnett College (Chapter 6).

Graciela Perera is associate professor of computer science at Northeastern Illinois University (Chapter 8).

Todd Pourciau is dean for innovative learning and academic support at Baton Rouge Community College (Chapter 1).

Nicolas W. Proctor is professor of history at Simpson College (Chapter 4).

Jessie Reed is a graduate student of psychology at Spalding University (Chapter 2).

Joe Reinsel is assistant professor of media art at the University of Michigan-Flint (Chapters 1 and 10).

Gina Riggio is adjunct science instructor at Delaware Technical Community College (Chapters 1 and 4).

Arthur Roberts is assistant professor of pharmaceutical and biomedical sciences at the University of Georgia (Chapter 6).

Rebecca Roberts is associate professor of biology at Ursinus College (Chapter 2).

Lisa Ruch is professor of English and communications and chair of liberal studies at Bay Path University (Chapter 8).

Jeffery Schwehm is coordinator of the Center for Excellence in Learning and Teaching at Concordia University (Chapter 1).

Ajay Sharma is assistant professor of veterinary diagnostic imaging in the College of Veterinary Medicine at the University of Georgia (Chapter 8).

Michael Shepard is professor of practice in cultural sustainability and environmental studies and an instructional designer at Goucher College (Chapter 3).

Andrea Skellie is public relations specialist in the Office of Admissions at the University of Georgia (provided Figure 11.2).

Anthony Smith is visiting assistant professor of business law at Indiana University South Bend (Chapter 1).

Bonni Stachowiak is associate professor of business management at Vanguard University and host of the Teaching in Higher Ed podcast (Chapter 9).

Robert Talbert is associate professor of mathematics at Grand Valley State University (Chapter 5).

Laura Tejada is assistant professor of counselor education in the Daniel L. Goodwin College of Education at Northeastern Illinois University (Chapter 4).

Denise Thorsen is associate professor of electrical and computer engineering at the University of Alaska Fairbanks (Chapter 7).

Susanna Throop is codirector of the Teaching and Learning Institute and associate professor of history at Ursinus College (Chapter 4).

Leslie Vincent is instructor of mathematics at Delaware Technical Community College (Chapter 2).

Linda Wanless is assistant professor of technology at Michigan Technological University (Chapter 7).

David R. Wessner is professor of biology at Davidson College (Chapter 3).

Jack Williams is professor of osteopathic medicine at the University of New England (Chapter 3).

Robin Black Wilson is assistant professor of education at Goucher College (Chapter 8).

DeDe Wohlfarth is professor of psychology and director of the child, adolescent, and family emphasis area in psychology at Spalding University (Chapters 2 and 4).

Hu Womack is an instruction and outreach librarian at Wake Forest University (Chapter 10).

Introduction

Designing for the Brain in the Body

THIS BOOK INVESTIGATES how we might apply new technology and research on how the brain learns to redesign courses and classrooms. Decades of research have brought an explosion of knowledge about how human evolution shaped the way we process, think, and remember. That research informs this book, but the focus here is on practical and discipline-specific applications for faculty. At the same time that psychology and research have given us new insights into student learning, students now have much more to learn and new technologies that help, or inhibit, how they learn. We are already in a new learning economy, where, thanks to this same explosion of knowledge creation and technology, most of what students will need to learn, they will need to learn *after* they leave our classrooms. What we know in our disciplines will remain important, but what we know about student learning and development will also grow in importance. The future belongs to self-regulating, lifelong learners, and we need to know how to create them.

As faculty, we of course have spent a lot of time in school, and we assume that gives us some insight into how people learn. Sadly, the opposite is probably true. We may have understood the value of paying attention even when bored, long sessions of single focus without distraction, distributed repetition, the futility of cramming, discovering why the professor assigned the reading, the importance of rewriting notes, and probably naps. All of these are now proven learning enhancers, but none of them are obvious. If we are to turn students into lifelong learners (by far, the most important outcome of college in the learning economy and the Internet age), we need to be explicit in designing environments that help students learn for themselves.

Terry Doyle (2008, p. 25) sums it up this way: "The one who does the work, does the learning." That does not mean teachers only need to put content out there and let students work; if that is all you do, the Internet does it better. Rather, it means that *the value of the teacher is in the way he or she can stimulate good behaviors in students: pedagogy is a design problem.* The fitness coach does not do our exercise for us but still provides enormous value. More exercise equipment will not increase your fitness, in the same way that more content will not increase your learning (faculty being the exception). Normal learners need a teacher who understands their anxieties and what motivates them and can then create structures that will allow them to succeed.

Learning Behaviors: The Brain in the Body

Sleep, water, exercise, eating (diet), and time (SWEET) plus a few study habits may matter as much as our pedagogical methods or classroom technology. We know a lot about the good behaviors of learning, and we can learn the basic science with excellent books from James Zull (*The Art of Changing the Brain: Enriching the Practice of Teaching by Exploring the Biology of Learning*, 2002, and *From Brain to Mind: Using Neuroscience to Guide Change in Education*, 2011) and Brown, Roediger, and McDaniel (*Make It Stick: The Science of Successful Learning*, 2014). Terry Doyle and Todd Zakrajsek's *The New Science of Learning: How to Learn in Harmony with Your Brain* (2013) has even turned this research into a practical manual for students, but how do we best apply this research to redesign classrooms and colleges? (See Chapter 12 in this book.)

Kuh, Kinzie, Schuh, and Whitt (2005) and Chambliss and Takacs (2014) have identified a number of high-impact pedagogical and institutional practices, many of them small or low-cost changes, that have a disproportionate impact on student learning. Understanding that our brains are encased in physical bodies and that stable blood glucose and protein are essential for connecting brain cells provides us with even more ways to improve learning. We know, for example, that most of us are mildly dehydrated when we wake up, but the brain needs plenty of water for better learning. Perhaps two tall glasses of water before the first morning class is another high-impact practice?

Dement and Vaughan (1999) helped us learn about sleep deficits and how hard they are to detect, and additional studies have provided insights that likely have ramifications for learning. As an example, we now know that when we go two straight weeks with only 6 hours of sleep a night, we are actually as impaired as those who had not slept for the last 48 hours (Van Dongen, Maislen, Mullington, & Dinges, 2003). Without that last 2 hours of sleep, we just write over the short-term memory the next day and remember very little from the previous day. We have known for decades that adults need 7.5 to 9.0 hours a night of sleep, but we now know that our memories move from the hippocampus (short-term storage) to the neocortex (long-term memory) mostly in the last 2 hours of the night (Walker, Stickgold, Alsop, Gaab, & Schlaug, 2005). Sleeping with the smell of roses (and perhaps other pleasant smells) after studying improves this process (Rasch, Buchel, Gais, & Born, 2007), as does studying just before bed or taking a break after studying (Dewar, Alber, Butler, Cowan, & Della Sala, 2012). Similarly, high-performance athletes and musicians are much more likely to interleave practice with breaks. We have also learned that the brain prioritizes what we think is important: students who studied new material before bed and knew it was going to be on a test remembered substantially more than those told they would not be tested on the material (Wilhelm et al., 2011). Is there any way we can apply that knowledge to how we design our courses?

Research on the learning benefits of sleep and naps has exploded since about 2000 ("Napping May Not," 2009). A short nap, 8 hours after you wake up, is much better at helping you pay attention than an extra 20 to 30 minutes of sleep each night (Maas & Robbins, 2011). Short naps (20–30 minutes) and breaks immediately after learning also help stabilize memory (Doyle & Zakrajsek, 2013). We know that breaks and naps are important for processing and that the brain also connects by proximity, especially time. This suggests that back-to-back classes are a bad idea for most learners. Would it be a good idea for higher education to reexamine its course grid?

Research on learning and movement should also have profound implications for how we design our campuses and classrooms. Our brain evolved to learn while in motion, and 80% of the brain's neurons are located in the cerebellum, the large structure on the back dedicated to motor coordination. Our survival is now less dependent on the way we move through our environment, and a growing body of research investigates the relationship between our increasingly sedentary lifestyles and depression. In *The Case for Working With Your Hands*, Matthew Crawford (2011) makes a compelling argument that the massive increase in the reporting of depression—10 times more at the end of the 20th century than at the beginning (Blakeslee, 2004)—and the even more massive increase in the use of chemical antidepressants—up 400% between 1988 and 2008 (Kuehn, 2011)—is related to less challenging contexts for our brains. Manual labor is not necessarily less cerebral, and the mental health benefits of chores and daily activity have long been recognized. Gardening or knitting was prescribed for women with anxiety in the 19th century (Lambert, 2015), but new studies confirm that knitting and crafting increase cognitive functioning, reduce stress, and increase dopamine production (Riley, Corkhill, & Morris, 2013). New depression treatments that use coordinated movement are 50% more effective than treatment with antidepressants alone (Lambert, 2015). Handwriting and manual note taking also seem to have benefits (Mueller & Oppenheimer, 2014), and given that so much of our motor coordination involves our hands, this should be no surprise. Typing also involves the hands, so it may be that we can eventually find even more productive ways to take notes with technology, but it is unlikely that "hands-free" learning will ever be optimal.

We have long known that students prefer learning by doing. But now we also understand that doing means movement (many of the techniques in Chapter 7 get students moving). Mild exercise creates the protein BDNF, which collects in pools near brain synapses to stimulate every aspect of learning, which is mostly about growing connections between nerve cells (Ratey, 2013). Mild movement, like walking, sitting on a balance ball, or working at a stationary bike, all seem to improve learning. Very recent research suggests that exercising four hours after learning also improves retention of that content (Van Dongen, Kersten, Wagner, Morris, & Fernández, 2016).

We can now finally put to rest the false notion that some people are primarily audio, visual, or kinesthetic learners (Pashler, McDaniel, Rohrer, & Bjork, 2008). We all learn better and remember more when the senses are combined (Moreno & Mayer, 2007; Shams & Seitz, 2008), and we all learn more and more quickly from visuals (Medina, 2014). It is no accident that when we understand something, we say "I see." "The brain's ability to visualize is arguably the most significant aspect of cognition" (Zull, 2002, p. 138), which is why translating ideas into graphs and pictures works as an effective study technique. Reading is the slowest way to get information (Dehaene, 2009), but faculty were often the ones who figured out that annotations (not underlining), elaborations, and lack of distractions help enormously (Brown, Roediger, & McDaniel, 2014). Elaborations are efficient because they retrieve, reuse, and restore, so visual elaborations (e.g., concept maps) are another powerful study tool (Novak & Cañas, 2008: both are discussed in Chapter 6).

Ultimately, the nature of your desired learning outcomes should largely dictate the modality you might choose to use as you teach (see Chapter 11). For instance, imagine the two of us had never played tennis before, but Eddie was given a week to review a tennis-for-beginners book and José was given an hour's lesson with a tennis pro. All other things being equal, who would you think would likely win their first tennis match? So if you want your students to be able to perform dissections of animals, reading about how to do it or watching video demonstrations are not the most effective approaches to helping them achieve that outcome. Having scalpel in hand in front of a real specimen with some guidance and feedback along the way is the best choice of strategy.

Focus and Motivation

A significant body of evidence shows that humans do not possess the cognitive, behavioral, or cortical structures to effectively multitask (Watson, Terry, & Doolittle, 2012). We are, however, really good at doing one thing at a time. For most, multitasking is really just switching between tasks (Medina, 2014), but it doesn't appear we are good at that either (Strayer, Cooper, Turrill, Coleman, & Hopman, 2015). So one question, then, is this: Can we structure learning environments and assignments to help students study in longer, more engaged blocks? How do we encourage students to invest the appropriate amount of time in preparation for class, for instance (see Chapter 6)? Investment is a key concept. Emotions are also linked to memory and learning (Immordino-Yang, 2015), so emotional investment (what we call "entry point" in Chapter 2) is key. Connecting these concepts, it's not surprising that people remember a concept that is attached to a dramatic image (Perrin et al., 2012)

We know students learn more when they pay attention, but note that phrase: "pay attention." Focus costs us something, and Langer (1989) notes how easily we can overfocus. When we "pay attention," we give up something else (that might be more interesting). More interesting and less stressful teachers and classrooms can help (discussed in Chapter 7). Sensory information is sent simultaneously to two parts of the brain: the sensory cortex and the amygdala, our emotional control center. Yes, everything we want our students to learn is also checked for potential threat (Zull, 2002). When we perceive something as dangerous, we react instinctively, shutting down our cognitive processors. Emotional engagement, low stress, and feeling safe and supported are all important for learning (and feature in the techniques discussed in Chapter 4). While colleges often talk about "disturbing students," note that too much disruption shuts down learning. The same is true for the balance between too easy and too hard. We need to get more students into the "pleasantly frustrating" zone (see Chapters 8 and 11), but ultimately, we all have to learn something boring at some point in our lives (boredom is the opposite of "pleasantly frustrating"; it happens when something is not personally engaging and perceived as trivial or impossible). Those who do the work, who find a way to engage, are the ones who learn. Paraphrasing Richard Bach (1977), learning success requires sacrificing boredom.

People who understand and can use delayed gratification do better in almost every aspect of life (Mischel, Shoda, & Rodriguez, 1989), and we also now understand that our belief in our ability to learn—our mindset—is equally critical in determining what we can learn (Dweck, 2007). We've learned that praising hard work instead of talent or ability helps (Dweck, 2007), but we've had difficulty figuring out how to get students to push through the boring bits (Duckworth, 2016). Fitness coaches understand this problem.

What a fitness coach knows about your body is key. For instance, holding stretches for less than 30 seconds does not allow your muscles time to reap the full benefit. A good fitness coach also reminds you that hard work is the only real solution to better fitness. Similarly, teachers should be able to tell you about various ways in which your brain learns best. In general, students who can work even when they are bored and who understand how to pay attention do better. It has been noted that mind wandering shows a failure of executive control (Schacter & Szpunar, 2015; Seli, Smallwood, Cheyne, & Smilek, 2015), but we shouldn't be surprised by this "failure" in many of our students. Full brain maturation doesn't occur for most humans until around the age of 25 (Aamodt & Wang, 2011). It's not a random choice that most car rental companies require renters to be at least 25 years old. This doesn't mean that it's impossible to control mind wandering. Langer (1997) and, more recently, Barbezat and Bush (2014) suggest that mind wandering can be harnessed through mindfulness practices. Certainly, strategies that foster self-regulation can help students work through bouts of boredom and increase appropriate focus.

Mischel and Ayduk (2004) now believe that the key to delayed gratification in five-year-olds, and perhaps in all of us, is distraction. When we know we need to wait, using strategies that make the time go faster seems to help. That appears connected to the most recent research that having a higher purpose or mission (or helping students remember why they are working so hard) greatly improves persistence (Yeager et al., 2014). Reminding students not only that learning is work but that this work is directly connected to their own personal goals helps. The more transcendent the goal, the better. Students will work because they need to pass your class, but they will work harder if they understand it will save the lives of their patients or help them get a job later. It is why fitness trainers start by getting to know you and not first watching you sweat.

Getting students to enjoy learning for its own sake is probably another mistake based (again) on faculty using themselves as models. Learning for pleasure, especially in formalized classroom settings, is perhaps not as normal as we might assume. Human evolution suggests that we learn what is most important to us, and our brains prioritize constantly what we should retain and what we can discard. Asking students to "find something interesting" in the reading helps recall; they may not find it pleasurable, but that's okay. Fitness coaches like to work out, often obsessively, and they recognize that they themselves probably do not need a motivation coach. Their clients have come precisely because they do not like to work out. In many ways, that's an apt metaphor for you and your students.

Our job as faculty is to understand how the brain learns, what motivates students, and how to create environments that encourage good learning behaviors on the part of students. We need then to assess progress, provide feedback, and encourage more work. It is a bit like helping people use a gym, except that our design issue is largely psychological instead of physical. Faculty are cognitive coaches.

Learning and Technology

A fitness coach understands the human body and the individual subject, but also the equipment in the gym. Technology is bringing new tools and new competition to higher education, but it is also changing the basic rules about how we operate as human beings: the meaning of *friends* has changed forever. Technology or equipment, of course, is only a tool, not an educational strategy. While our use of technology will surely increase, our goal remains more learning. For this, colleges and universities will need to design much better environments (see Chapter 12) that include vastly more thorough understandings of both how technology works and how learning works.

Internet technologies have changed our relationship with knowledge. While most of us remember a not-so-distant past of knowledge scarcity (where the simple arrival on a campus increased our access to knowledge).

Current students have no concept of this. The world is now knowledge rich, and students can access more information from their phone than in any college library. The Internet is overloaded with data. I can, for example, get information on every flight every day to every place, but the app on my phone limits that information to what is relevant and useful today: Is my flight on time, and how long will it take me to get to the airport given current traffic conditions? College should be like an app for the mind.

As faculty, if we are primarily concerned with transmitting content, our value will continue to decrease. The Internet contains a much broader selection of lectures, demonstrations, animations, and examples, on more subjects, in more languages, and with a greater variety of approaches, methods, and pedagogies, than any professor, department, or even entire university could provide. If, however, we are more concerned with faculty-student interaction; the design and sequence of learning experiences; the application, analysis, and synthesis of information; the motivation of students; and especially the increasing complexity of student mental models, then the value of what we do will increase.

While all colleges talk about the importance of critical thinking, higher education is largely structured around the delivery of content. The way we furnish classrooms, structure curriculum, train future professors, organize syllabi, and assess student learning prioritizes current disciplinary knowledge. All of these are holdovers from a time when opportunities for learning were scarce, but in the future, there will only be more things and more ways to learn. Access to content and courses will be cheap and plentiful. As we know already from the early massive open online courses (MOOCs), knowing how to learn new content (and, more important, how to integrate new ideas) is a necessary prerequisite for MOOC success. The point of college is increasingly to prepare the mind for the unknown, to prepare students to be lifelong learners in diverse contexts.

While knowledge is required for thought, content is a means and not the end. Our real goal is to improve how students process and integrate new information. We want to change them. While what we have to teach them may get them a first job, it will not—on its own—get them a second job that may not yet even exist. We want our students to be able to learn new things, analyze new knowledge, integrate it into their thinking, and occasionally change their minds when necessary. Employers say they want employees who can solve complex problems with people who are different from them (Hart Research Associates, 2013). This seems entirely in harmony with what colleges say we do. The disconnect is that while we hope to accomplish these two things simultaneously, we often spend more time on content than on critical thinking. We, in higher education, tend to accuse employers of not really meaning what they say and overvaluing certain majors or graduates from elite schools. Would this still be the case if we could really deliver what employers say they want? Companies like Google say they are no longer going to accept these proxies (content training or admission standards) in place of creative and critical abilities (which they will measure themselves). What if we could demonstrate that our liberal arts graduates have these skills?

Technology can be a partner in changing this. The technology that makes knowledge so easily accessible has also made the ability to analyze that information more important. Furthermore, with greater access to content now freely available, we should have more time in the classroom for the pedagogy of critical thinking. Teaching critical thinking is hard and labor intensive; technology has also made course design and pedagogy more important. If you think of a syllabus or a course as being a list of topics or content to be mastered, you are doing only half of your job, and that is the part of the job that is being devalued.

The good news is that that the greatest value of a physical university will remain its face-to-face (naked) interaction between faculty and students. The first role of technology therefore is to create more time and more opportunities for teaching naked. At a basic level, new technology can increase student preparation and engagement between classes and create more time for the (naked) in-class dialogue that makes the campus experience worth the extra money it will always cost to deliver. The most important benefits to using technology occur *outside* the classroom.

Pedagogy as Design

Education is ultimately a design problem: the goal is to create structures and processes that will encourage students to engage in the behaviors that lead to learning. In the end, students must do the work, but that does not mean that we are simply content providers. Instruction is not teaching; it is designing.

We often think of design as just "style," but designers also frame and solve problems, assess sequence, integrate user needs, anticipate extremes, and improve systems. Design thinking and techniques are now being applied in everything from medicine to public policy. Education is indeed a design problem. While students are the "products" of education, they are also undeniably the "users," and we are designing systems that will frame their goals, guide them, and anticipate problems along the ways. In truth, technology has increased the need for teachers to think of pedagogy as design.

Using more technology increases your credibility with students but by itself does not increase learning. Students are often quite able to use the technology that they find useful or entertaining, but they are not proficient in using technology to access information, and we especially need to think much more carefully about how they process and integrate what they access.

Dee Fink (2013) has developed an integrated model of course design that connects learning outcomes, activities, and feedback to create significant learning experiences. Technology has given us more options for how we sequence these activities, created more options for feedback and support, and made class time (the most expensive and least scalable piece) even more precious.

"Inverting" or "flipping" assumes there are two parts to be exchanged, but using Fink's model, it becomes clear that teaching naked also needs to

---

FIGURE I.1

A Thumbnail Summary of the Essentials of Human Learning and the Teaching Naked Design Process

The Science	The Student Experience	The Teaching Naked Design Process
Concrete and personal (matters to me, examples)	**Motivation**	**Instructions and entry point** (concrete and personal)
Knowledge is necessary (but not sufficient)	**Exposure** (Content)	**Content for first exposure** (read/watch/do)
Retrieval and self-testing (online exams, games)	**Recall**	**Exam to evaluate** (retrieval)
Elaboration (connections, analogies, writing)	**Elaboration**	**Writing to reflect** (elaborate, contextualize)
Abstract (extracting rules, larger context, mental models)	**Reflection**	**Cognitive wrappers to self-regulate** (abstract)
Failure (add difficulty, attempts before solutions, feedback)	**Complication**	**Class to challenge** (failure, complicate)
Interleaving (varied practice, space out practice)	**Reflection**	**E-Communication to reinforce** (connections, spacing)

Source for Science: Brown, Roediger, and McDaniel (2014).

be thought of as a cycle, looking more broadly at the choices of sequence and design and at how technology expands the opportunities for interactivity. Using new communication technologies, rethinking our assignments, and creating online quizzes and games can ensure that students finally come prepared to class for the more challenging activities and interactions that most spark the critical thinking and change of mental models we seek.

Our design processes were equally influenced by the new research on how the brain learns and by key ideas from *Make It Stick: The Science of Successful Learning* (Brown et al., 2014) and by thinking about how these track with the student experience. The science and how we translated this into pedagogy are summarized in Figure I.1. Learning is more likely to stick when it is:

- *Concrete and personal.* Our brains prioritize. We are less likely to be bored or to prioritize other learning when we understand how this learning matters specifically to us. We like examples, but they help only if the examples are relevant to us.

- *Knowledge is necessary.* All colleges say they teach critical thinking, but this is not a purely abstract technique: we need to think about *something*. At the same time, rote memorization neither sticks nor advances thinking because it is often disconnected from existing schemas and mental models. Bloom was right: when we analyze, apply, and critique new knowledge, it is both more likely to stick and to change us.

- *Retrieval and self-testing.* Retrieval is essential to learning, and the more the better. We have become confused: tests are actually a great learning tool (and not just an assessment tool). The problem with tests are the stakes: high stakes lower performance. Game designers understand this and provide lots and lots of low-stakes retrieval (video games are really a series of microtests with continuous variation and addition of new material after mastery).

- *Elaboration.* We learn by connecting and comparing new information to what we already know. Translating content into your own words and explaining it to others in different contexts and with new analogies is much more effective than simple repetition. Highlighting creates false fluency. Exposure and rereading make things look familiar, but that is not deep learning. Writing, for example, is an effective way to process and elaborate.

- *Abstract.* Extracting the larger rules and concepts and putting them into a wider context is equally important. If we want learning to improve the complexity of students' mental models, we need to make sure they are working on their own to abstract and contextualize.

- *Failure.* We learn more from failure than success, and now it turns out that even the praise for success ("You must be smart") is damaging. Understanding that learning is work is as important as the opportunity to "learn from your mistakes." Encouraging multiple attempts, providing students productive environments for failure, and understanding how to give constructive and timely feedback are critical.

- *Interleaving.* We learn better when we space out and mix up the kinds of learning. Distributed and varied practice improve learning. Knowing when to take a break or a nap helps too.

Teaching naked is a design process that translates this learning science onto the new opportunities for sequence and contact that new technology has provided (see Figure I.2). Since it is only students who can do the learning, this pedagogy is a way to design a process that encourages good learning behaviors for students.

This book is organized around these stages, generally with a chapter devoted to each. There are additional chapters about setting learning goals (Chapter 1), providing feedback (Chapter 9), integration (Chapters 11 and 12), and preparing yourself for these challenges (Chapter 13). Each chapter begins with some research and a compelling case for each part of the design cycle and then provides step-by-step instructions, examples, and further resources for each stage.

The sequence as teachers design and students encounter, however, is different. The design process starts with the end: What do we want to accomplish?

FIGURE I.2

The Teaching Naked Design Process

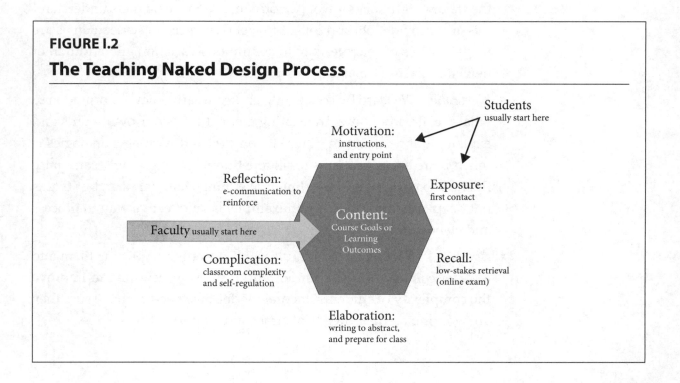

While faculty generally start with thinking about goals and content (the inside of the hexagon in Figure I.2), students start with motivation, an entry point, or their own first exposure and then move around the outside of the hexagon in Figure I.2. Students begin literally as outsiders. The opening chapters in *Teaching Naked Techniques* therefore appear in the order that faculty in the midst of the design process will need to consider them. So the book starts with outcomes (Chapter 1) and content (Chapters 2 and 3), and then it considers the entry point for students (Chapter 4). Part of the point of this intentional design process is to design a specific entry point (Chapter 4) and not just hope the students take us up on our suggested first exposure.

The following sections set out the sequence as students will encounter it in your course.

Instructions and Entry Point: Concrete and Personal

It is not enough to want (or insist) that students care about your subject. Engagement and learning start with what matters to students. This is the entry point, the topic of Chapter 4. If you understand what matters to students, you have a better chance of getting them to see what matters to you. You don't need to be an expert in popular culture, but you need to know something about their hopes and fears. This will help you connect with them, but it also gives you tools for motivating them (and that is most of the job really). Don't start by writing "Wagner" and "gesamtkunstwerk" on the board. Ask them why music matters to them.

Minor alterations in your instructions can make a big difference. Instead of asking your students simply to "read," "look," "solve," or "practice," suggest that students "find something interesting in the text," "look at the picture from different perspectives," or "practice the scales in a variety of ways." Intention improves retention and memorization.

Online lecturers and professors are often famous content experts, but they are unlikely to know the particular interests, anxieties, beliefs, and curiosities of their students. Remember that motivation was not *your* problem; you liked school so much that you are still here. You understood why professors assigned so much reading; you even liked it. You are not the typical student. Knowing what motivates or worries your students and how to engage them with the content is a huge advantage of campus teachers, and its value will only increase.

Content for First Exposure: Knowledge

Try searching for content in your courses as if you were a student trying to avoid going to class (forget your personal eagerness for school). Chapter 2 will start you with a Google search (and note the ability to search just for videos), but then make sure you know Open Yale, edX, iTunesU, Khan Academy, CrashCourse, PhET, Utubersidad (with Spanish-language academic lectures), Academic Earth, and Merlot.org just for openers. For most subjects, the Internet offers a much broader range of lectures, explanations, examples, different analogies, songs, animations, games, and unique ways to learn than you and your colleagues might invent in a lifetime.

If you don't want to spend a lifetime trolling through millions of online lectures, then set up a free wiki (try PBworks or your campus course management system) or a course Pinterest page and ask your students to create a community study guide using the resources they find. If you offer to make up your final exam from this wiki, you will add an incentive, and they may be willing to share their sites. Chapter 3 will also help you create your own content.

Critical reading is still an important skill, but you need to teach this *as* a skill. Start by assigning shorter portions (especially in the first year), and help students read them in more depth. Tell them why they are reading in advance, and then discuss and use all of what you assign until students get better at digesting reading on their own. Reading is more work than a video, so you will need an even better entry point to motivate them. If reading is important for your department, you need a progressive multi-course, multiyear plan that teaches students how to do this.

Exam to Evaluate: Retrieval

You can encourage students to read the article or watch the video by creating online exams before every class (see Chapter 5). Giving students just a few "thought" or "study" questions before every class can guide their learning and give you feedback on what they are thinking. It also offers feedback to students that provides intention for the next reading and gives them some control over their learning (all research-based pedagogies). Many forms of questions can be graded automatically in your course management system, so both students and you can see the results instantly. If these quizzes are due one hour before class, you will then have results that may shape your use of class time. You can condition students from the first day of class by posting the syllabus online and having a syllabus quiz due before the second class.

Writing to Reflect: Elaborate, Contextualize

Ask students to write short paragraphs or arguments about the reading or video content on index cards, identify the weakest argument or most controversial claim in the article, correct three mistakes in the Wikipedia article they read, argue for the importance of a theme left out of the CliffNotes video on *Hamlet*, or copy a quote and explain why they think it is essential for the persuasiveness of the reading (see Chapter 6). Students then bring these index cards to class and swap with a neighbor, who reads the card and maybe turns it over to write a rebuttal, paraphrase the argument, or provide another perspective.

Vigilance about the veracity or persuasiveness of everything you find on the Internet is an essential skill. Scholars are trained to be skeptical, but too often we reserve this complex skill for after the basics (and when rigidity of disciplinary thinking has been calcified). But now that the bar to publish on the Internet is essentially set at zero, providing "trusted" sources like textbooks may evoke a false comfort that ironically exists only in the ivory tower. Employers will be grateful for graduates who question sources.

Before class is also a good time for students to create diagrams, imagine alternative theories, find relevance, explore connections, outline proposals, summarize data, and provide solutions to problems. These do not have to be long assignments, but it is key that students are thinking, evaluating, and synthesizing before class.

Class to Challenge: Failure, Complicate

Now you face a room full of prepared students with time for discussion, applications, active learning, role playing, or problem solving. Can you structure your class more like a lab or studio now (see Chapter 7)? Try applying something prepared as homework to a new situation. Have students prepare a presentation for a meeting in New York City; then at the start of class, tell them that the meeting has been moved to Tokyo, the original data were flawed, or the client wants something different, and give them 15 minutes in class to figure out how to alter the presentation. If you are ready for more adventure, try playing or designing a classroom game.

Now you can really learn what students think and how they process. Your preparation will become more about the design of an experience than the covering of content—and remember that more content, more reading, and more "exposure" do not result in more learning. Especially in introductory courses, less content and more focus on how to study and apply can create more motivated learners for upper-division courses. Nothing kills academic motivation like a freshman survey course that skims the surface all semester. Even if your class is large, perhaps you meet with students only in smaller groups and never as a large class (since you no longer need to cover the content).

Cognitive Wrappers to Self-Regulate: Abstract

The goal of college is to help students develop more complex mental models. This is mostly a process of helping students learn to self-regulate their own learning process.

A great way to do this is to use cognitive wrappers, a generalized approach based on Marsha Lovett's exam wrappers in STEM fields, explored in Chapter 8. When handing back a paper, a problem set, an exam, or the audition results, also provide students with a single sheet of paper that asks them to reflect on three things: (1) how they prepared, (2) where they lost points, and (3) how they might prepare differently next time (there is a free template at TeachingNaked.com). Students themselves will start to see that these three things might be connected.

Do not grade them: simply allow students time to do them in class repeatedly. You can collect them and hand them out before the next test, paper, or audition. Wrappers are much more effective when used simultaneously in very different classes or situations, and students start to think about how preparation and study habits might need to be customized for different tasks. This leads to better metacognition—what John Dewey described as thinking about your own thinking.

E-Communication to Reinforce (Connections and Spacing)

Social media can be teaching tools, allowing students to connect ideas to other ideas. Chapter 10 suggests that you ask students to use your Twitter hashtag (#mycourse) and each week find one connection (Web link) that they can post. Twitter is all about connections, and students often don't even look for the connections between your class and the outside world. In fact, if you don't ever contact students outside class, you are reinforcing the idea that the information in your class is not relevant to the "real world." First, connect.

Social media are also places where you can show your passion (students perceive your messages as supportive and motivating), but oddly, they also give you a way to demonstrate the power of slow thinking. Students think that because you are smart and know lots of things, you must always know the answer. They will be shocked and surprised when instead of answering a question in class, you want to "think about that question" or "first do more research" and then respond in an e-mail to the entire class. Time for reflection and interaction is a casualty of the digital age, but you can help reclaim this time.

There are many useful ways to think about course design. The Teaching Naked design process provides a structure for thinking about units, classes, and courses that incorporates both technology and good learning behaviors (see the figures in Chapter 11).

Ultimately we need to apply these same design principals to everything on campus (Chapter 12). We have inherited a system designed for students from a different time and with different assumptions and capabilities; they have different aims and live in a world with different technology. Our early designer ancestors did not have the benefit of copious educational research as the system was put into play. Given what we now know, we need to redesign higher education.

References

Aamodt, S., & Wang, S. (2011). *Welcome to your child's brain: How the mind grows from conception to college*. New York, NY: Bloomsbury.

Bach, R. (1977). *Illusions: The adventures of a reluctant messiah*. New York, NY: Dell.

Barbezat, D. P., & Bush, M. (2014). *Contemplative practices in higher education: Powerful methods to transform teaching and learning*. San Francisco, CA: Jossey-Bass.

Blakeslee, T. (2004). *The attitude factor: Extend your life by changing the way you think*. Lincoln, NE: iUniverse.

Bloom, B. S., ed. (1956). *Taxonomy of educational objectives. The classification of educational goals. Handbook I: Cognitive domain*. New York: David McKay.

Brown, P. C., Roediger, H. L. III, & McDaniel, M. A. (2014). *Make it stick: The science of successful learning*. Cambridge, MA: Belknap Press of Harvard University Press.

Chambliss, D. F., & Takacs, C. G. (2014). *How college works*. Cambridge, MA: Harvard University Press.

Crawford, M. B. (2011). *The case for working with your hands, or, why office work is bad for us and fixing things feels good*. New York, NY: Penguin Viking.

Dehaene, S. (2009). *Reading in the brain: The science and evolution of a human invention*. New York, NY: Penguin.

Dement, W., & Vaughan, C. (1999). *The promise of sleep: A pioneer in sleep medicine explores the vital connection between health, happiness, and a good night's sleep*. New York, NY: Random House.

Dewar, M. T., Alber, J., Butler, C., Cowan, N., & Della Sala, S. (2012). Brief wakeful resting boosts new memories over the long term. *Psychological Science, 23*, 955–960.

Doyle, T. (2008). *Helping students learn in a learner-centered environment: A guide to facilitating learning in higher education*. Sterling, VA: Stylus.

Doyle, T., & Zakrajsek, T. (2013). *The new science of learning: How to learn in harmony with your brain*. Sterling, VA: Stylus.

Duckworth, A. (2016). *Grit: The power of passion and perseverance*. New York: Scribner.

Dweck, C. (2007). *Mindset: The new psychology of success.* New York: Ballantine Books.

Fink, L. D. (2013). *Creating significant learning experiences: An integrated approach to designing college courses* (2nd ed.). San Francisco, CA: Jossey-Bass.

Hart Research Associates. (2013). *It takes more than a major: Employer priorities for college learning and student success.* Washington, DC: Association of American Colleges and Universities. Retrieved from https://aacu.org/sites/default/files/files/LEAP/2013_EmployerSurvey.pdf

Immordino-Yang, M. H. (2015). *Emotions, learning, and the brain: Embodied brains, social minds, and the art of learning.* New York, NY: Norton.

Kuehn, B. M. (2011). Antidepressant use increases. *Journal of the American Medical Association, 306*(20), 2207. doi:10.1001/jama.2011.1697

Kuh, G. D., Kinzie, J., Schuh, J. H., & Whitt, J. H. (2005). *Assessing conditions to enhance educational effectiveness: The inventory for student engagement and success.* San Francisco, CA: Jossey-Bass.

Lambert, K. (2015). Do or DIY. 21st Century Enlightenment. *Royal Society for the Encouragement of Arts, Manufactures and Commerce. Journal Issue 1,* 2015. 20–24.

Langer, E. J. (1989). *The power of mindful learning.* Cambridge, MA: Da Capo Press.

Langer, E. J. (1997). *Mindfulness.* Cambridge, MA: Da Capo Press.

Lovett, M. C. (2013). Make exams worth more than the grade: Using exam wrappers to promote metacognition. In M. Kaplan, N. Silver, D. LaVague-Manty, & D. Meizlish (Eds.), *Using reflection and metacognition to improve student learning: Across the disciplines, across the academy* (pp. 18–52). Sterling, VA: Stylus.

Maas, J. B., & Robbins, R. S. (2011). *Sleep for success! Everything you must know about sleep but are too tired to ask.* Bloomington, IN: AuthorHouse.

Medina, J. (2014). *Brain rules: Twelve principles for surviving and thriving at work, home, and school* (2nd ed.). Seattle, WA: Pear Press.

Mischel, W., & Ayduk, O. (2004). Willpower in a cognitive-affective processing system: The dynamics of delay of gratification. In R. F. Baumeister & K. D. Vohs (Eds.), *Handbook of self-regulation: Research, theory, and applications* (pp. 83–105). New York, NY: Guilford Press.

Mischel, W., Shoda, Y., & Rodriguez, M. I. (1989). Delay of gratification in children. *Science, 244*(4907), 933–938.

Moreno, R., & Mayer, R. (2007). Interactive multimodal learning environments. *Educational Psychology Review, 19,* 309–326.

Mueller, P. A., & Oppenheimer, D. M. (2014). The pen is mightier than the keyboard: Advantages of longhand over laptop note taking. *Psychological Science, 25*(6), 1159–1168.

Napping may not be such a no-no. (2009, November). *Harvard Health Letter.* Retrieved from http://www.health.harvard.edu/newsletter_article/napping-may-not-be-such-a-no-no

Novak, J. D., & Cañas A. J. (2008). *The theory underlying concept maps and how to construct them*. Pensacola: Florida Institute for Human and Machine Cognition. Retrieved from http://cmap.ihmc.us/Publications/ResearchPapers/TheoryUnderlyingConceptMaps.pdf

Pashler, H., McDaniel, M., Rohrer, D., & Bjork, R. (2008). Learning styles: Concepts and evidence. *Psychological Science in the Public Interest, 9*(3), 105–119.

Perrin, M., Henaff, M.A., Padovan, C., Faillenot, I., Merville, A., & Krolak-Salmon, P. (2012). Influence of emotional content and context on memory in mild Alzheimer's disease. *Journal of Alzheimer's Disease, 29*(4), 817–826. doi:10.3233/JAD-2012-111490

Rasch, B., Buchel, C., Gais, S., & Born, J. (2007). Odor cues during slow-wave sleep prompt declarative memory consolidation. *Science, 315*(5817), 1426–1429.

Ratey, J. J. (2013). *Spark: The revolutionary new science of exercise and the brain*. New York, NY: Little, Brown.

Riley, J., Corkhill, B., & Morris, C. (2013). The benefits of knitting for personal and social wellbeing in adulthood: Findings from an international survey. *British Journal of Occupational Therapy, 72*(2), 50–57.

Schacter, D. L., & Szpunar, K. K. (2015). Enhancing attention and memory during video-recorded lectures. *Scholarship of Teaching and Learning in Psychology, 1*(1), 60–71.

Seli, P., Smallwood, J., Cheyne, J. A., & Smilek, D. (2015). On the relation of mind wandering and ADHD symptomatology. *Psychonomic Bulletin and Review, 22*(3), 629–636.

Shams, L., & Seitz, A. R. (2008). Benefits of multisensory learning. *Trends in Cognitive Sciences, 12*(11), 411–417.

Strayer, D. L., Cooper, J. M., Turrill, J., Coleman, J. R., & Hopman, R. J. (2015). *The smartphone and the driver's cognitive workload: A comparison of Apple, Google, and Microsoft's intelligent personal assistants*. Washington, DC: AAA Foundation for Traffic Safety.

Van Dongen, E. V., Kersten, I. H. P., Wagner, I. C., Morris, R. G. M., & Fernández, G. (2016). Physical exercise performed four hours after learning improves memory retention and increases hippocampal pattern similarity during retrieval, *Current Biology, 26*, 1–6. doi: http://dx.doi.org/10.1016/j.cub.2016.04.071

Van Dongen, H. P. A., Maislin, G., Mullington, J. M., & Dinges, D. F. (2003). The cumulative cost of additional wakefulness: Dose-response effects on neurobehavioral functions and sleep physiology from chronic sleep restriction and total sleep deprivation. *Sleep, 26*(2), 117–126.

Walker, M. P., Stickgold, R., Alsop, D., Gaab, N., & Schlaug, G. (2005). Sleep-dependent motor memory plasticity in the human brain. *Neuroscience, 133*(4), 911–917. doi:10.1016/j.neuroscience.2005.04.007

Watson, C. E., Terry, K., & Doolittle, P. E. (2012). Please read while texting and driving. In J.E. Groccia & L. Cruz (Eds.), *To improve the academy, vol. 31* (pp. 295–309). Hoboken, NJ: Wiley.

Wilhelm, I., Diekelmann, S., Molzow, I., Ayoub, A., Mölle, M., & Born, J. (2011). Sleep selectively enhances memory expected to be of future relevance. *Journal of Neuroscience, 31*, 1563–1569. doi:10.1523/JNEUROSCI.3575-10.2011

Yeager, D. S., Henderson, M. D., D'Mello, S., Paunesku, D., Walton, G. W., Spitzer, B. J., & Duckworth, A. L. (2014). Boring but important: A self-transcendent purpose for learning fosters academic self-regulation. *Journal of Personality and Social Psychology, 107*(4), 559–580.

Zull, J. E. (2002). *The art of changing the brain: Enriching the practice of teaching by exploring the biology of learning.* Sterling, VA: Stylus.

Zull, J. E. (2011). *From brain to mind: Using neuroscience to guide change in education.* Sterling, VA: Stylus.

Chapter 1

Transparency and Clearer Targets

WE FACULTY ARE odd. We like school so much we are still here. This makes it easy for us to forget that school is a strange and mysterious place for most students. Not only is it a place from which they hope to leave and never come back (that is generally considered the "normal" view of the world), but it is a place with a unique set of rules. These rules have become obvious to faculty but often appear completely opaque to students as they first encounter them. This disconnect is exacerbated with first-generation students who often lack the network of experienced adults who can answer their questions regarding how all of this is supposed to work.

We know that transparency improves learning, that the more we share about why we have chosen our teaching practices the better students perform, and that these effects are disproportionately greater for students who do not have another source to ask regarding these practices (Winkelmes, 2013). Why do faculty assign only the odd- or even-numbered problems? Why do faculty have us work in groups? Why do faculty scribble all over my paper when they hand it back? These are serious concerns about the code of academia, and the answers are often obvious only to those of us who live here.

Research suggests that faculty can help by explaining to students what they are to do, why we want them to do it, and how it will help them learn (Jonsson & Svingby, 2007). Try being this explicit with students: "Each time you repeat the task with small variations, your brain makes different connections. Practice makes perfect, as you may have experienced in a video game."

This is especially true on the macrolevel: What are the goals for this class? For most students, the goal is to get an A. If you want your students to aspire to more than this, you need to articulate what else they might want and how it might relate to their longer-term goals. You may also have to outline the steps necessary to reach these goals, clarify what A work looks like, and what behaviors are likely to result in success. Better pedagogy begins with transparency.

Learning Outcomes

When most of us taught our first class, the name of the game was content coverage. We didn't really know how to approach teaching any other way. We tried to get a sense of what content likely belonged in our course, and then we would divide the content into chunks that could then be further divided into days. We'd prepare to share that content with our students with perhaps little thought regarding what they were to do with that content beyond the life span of our introductory course. There are, of course, far better strategies to use to design a course, and the best place to start is with the articulation of learning outcomes.

Bloom's taxonomy of educational objectives (1956) was designed for higher education, but it is now pervasive in curriculum design; even dog trainers use a version of this structure. Anderson and Krathwohl (2001) revised the taxonomy into the form most widely used today. The taxonomy classifies cognitive skills into six levels of increasing complexity. Like a video game, each higher level assumes mastery of all of the previous levels.

- *Remembering:* Retrieving, recognizing, and recalling relevant knowledge from long-term memory

- *Understanding:* Constructing meaning from oral, written, and graphic messages through interpreting, exemplifying, classifying, summarizing, inferring, comparing, and explaining

- *Applying:* Carrying out or using a procedure through executing or implementing

- *Analyzing:* Breaking material into constituent parts, determining how the parts relate to one another and to an overall structure or purpose through differentiating, organizing, and attributing

- *Evaluating:* Making judgments based on criteria and standards through checking and critiquing

- *Creating:* Putting elements together to form a coherent or functional whole; reorganizing elements into a new pattern or structure through generating, planning, or producing (Anderson & Krathwohl, 2001, pp. 67–68)

Bloom's levels are a common vocabulary in learning outcomes and the development of instructional activities. This taxonomy can help you articulate, for yourself and your students, what you hope students will accomplish in your course or from an activity. They can also guide the sequence of what happens in your course. These levels may be obvious to you, but they may be a revelation to your students. Helping them understand that there is a progression of thinking skills that they will develop over time can do a lot to break down resistance to your content, your instructional approach, and even your course. Taking the time to consider what students will be able to do by the end of every course (and even every unit or class session) will improve everything about your design and help you prioritize which investments in new pedagogy will give you the most return for your time.

The increased specificity and the progression of cognitive skills can also help students understand what they are supposed to be learning, and this will help them make appropriate choices about their own approach to your course. Connecting content to levels of thinking can help clarify the order and purpose of specific activities for your students (Chapter 11 provides more on sequence and integration).

FIGURE 1.1

Fink's Taxonomy of Significant Learning

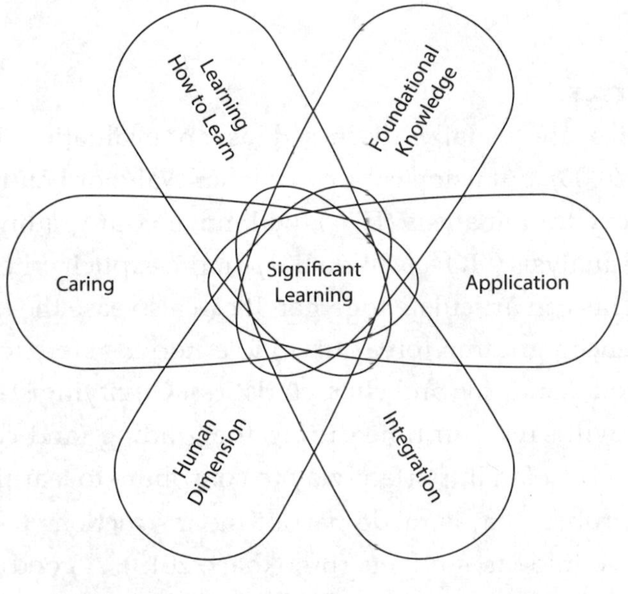

Source: Fink (2013) p. 30.

Dee Fink (2013) proposed another revision to Bloom's linear progression of six levels of cognitive learning with six kinds of related learning that enhance each other:

Foundational knowledge: The facts and principles that constitute course content.

Application: Problem solving, decision making, skills, or creative thinking.

Integration: Interdisciplinarity and the interactions among subjects matter.

Human dimension: Learn about themselves or how to interact with others in life.

Caring: Students change their feelings, interests, or values in relation to a subject.

Learning how to learn: How to we prepare students to continue learning? (Fink, 2013, p. 30)

The more of these six areas a course or program can promote, the more significant the overall learning experience will be for students. Articulating clear objectives that also make sense to students is a challenge, but as with all increases in transparency, it will be especially beneficial to students in the bottom half of your class.

Rubrics

Rubrics are usually discussed as an evaluation tool (see Stevens & Levi, 2005), but using rubrics, or what Walvoord and Anderson (1998) call primary trait analysis (PTA), will move your grading from unstated personal analysis ("It feels like a B") to more explicit criteria that you and your students can articulate together. It can also ease the transition from norm-referenced grading (on a curve) to criterion-referenced scoring (based on defined standards and characteristics). Clarifying standards and expectations will save you time during the grading (and complaining) process, but it is also an important way to contribute to learning (Selka, 2013).

A rubric that is made part of the instructions for an assignment provides a guide to students (Brookhart, 2013). A good rubric should clearly demonstrate to students your criteria and your standards; putting them into a table ensures that you provide both. Note that with the detailed and specific rubric in Table 1.1, the assignment is apparent almost without further instructions.

TABLE 1.1
College Writing Rubric Example

	Absent (0%)	Poor (40%)	Average (70%)	Good (90%)	Great (100%)
Thesis, ideas, and analysis (20%)	There is no thesis or focus.	The thesis is split or unclear. The paper wanders off topic.	The essay is focused around a single thesis or idea.	The thesis is interesting, and there is at least one original perspective in one of the points.	The thesis is original, and there are compelling ideas throughout.
Evidence (30%)	There is almost no detailed evidence to support the thesis.	There is some evidence, but in key places evidence is vague or missing.	There is supporting evidence for most of the claims, but some evidence may be unrelated or vague.	There is supporting evidence for all claims, but it is not as strong or complete in some areas.	There is a variety of support for every claim, and it is strong, concrete, and appropriate.
Organization (20%)	There is little or no organization.	There is some organization, but the paper is "jumpy." It does not have a clear introduction and conclusion, and paragraphs are not focused or are out of order.	The introduction, body, and conclusion are clear, but some paragraphs may need to be focused and/or moved.	Each part of the paper is engaging, but better transitions, more (or fewer) paragraphs, or stronger conclusion are needed.	Each paragraph is focused and in the proper order. The introduction and conclusion are complementary, and the transitions are excellent.
Language maturity (10%)	Frequent and serious grammatical mistakes make the meaning unclear.	Grammatical mistakes slightly interfere with the meaning of the paper.	The writing is clear, but sentence structures are simple or repetitive. There are repeated grammar errors.	The language is clear, with complex sentence structure, but the paper contains minor grammatical errors.	Creative word choice and sentence structure enhance the meaning and focus of the paper.

(continued)

TABLE 1.1 *(continued)*

	Absent (0%)	Poor (40%)	Average (70%)	Good (90%)	Great (100%)
Style/voice (10%)	Writing is very general with no sense of either the writer or audience.	Writing is general, with little sense of the audience or communication of the writer's voice or passion.	The essay addresses the audience appropriately, with some examples of creative expression.	The essay addresses the audience appropriately and is engaging with a strong sense of voice.	There is a keen sense of the intended audience and the author's voice, and the writing conveys passion.
Citations (10%)	The material is presented almost entirely without citations.	There are some citations, but they are either incomplete or inappropriate.	The citations are good, but there are not enough of them	All evidence is cited, but with minor format errors.	All evidence is well cited in appropriate format

Source: Bowen (2012, Table 7.1, pp. 164165).

Rubrics improve transparency and give students a target. Students (especially first-generation college students) are deeply confused about grading and what you want. When you say "critical thinking," they hear "trick question." They genuinely believe that writing papers (and school in general) is largely about figuring out how to please different, highly individual, and often quirky people called professors. They do not see this as standards. Students complain that it takes half the semester to discover what individual faculty want. One of the most common complaints is that a student will use the format, style, or type of writing they learned in an earlier class and then get a poor grade on the first paper in the next class for doing what they thought was rewarded previously. A rubric can give students guidance for the first writing assignment, without having to wait for the grade. Rubrics can be highly personal. If you have unusual demands, a rubric is critical in helping your students understand what you want them to do.

Your criteria (the first column on the left) should indicate your priorities and weights. If a creative thesis is more important than a bibliography, then it should be worth more points. If you do not care about voice, eliminate it from the rubric. Across the top are the standards for each criterion: these could be A, B, C, D, and F, descriptive levels, or percentages. Start by writing standards for the highest level of performance and keep them high to provide clarity and give students a target.

Checklists

Another common mystery in academics is how to accomplish a basic task. As faculty, we figured out that more research led to better papers and that we needed to start with reading and a trip to the library. That is hardly obvious, especially in the Internet age. A checklist is a narrative description of the process for producing good work, and it can help your students know the steps you anticipate.

While you should acknowledge different preferences in work styles, we know now that there are "fundamental problems with regard to both the diagnosis of learning styles and the alignment of instruction to these styles" (Kirschner & Merriënboer, 2013, p. 173). For instance, learning the piano is a kinesthetic process and can't be done through just listening, reading, or watching, regardless of one's purported learning style. We now know that there isn't evidence that supports using learning styles conceptions in any way in instruction (Pasher, McDaniel, Rohrer, & Bjork, 2008), and we can jettison that idea in favor of evidence-based practices. We now know that most learning is about putting in the work; it's about cognitive processing. Many first-year and first-generation students simply don't know which work will be most useful or in what sequence to do it, and that's why providing a checklist that offers an order of progressions for students can have a strong impact.

Advance Organizers

Similar to checklists, advance organizers can help students figure out how to be successful as they work through a module, class, or assignment by allowing them to see what is most important and how things relate to one another. This isn't a new notion. Ausubel (1968) recommended using advance organizers to bridge the gap between what our students already know and what they need to know to be ready to complete a task. They provide students with advance warning of the content that is to come, which enables them to begin to make connections between what they already know and the new information you are providing for them. They facilitate the construction and expansion of mental models and are an excellent first step as you begin to introduce new ideas to students.

An advance organizer can be as simple as providing students with that day's learning outcomes at the start of class or an outline that shows the order in which topics will be explored over the next hour or week, for example. A rubric can also function as an organizer for students. A more elaborate advance organizer might be a visual or graphic that shows how concepts are related to one another, evoking what students already know and connecting those ideas to what is to come. This would be provided at the start of instruction and referenced often to make explicit the relationship of ideas. Yet another advance organizer strategy would be in the form of guidance for students. For example, suggesting that they skim a chapter, or at least look at the section headings, before they read can help them begin to organize new material and make connections to what they already know prior to jumping into the content.

Common Language

Another academic practice faculty take for granted is terminology. We know that while we like to talk about critical thinking, Professor Jones prefers the phrase *mindful learning* and Professor Smith says *discernment and analysis*. We know that these are related concepts. In fact, we are so used to these concepts that we often forget to label them at all. Using labels helps students to clarify that this week's paper, class discussion, problem set, or group activity involves an important and transferable skill called *critical thinking* (or whatever common term your department or college chose to use).

Students are not as good at connecting concepts from week to week, or course to course, as we think they are. Using consistent labels and being clear about how they are related to the larger learning goals is another form of transparency that will disproportionately support first-generation and other underrepresented students (Winkelmes, 2013).

This is the most basic preliminary work you should do before designing a course. There are obviously longer and better resources available for each of these topics (see the References at the end of the chapter), but we have included this brief introduction here because even a little bit of advance work will greatly enhance your design process. Both you and your students are more likely to hit the target if you articulate where you want them to aim.

Step-by-Step Guide

Step 1: Clarify for Yourself What You Want Students to Learn

What are the most important things you want students to be able to do in five years? Know that students often remember nothing about a class after five years, so this is a not a trivial exercise.

Step 2: Write Learning Goals for Your Students

Use Bloom's or Fink's taxonomy to write course learning goals and test them with students for clarity:

Remembering (know, define, repeat, describe, identify, recall, list, tell, locate match)

Understanding (comprehend, classify, convert, explain, summarize, predict, discuss, compare)

Applying (demonstrate, modify, arrange, solve, relate, apply, examine, classify, illustrate)

Analyzing (infer, estimate, order, separate, subdivide, distinguish, contrast, categorize)

Evaluating (critique, justify, discriminate, support, conclude, judge, verify, assess, argue)

Creating (synthesize, design, formulate, revise, construct, compose, invent, imagine, propose) (Bloom, 1956)

Consider these examples:

Example 1: Students will learn about the importance of scientific, social, artistic, or political innovations or discoveries.
In this course/major, students will learn to:

- List important discoveries from the past
- Explain the basic disciplinary concepts underlying each discovery
- Apply the concepts of the discipline to classify discoveries
- Analyze novel aspects of each discovery
- Evaluate which current discoveries will have the greatest impact
- Design a strategy to address an important unanswered question in the field

Example 2: Students will learn about musical styles and historical periods.
In this course/major, students will learn to:

- Define the different conventions operating in each style or period
- Compare examples of each style or period
- Classify key practitioners using examples
- Infer the style of unknown practitioners using typical characteristics
- Judge if the most typical exemplar is the most interesting
- Construct an argument as to how and why certain thinkers, artists, or authors cross boundaries

Example 3: Students will learn about entrepreneurship.
In this course, students will learn to:

- Identify reasons to start a new business
- Understand the elements of and rationale for a business plan
- Critique successful and failed business plans
- Create a business plan for a new venture

Example 4: Students will learn about creative autobiographical writing as a journey of self-discovery.
In this course, students will learn to:

- Define their own reasons for writing
- Discuss writing that inspires them
- Demonstrate the ability to communicate what most matters to them

- Judge the best ways to improve their own writing
- Revise their own writing

Step 3: Create Rubrics

Create a rubric for each goal that will provide students with a model and give you a fair and quick way to provide feedback. You can modify rubrics later for individual assignments, but making sure you can identify the goals and how you will recognize them is a good first step.

Step 4: Consider a Checklist for an Assignment

A checklist is a good complement to a rubric. It is a list of steps that you recommend students follow to do good work. Another option is to ask students to create their own checklist and revise it as they work through several sets of similar assignments.

Example: Checklist for a Problem Set

1. Reread the learning outcome for this unit [or problem set].

2. Read [or view] the content explanation.

3. Summarize the key technique or concept in your own words at the top of your paper.

4. Complete all of the problems where you feel confident. *Skip the problems that have you stumped after 5 minutes.*

5. Get together with a friend [perhaps assigned] in the class and compare your summaries of the concept and which problems you thought were easy. [This might also be managed in a virtual community; see Chapter 10.]

6. Investigate any discrepancies in your answers. Note this is a fundamental tenet and process of the scientific method: peer review. If you correct a mistake, that is fine; just make a note of this in the margin.

7. See if you can manage one of the difficult problems together.

8. Note your collaboration and what stumped you about any problems you could not complete.

Step 5: Consider an Advance Organizer for Class

Provide the learning goals to your students at the beginning of each class as a standard part of your practice. Begin your lesson by briefly discussing the learning goals and explaining how they fit together. For complex ideas, consider building a visual to show the relationships among the various components. Depending on your topic, Venn diagrams may be an easy way to show relationships, but you may also want to consider something more elaborate, like a concept map (see Chapter 6).

Examples

In each chapter of this book, we present specific examples of how these best practices have been modified and applied in various fields in a range of courses at different types of higher education institutions.

Goal Sheets

Sarah Leupen, University of Maryland Baltimore County

To clarify goals, Sarah provides what she calls "goal sheets" based on chapter and course goals. Students are given these documents, and they guide the instruction in the course and student work as they progress through the course. She notes that some of these goals are quite difficult; however, her students "perform well since they know what they are expected to do."

Course Goals as an Organizational Structure

Anthony Smith, Indiana University South Bend; Jeffery Schwehm, Concordia University

Some faculty include students in the process of goal setting, which can have the additional benefit of increasing student motivation and engagement, as well as ensuring greater clarity regarding the goals (Hugg & Wurdinger, 2007). Others deeply integrate goals into the instructional activities of the course to ensure that the students always have an eye toward the purpose of various course activities. Anthony uses course goals as an organizational structure for his course. He revisits the goals throughout class by referencing them as he provides examples and the students work through his course's framework. Jeffery ensures his students clearly understand the goals by quizzing them prior to his chemistry activities. Students must make connections between the goals and the purpose of the upcoming activity.

Reinforcing Learning Outcomes

Peter Scott Brown, University of North Florida

Similar to goals, well-crafted learning outcomes that use structures and formats provided by Fink and Bloom can ensure that students know what they are supposed to learn before, during, and after learning events. Peter explicitly states these in his syllabus, during class, and during interactions with students outside class. Such approaches ensure instructional alignment between the outcomes and what takes place during instruction, and students benefit throughout such an approach because they are continually refocused to what is important.

Progressive Learning Outcomes

Chris Mortensen, University of Florida

The creative use of learning outcomes can be used to assist students as they move to more complex cognitive skills, as described by Bloom's taxonomy. Chris implements active learning approaches toward specific learning objectives. These activities are first designed to ensure that students master foundational information before they move to evaluating information and then applying it in new, real-world contexts.

Sequencing Learning Outcomes with Activities

Oana Godeanu-Kenworthy, Miami University; Joe Reinsel, University of Michigan–Flint

Oana, in her course entitled America: Global and Intercultural Perspectives, sequences learning activities with the goal of increasingly moving students to higher-order learning outcomes. A series of brief, lower-level assignments are used as precursors to formal and informal writing assignments. These writing assignments are tailored to target midlevel Blooms outcomes as students journey toward a final project that brings them to acts of evaluating and creating.

As suggested here, final projects are often an exceptional approach for pursuing higher-order learning outcomes. Joe, in his Games and Virtual Art course, specifically focuses on Bloom's "creating" and Fink's "learning how to learn," with the course target being the final project. Students research and create a number of gaming structures and mock-ups as they progress in their collective development of a working prototype of a game that is then played by the class at the end of the semester. Notions of higher-order learning influence course structure and mirror what the professor hopes students can do at the end of the course.

Rubrics

Gina Riggio, Delaware Technical Community College

Best practices in rubric implementation abound across higher education, and one such practice is to provide students with the rubric you will be using to grade assignments. Gina does just that. She provides an empty rubric and then shows the students how she fills it in, section by section, so that they know how she calculates grades. Grading becomes far less subjective, and transparency in grading enables students to know how they can earn an A.

Students Using Rubrics

Tawnya Means, University of Florida

In her Business Telecommunications course, Tawnya has her students complete grading rubrics for their projects prior to turning them in as a required component of assignment submission. This provides students with an opportunity to be reflective regarding their work and to make revisions based on true project expectations prior to submission. This also reduces surprises that might result when students receive their graded work.

Common Language

Todd Pourciau, Baton Rouge Community College

Repetition is an excellent strategy for incorporating terminology and establishing a common language in a course, and a challenge is often how to incorporate notions of repetition in meaningful ways. Todd ties core concepts and language from his learning outcomes to the topics of career searches and future job advancement. Video projects are a component of his College Success courses, and students must write scripts and record projects that incorporate key vocabulary while also improving their critical thinking and communication skills. Through this approach, students not only come to understand key vocabulary; they also are able to apply it in appropriate situations and contexts. This ensures that true assimilation of this language has occurred in his courses.

Key Concepts

- Make learning goals transparent to students. This improves their learning and benefits first-generation and underrepresented students in significant ways. Openly share the "why" of everything you do with your students.

- Incorporate Bloom's and Fink's approaches to ensure that your course has progressive or integrative learning outcomes.

- Use Bloom and Fink to clarify your cognitive and noncognitive goals. This explanation will provide greater clarity to students regarding where to focus their energies and time.

- Create rubrics as you develop assignments to help articulate your expectations. Specify both criteria and standards.

- Give grading rubrics to your students in advance as you provide and discuss assignments.

- Try a checklist that details your suggested process for completing an assignment as a complement to your rubric (which focuses on the outcome).

- Use consistent language, and be clear about how these terms relate to learning outcomes. This form of transparency will foster student assimilation of foundational language within a course.

Further Resources

Association of American Colleges and Universities. (2009). *VALUE rubrics*. Retrieved from https://www.aacu.org/value

VALUE (Valid Assessment of Learning in Undergraduate Education) is a campus-based assessment initiative sponsored by the Association of American Colleges and Universities as part of its Liberal Education and America's Promise initiative. These rubrics are freely available to help campuses guide and assess student work in a variety of areas.

■ ■ ■

Angelo, T. A., & Cross, K. P. (1993). *Classroom assessment techniques: A handbook for college teachers* (2nd ed.). San Francisco, CA: Jossey-Bass.

This book provides a range of practical resources for those looking for new ideas regarding classroom assessment. It also provides a number of detailed case studies that make explicit how classroom assessment should work in a range of classroom settings.

■ ■ ■

Center for Excellence in Learning and Teaching. (2011). *A model of learning objectives*. Iowa State University. Retrieved from http://www.celt.iastate.edu/teaching/effective-teaching-practices/revised-blooms-taxonomy

Even if you are already very familiar with Bloom's taxonomy, you will find this interactive, three-dimensional tool and associated extra materials enlightening. The overlay of the "knowledge dimension" will be a new way to consider Bloom's for many.

■ ■ ■

Eberly Center for Teaching Excellence and Educational Innovation. (2016). *Grading and performance rubrics*. Retrieved from https://www.cmu.edu/teaching/designteach/teach/rubrics.html

This Carnegie Mellon site provides a number of robust sample rubrics for a range of assignment types. They are downloadable in the .doc format, which means that you can edit and adjust them to fit the scoring needs of your assignments.

■ ■ ■

Gustafson, K. L., & Branch, R. M. (2002). *Survey of instructional design models* (4th ed.). Syracuse, NY: ERIC Clearinghouse on Information and Technology. Retrieved from http://files.eric.ed.gov/fulltext/ED477517.pdf

There are more ways to approach instructional design than just the ADDIE (Analysis, Design, Development, Implementation, and Evaluation) model, and this book, freely available online as a PDF, provides a number of ways to approach the design process.

■ ■ ■

Kheiry, M., & Tarr, T. (2014). *Writing student learning outcomes*. Indianapolis, IN: IUPUI Center for Teaching and Learning. Retrieved from http://ctl.iupui. edu/Resources/Planning-the-Learning-Experience/Writing-Student-Learning-Outcomes

This brief site walks you through the process of writing student learning outcomes and shares a number of examples of these from a range of disciplines. It also provides a list of action verbs that will help guide you in writing outcomes that are both observable and measurable.

References

Anderson, L. W., & Krathwohl, D. R. (Eds.). (2001). *A taxonomy for learning, teaching, and assessing: A revision of Bloom's Taxonomy of Educational Objectives*. New York, NY: Longman.

Ausubel, D. P. (1968). *Educational psychology: A cognitive view*. New York, NY: Holt, Rinehart and Winston.

Bloom, B. S. (Ed.). (1956). *Taxonomy of educational objectives, handbook I: The cognitive domain*. New York, NY: McKay.

Bowen, J. A. (2012). *Teaching naked: How moving technology out of your college classroom will improve student learning*. San Francisco, CA: Jossey-Bass.

Brookhart, S. M. (2013). *How to create and use rubrics for formative assessment and grading*. Alexandria, VA: Association for Supervision and Curriculum Development.

Fink, L. D. (2013). *Creating significant learning experiences: An integrated approach to designing college courses* (2nd ed.). San Francisco, CA: Jossey-Bass.

Hugg, R., & Wurdinger, S. (2007). A practical and progressive pedagogy for project based service learning. *International Journal of Teaching and Learning in Higher Education, 19*(2), 191–204.

Jonsson, A., & Svingby, G. (2007). The use of scoring rubrics: Reliability, validity and educational consequences. *Educational Research Review, 2*, 130–144.

Kirschner, P. A., & Merriënboer, J. J. G. (2013). Do learners really know best? Urban legends in education. *Educational Psychologist, 48*(3), 169–183.

Pasher, H., McDaniel, M., Rohrer, D., & Bjork, R. (2008). Learning styles: Concepts and evidence. *Science in the Public Interest, 9*(3), 103–119.

Selka, M. J. G. (2013). *Rubric assessment goes to college: Objective, comprehensive evaluation of student work.* Lanham, MD: Rowman & Littlefield.

Stevens, D. D., & Levi, A. J. (2005). *Introduction to rubrics: An assessment tool to save grading time, convey effective feedback, and promote student learning.* Sterling, VA: Stylus.

Walvoord, B. E., & Anderson, V. J. (1998). *Effective grading: A tool for learning and assessment.* San Francisco, CA: Jossey-Bass.

Winkelmes, M. A. (2013). Transparency in teaching: Faculty share data and improve students' learning. *Liberal Education, 99*(2). Retrieved from https://www.aacu.org/publications-research/periodicals/transparency-teaching-faculty-share-data-and-improve-students

Chapter 2

Finding Online Content for First Exposure

NOT SO LONG ago, information was scarce but relatively reliable. Students seeking information would consult textbooks and encyclopedias and go to lectures and the library. Now students carry around a device (or two or three) that has access to much more content than any college library or classroom but is mostly full of unreliable opinion, junk, and cat videos. Virtually overnight, our relationship to knowledge has changed.

In moving from an information-scarce world to an information-rich one, we have also moved from mostly reliable to mostly unreliable sources. Even those of us who still keep hard-copy research journals on our shelves use the easy access and low-reliability Internet sources on a daily basis. The value of professing and knowing has gone down, while the importance of interrogation, discernment, and analysis has skyrocketed.

Colleges claim that we are teaching students to think, but then we pre-select and distribute reliable hard-copy sources (textbooks) to students for the last time in their lives. Once students graduate, there will be no more textbooks, and students will be asked to find reliable information for themselves, quickly, and out of a sea of rubbish on the Internet. Even a visit to the library used to involve the card catalogue—which meant thinking first about what was really required and what subject heading was mostly likely to lead us there. Now Google or Siri make many of those first-cut decisions.

Decades ago, José asked students in his jazz history class to go to the music library and listen to Bud Powell and Red Garland play the piano in different bands and see if they could learn to tell the difference. José explained that it would be easy to find each pianist playing with his own trio, but that if they wanted to hear these artists play in larger bands, they would need to find a band where each was only a sideman. This required looking in books (and discographies perhaps), but ultimately students would discover for themselves that Powell was more likely to be found with Charlie Parker and Dizzy Gillespie and Garland with Miles Davis and

John Coltrane. This was confusing and messy, and so eventually a few "good" examples were simply left on a cassette tape in the library. Later these became CDs or a set of files on Blackboard. Students could now easily find exactly the right content but were finding nothing else and having no further sense of discovery and curiosity. In the process of making things easier and faster, students weren't a key to the learning experience.

Given the choice, few students today would be willing to rummage through the card catalogue and then wait to pull out books to read which musicians were playing with whom. Fast (and often virtually immediate) access is now assumed. So students welcome textbooks and lectures as being "easy" shortcuts instead of the complicated and problematic long road to often better and deeper learning. This is a disservice to them: very few jobs come with a textbook or manual. While it often seems that employers initially want employees preloaded with exactly the right skills and information, surveys (Hart Research Associates, 2013) are increasingly demonstrating that employers really want students who can work with new information, solve unstructured problems, and learn new things *for themselves*. The information needed for most jobs changes quickly, and being a voracious, self-regulated learner is the best defense against a changing job market and a world that creates information at a staggering rate, unfathomable to any previous generation. The jobs of the future are yet to be invented and will require information that has not yet been discovered. This information will be unavailable in any textbook for years (even in the latest e-book) and will probably arrive with contradictory information and disputed conclusions. Learning is messy, and textbooks create a false sense of security.

At the same time, textbooks and lectures have more information than students can or want to absorb, and they look for even faster shortcuts. Why get up and go to a lecture on a snowy morning when the laptop in bed has dozens, perhaps hundreds, of online lectures on the topic? Why read the book when there are shorter, funnier, and more entertaining video summaries online?

Students are also arriving on campus with less experience reading longer material and much more experience watching videos or reading on their phone. (See Figure 2.1 for the acceleration of cell phones as an academic device.) You will need to motivate and demonstrate why reading, especially longer and more difficult reading, is worthwhile (see Chapter 4), and you need to expect that many students will happily spend an hour looking for a 5-minute video summary rather than read a short article that might have taken 15 minutes to read. Most adults and even scholars do this routinely: we get a long report, but we look first for the abstract or executive

FIGURE 2.1

Student Use of Devices for Academic Work, 2012–2014

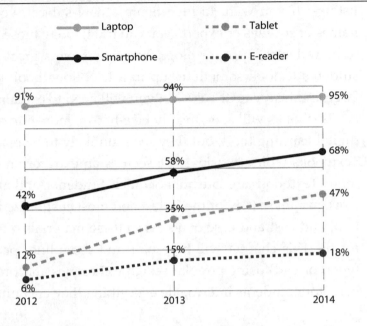

Source: Chronicle of Higher Education (2014).

summary to see if it is worth reading the entire thing. Or we flip to the end of journal articles and read the conclusion before deciding if this month's issue requires more time. And very few of us would go to the shelf and pick up a (probably out-of-date) travel book to find a good restaurant. Each of these activities involves a compromise: we forfeit some reliability and trust someone else's interpretation in exchange for some precious time. Why should we expect our students, who can examine both the amalgamated critic score and fan reviews on Fandango before paying for any movie, to be any different?

An important faculty job is to help students understand that turning information into knowledge is complicated and messy. We are here to increase the complexity of their mental models. Thinking requires information, but it is easy to fall into the pedagogical trap that students must first memorize, and then understand, and only then apply. We learn very few words out of dictionaries. We learn them out of the mouths of others, with a wild host of accents, inflections, and specific uses (Bakhtin, 1981). It is true that it may be faster to learn some aspects of a new language with a highly structured textbook than by wandering around in a new country, but most of us try a little of both.

Part of any learning is finding the best tools—often the tools that work best specifically for you. If you want to buy a house or a car, you ask friends which websites or apps have the most accurate information or the most listings. If you want to investigate a new subject, you look first for the names of surveys or experts you can trust; today those "experts" are likely to be websites, apps, or blogs. You may have a great reason for wanting students to look something up in a telephone book (or read an equally large and heavy textbook), but you will need to explain why.

Textbooks will soon mostly be e-books, more current and full of other digital learning tools, but they seem unlikely to be read more thoroughly. Textbooks will increasingly be seen as an extra or an option for learning more. Textbooks are safe but not quick. Students (and most adults) are now in a constant search for the fastest and most customized source of information, and cost and ease of access to these materials often make the choice for us. This chapter will help you find discipline-specific online content (good or bad) using popular search techniques and provide techniques to help your students interrogate everything they encounter.

Step-by-Step Guide

Both your teaching and student learning will improve if you take the time to discover where your students are actually going to get information. Many start by asking their phone, which will provide a host of sources likely to be inaccurate, opinionated, grossly flawed, one-sided, satirical, or worse. Nevertheless, flawed content often provides opportunities for critical thinking.

Step 1: Search for Video

Most professors have become adept at the quick Google search. We use it to find data points or references we have forgotten. We have our favorite websites and might even regularly use Google Scholar or Google Books to find references for quotes.

Students too know how to use Google for their own purposes, but finding a good party or the closest theater may have given them a false sense of Google's reliability. You want to know what your students are reading (and probably watching) instead of the texts you have assigned. Start by searching for the topics as you list them on your syllabus. (In the future when you prepare a syllabus, remember that students use your lecture or topic titles as search terms, so think carefully about how you label class sessions.)

Students may also try to abbreviate and shorten these titles. As you type in Google, an algorithm tries to guess what you will type next by comparing the words you have typed against all other searches, but also by knowing where you are located (if you are in Paris, Texas, looking for restaurants, you generally don't want Google to suggest restaurants in Paris, France) and also by remembering what you specifically have searched for before (You can change this, but only by having and logging into your Google account). So if you type in "hot" and you travel a lot, Google may guess that you are looking for "hotels." If you live in Phoenix during a heat wave, Google might guess you are looking for weather. If "hot photos" is suggested, you might reconsider what else you are doing on your work computer.

Google is designed to give you information you want, which is generally useful, but this also builds in even more confirmation bias into the results. Try Googling your own name on your computer and then borrow a friend's computer and try it again. Different people may get very different results from the same search.

Most people, including students, are likely to click on the first suggestion or at least on the first page. There are many variables in the click probabilities of each Google position, and this is a major business, but, on average, nearly 60% of organic clicks go to the first position. There is, of course, variance by culture and country. Germans are more skeptical (52.3%), for example, but French (67.7%) and Spanish (77.2%) users are more likely to click on the first position (Beus, 2015). People are also more likely to get distracted or look for the most popular results. "Feminist theory" might become "feminism explained," and that too changes the results. (In this case, the first hit is a wildly popular satire video.)

There are two ways to get a better sense of what your students are watching. First, try a Google search for your topic, but sort your results by "videos" rather than "all" (one of the buttons just beneath the search box; see Figure 2.2). Note that in a video search, the length of YouTube videos appears in the thumbnail. If the first hit is under 10 minutes and popular, this is a likely candidate for many students to watch. If you then click on "Search Tools" at the far right of the same row, you will get another row of options, including a drop-down menu headed "Any duration." If you click "Short (0-4 min.)," you will find other likely suspects for short videos your students may be watching.

A second way to find what students are studying or watching is to ask them. CollegeHumor.com will likely be their first answer, but dig a little

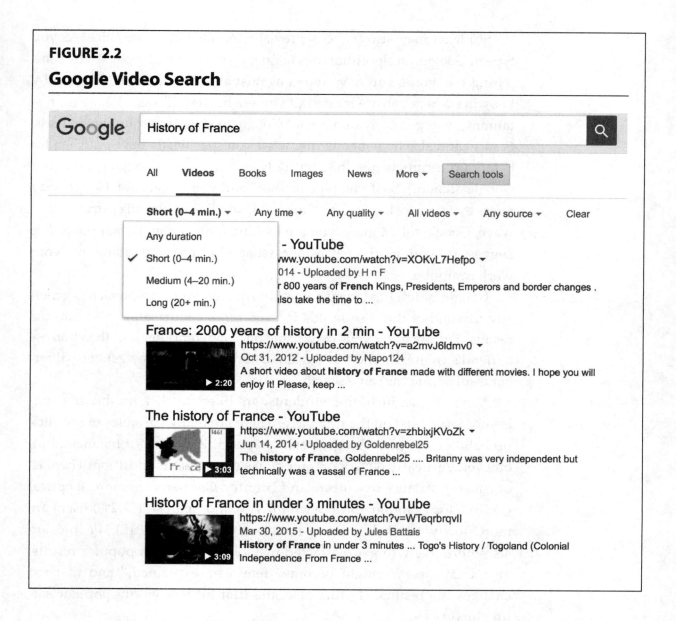

FIGURE 2.2

Google Video Search

deeper. What they share may not be the most reliable information, but it is easier and faster. Set up a wiki site for your course or another forum, like your learning management system (LMS), Facebook, or Pinterest, where students can share the videos as they find them.

Step 2: Find Better Content

The quality of information and production varies greatly on the Internet. Many universities have now made high-quality and well-produced lectures, content, and learning tools available online for free. The Further Resources section at the end of this chapter provides a small sample of the many open source and free resources available. The sources of courses (e.g., Coursera, edX) are also a source of individual lectures, but you may need to guide students to them. Khan and CrashCourse are also used extensively in high school, and your students may be familiar with them. Many of these also present content in other languages, as do Khan, Utubersidad, Merlot, edX, and Coursera, for example.

If videos seem useful and well done, students will watch them longer. You can indeed suggest the most useful content to them by setting up a page of links in your (online) syllabus or, better yet, in a course website or LMS.

Students are keenly aware they learn in different ways at different times and that there are multiple ways to organize and learn the same material. That is precisely how Khan and the other online tutorials got started: your math teacher seems useless to your learning, so you find someone else who "speaks your language." Just as you might characterize different styles of textbooks as "a more cultural approach," "just the facts," or "lots of charts and pictures," you might do the same for videos. Once students find a source that offers explanations that seem to click for them, they will go back every week to the same source.

Another way to find content in your discipline is to explore materials that are often termed *open education resources* (OERs). Partially envisioned as a strategy to reduce the cost of higher education, a wide range of free, high-quality OERs can be found in this domain. Possibly the best repository of such materials is at Rice University. It's called OpenStax College (also below) and is a nonprofit funded through grants from the Hewlett Foundation, Gates Foundation, and others and provides fully realized, faculty-authored, peer-reviewed textbooks online for free of comparable quality to books produced by traditional publishers (Grinberg, 2014). OpenStax College is targeting introductory, high-enrollment courses found on all college campuses. As a result, you and your students have access to free textbooks in physics, psychology, biology, U.S. history, economics, and more. You can deep-link to specific content within these textbooks or replace your textbook entirely.

Step 3: Investigate Games and Other Learning Tools

While video lectures are the easiest to find, many more types of learning tools and associated strategies foster rich engagement with course content. Games, demonstrations, animations, visualizations, and songs are among the range of options available beyond what we often do in our classes. In truth, notions of gaming for learning have a lengthy empirical pedigree (see Cameron &

Dwyer, 2005; Dekkers & Donath, 1981; Saunders, 1997), and Merlot.org offers a tremendous collection of learning tools, including games, curated and rated by other faculty. You can also find free games at PhET, SeriousGames.net, Education Arcade, TheProblemSite.com, FreeOnlineGames.com (or FOG .com), GameNode.com, and MiniClip.com.

ITunes is another easy way to find out what tools are out there. An iTunes search gives results in a number of categories (songs, artists and albums, apps); it also searches iTunesU where it reveals more traditional course content and lectures. So there may be a lecture, course, or podcast on your subject, but you'll find a range of iPad and iPhone apps for, say, "baroque art" or "The Krebs Cycle."

Significant research shows that providing variety in instructional delivery captures attention and helps students focus on content (Willingham, 2009). PhET at the University of Colorado is an excellent example of alternative content delivery through interactive simulations for science and math. Built on research-based approaches, these simulations are available for free to anyone with an Internet connection. Engaging content can also be delivered in the form of songs, and YouTube abounds in such opportunities. As but one example, see A Capella Science's *Bohemian Gravity!* This video replaces the lyrics of Queen's "Bohemian Rhapsody" with an explanation of string theory.

Step 4: Add Analysis

We want our students to be skeptical of everything they find on the Internet, so bad content can actually be very useful in course settings. Ask students to respond to everything they watch or read. Try using index cards and ask a simple question—for example:

- Find two mistakes in the video.

- Is the video factual, expert judgment, opinion, or satire? How do you know?

- Does the author make assumptions? Which ones?

- How might you rewrite this with a different point of view?

This works equally well for Wikipedia or a Harvard lecture. In class, students trade their index cards with neighbors, who analyze the responses and provide comments, further analysis, or rebuttals. This approach ensures deep engagement rather than passive viewing of online video content.

Examples

Assigning Khan Videos

Gretchen Kreahling McKay, McDaniel College

Gretchen had found that her introductory art history course was not living up to the aspirations she had for it. Art history courses sometimes lend themselves to a pattern of repetition of lecturing and tests, but Gretchen discovered the Khan Academy's Smarthistory website, which includes "more than 1500 videos and essays on art from around the world and across time" (Khan Academy, 2015). Using those materials, she assigns five to seven works of art per class for her students to explore using this site. She then quizzes students on one of them each class to ensure they keep up with the readings and videos. Class time is now often used to play short Reacting to the Past games (see Chapter 7). Big questions, such as, "What does it mean for a civilization to switch from hunting and gathering to farming?" are examined through the lens of the art created during that point in history. For Gretchen, assigning videos meant that class time moved away from lecturing toward active strategies that foster higher-order exploration of traditional art history topics.

Scientific Videos

Rebecca Roberts, Ursinus College

Employing videos for learning can be applied in experiential settings as well. In Rebecca's scientific research laboratory, she engages first-year students through seniors in undergraduate research. To help her students better understand the various ways scientists communicate and think, she assigns readings from the literature, but she also assigns podcasts from The Endocrine Disruption Exchange (TEDX). Students listen to and then develop a bulleted summary that they turn in. During lab team meetings, students then provide informal oral presentations about the scientific issues they discovered through their podcast. By engaging with these podcasts, students access current findings and participate in discourse that models true scientific practice.

Finding Better Content

Janine Bowen, Goucher College

Janine uses key content she has found online to curate material for her organizational behavior courses. She uses actual events, such as the fatal ascent to Mount Everest in 1996, to explore such key course concepts as sunk costs, regency effects, and leadership behavior, among many others. Rather than assigning a reading on an account of these events, she has her students watch excerpts from a *Frontline* video as well as a Harvard Business School seminar on the topic. Hearing from expedition survivors reveals the strong emotions attached to this case, and such first-person narratives make the importance of course concepts palpably clear.

Students Curate Content

Leslie Vincent, Delaware Technical Community College

You don't have to be the one locating and curating all of the content for your courses. Leslie, in her information technology course on network defense and countermeasures, asks students to locate recent articles or video presentations that relate to the assigned readings from the textbook. The materials students locate are then the foundation of brief presentations in class. As Leslie designed this assignment, she expected resistance; however, she found that students were consistently prepared to engage in class each day. They were also better able to discern how course content related to real-world settings. Due to the effectiveness of the student-led presentations and discussion, Leslie often finds herself revising planned lectures on the fly or jettisoning them altogether in favor of richer class discussions.

Adding Analysis

DeDe Wohlfarth, Paul Morgan, Regina Majestro, and Jessie Reed, Spalding University

Four colleagues at Spalding University have developed an ingenious way to use videos and analysis in their abnormal psychology courses. Students had shared that they found it very difficult to truly recognize the disorders under consideration through the material they were provided through readings and lectures. Working collaboratively, these faculty began exploring YouTube and discovered a number of videos displaying human psychopathology. Students were able to observe, and then recognize, a wide range of human behavior. Through this process of viewing and analyzing, they became adept at recognizing normal and abnormal behavior.

Over time, they extended this strategy into new approaches. In some cases, students were placed into groups and asked to rate the behaviors they observed in assigned videos on a continuum from normal to abnormal. They were then asked to discuss their ratings in online chats with other students in the course. These videos have been used as the foundation for in-class debating scenarios where students sought to make diagnoses based on what they had observed in the videos.

Their success with this approach in abnormal psychology has led these faculty to try similar strategies in other courses. For instance, in social psychology, videos of political speeches are used to analyze which persuasive concepts are used to influence an audience. This process of coupling videos with analysis has provided a concrete foundation on which students can learn, collaborate, perform, reflect, and receive feedback.

Key Concepts

- Resist the initial impulse to create all course content yourself. You can save time and enrich learning by capitalizing on what is available online.

- Search the way students do to find what they are using to study. Then create assignments that force students to be skeptical of these materials and analyze them. Critical thinking and information literacy are key skills that employers prize, and they are required for lifelong learning.

- Open online courses, video and lecture databases, and open education resources provide rich opportunities for locating high-quality material for your courses.

- Increase student engagement and preparation for class by varying content delivery strategies. Songs, simulations, and games are among the opportunities that can found and delivered online.

- Create a wiki or an assignment where students can share the videos and podcasts they like and think are useful in learning material in your course.

Further Resources

Entire Courses

Coursera, coursera.org

> Over 1,900 complete courses from Stanford, Penn, Duke, Johns Hopkins, and many other international institutions; for example, the Moscow Institute of Physics and Technology offers courses in Russian.

■ ■ ■

EdX, edx.org

> This Coursera counterpart from Harvard and MIT started with an $85 million investment from those institutions and now includes over 950 courses from the University of California, Berkeley, Georgetown, the University of Texas System, and a large collection of international institutions like the Sorbonne, University of British Columbia, Kyoto University, and the University of Hong Kong.

■ ■ ■

Open Education Database, oedb.org

> Over 10,000 free courses from MIT, University of Michigan, and Johns Hopkins University.

■ ■ ■

University of the People, uopeople.edu

> An accredited, tuition-free, online university that offers bachelor's degrees in business, computer science, and health science.

■ ■ ■

Udacity, udacity.com

> Free courses and nanodegrees mostly in technology and computer science and mostly created by tech companies.

Individual Lectures, Short Explanations and Demonstrations

CrashCourse, youtube.com/user/crashcourse

> A popular YouTube channel organized into courses of well-produced 15- to 18-minute videos about the humanities, math, and science.

■ ■ ■

Khan Academy, khanacademy.org

> One of the world's most visited educational websites (translated into 23 languages), founded by Salman Khan in 2006. With significant support from the Bill and Melinda Gates Foundation and Google, Khan now offers vast numbers of short videos organized into "playlists" in science, arts, humanities, economics, and extensively in math.

■ ■ ■

OpenYale, oyc.yale.edu

> Courses in many subjects from some of Yale's best-known faculty, with complete lectures on iTunes and YouTube.

■ ■ ■

TED, www.ted.com

> Now with over 2,200 talks in their archive, these lectures, almost all under 18 minutes, cover a wide range of the human experience.

■ ■ ■

Utubersity, utubersidad.com

> Eighteen thousand college lectures in both English and Spanish.

■ ■ ■

YouTube, youtube.com

> Mostly cat videos, but this is also where most academic videos are housed. A Google search will find most of this content, and it is an especially good place to look for science demonstrations, animations, and songs.

Open Education Resources

The Endocrine Disruption Exchange (TEDX), endocrinedisruption.org

> Podcasts and other materials that compile scientific evidence regarding low-dose exposure to chemicals that cause health and environmental problems.

■ ■ ■

Google Arts and Culture Project, google.com/culturalinstitute/beta/project/art-project

> A massive collection of high-definition images, virtual tours, exhibitions, and videos.

■ ■ ■

Merlot, merlot.org

> This is a vast curated collection of free open online teaching tools. You can search for edited games, experiments, lesson plans, websites, and more.

■ ■ ■

OnMusic Dictionary, dictionary.onmusic.org

> Launched as the Virginia Tech Multimedia Music Dictionary in 1999, the OnMusic Dictionary has been developed continually since then. It has been used by over 1,500 colleges and universities and is incredibly robust across all musical genres.

■ ■ ■

OpenStax College, openstax.org

> Funded through the work of several foundations, OpenStax at Rice University offers excellent free, open source, and peer-reviewed textbooks in popular subjects, largely core curriculum courses. These textbooks were written by faculty.

■ ■ ■

Open Education Consortium, oeconsortium.org

> Courses, textbooks, and more open source resources from a wide variety of international communities.

■ ■ ■

Open Textbook Library, open.umn.edu

> Free online textbooks in a wide variety of subjects from faculty around the world.

■ ■ ■

The Opera Platform, theoperaplatform.eu

> A rotating collection of high-definition current and free opera performances from the great opera companies of Europe

■ ■ ■

PhET, phet.colorado.edu

> Founded in 2002 by Nobel laureate Carl Wieman and supported by the Hewlett Foundation and the National Science Foundation, the PhET Interactive Simulations project at the University of Colorado Boulder offers hundreds of free interactive math and science simulations.

References

Bakhtin, M. M. (1981). *The dialogic imagination: Four essays by M. M. Bakhtin.* Ed. Michael Holquist, and trans. Caryl Emerson and Michael Holquist. Austin: University of Texas Press.

Beus, J. (2015). *Click probabilities in the Google SERPs.* Sistrix Research. Retrieved from https://www.sistrix.com/blog/click-probabilities-in-the-google-serps/

Cameron, B., & Dwyer, F. (2005). The effect of online gaming, cognition, and feedback type in facilitating delayed achievement of different learning objectives. *Journal of Interactive Learning Research, 16*(3), 243–258.

Dekkers, J., & Donath, S. (1981). The integration of research studies on the use of simulation as an instructional strategy. *Journal of Educational Research, 74*(6), 424–434.

Grinberg, E. (2014). *How some colleges are offering free textbooks.* Retrieved from http://www.cnn.com/2014/04/18/living/open-textbooks-online-education-resources/index.html

Growth in student use of devices for student work, 2012—2014. (2014, August 18). *Chronicle of Higher Education.* Retrieved from http://chronicle.com/article/Growth-in-Student-Use-of/147725/

Hart Research Associates. (2013). *It takes more than a major: Employer priorities for college learning and student success*. Washington, DC: Association of American Colleges and Universities. Retrieved from http://www.aacu.org/sites/default/files/files/LEAP/2013_EmployerSurvey.pdf

Khan Academy. (2015). *Cave paintings, contemporary art and everything in between*. Retrieved from https://www.khanacademy.org/humanities/art-history-basics/beginners-art-history/a/cave-painting-contemporary-art-and-everything-in-between

Saunders, P. M. (1997). Experiential learning, cases and simulations in business communication. *Business Communication Quarterly, 60*(1), 97–114.

Willingham, D. (2009). *Why don't students like school: A cognitive scientist answers questions about how the mind works and what it means for the classroom*. San Francisco, CA: Jossey-Bass.

Chapter 3

Creating Your Own Digital Content

MOST OF US do not write our own textbooks, but we often supplement and customize these materials. Technology makes it easy to mix and match textbook chapters or add content, such as Web pages and articles. In fact, this is often the baseline practice that faculty use in their course sites within learning management systems (LMS). The material that publishers develop is glossy and highly produced, which makes it both convenient and appealing. This is similarly true with digital content. And because the Internet is already full of quality videos, you will rarely be able to compete on production value. If you are going to develop video or audio content for your students, it should be unique, personalized for your students, interactive, and designed for multiple types of learners.

There are several types of recorded media content. For audio, you have simple audio files (i.e., podcasts) as well as feature-rich podcasts, which are often called "chapter podcasts" or "enhanced podcasts." For video, there are screen capture videos, webcam videos, classroom-based lecture capture options, and fully produced, high-quality edited videos. Depending on how the video is employed, the term *vodcast*, or *video podcast*, is sometimes used. Simple lecture capture (either audio or video) allows students to stop, rewind, or move forward. They like it, and it seems to improve learning, but this is not the best use of audio or video technology. The enhanced podcast, with multiple and redundant explanations, is a much better use of these technologies, in the same way that a video of a stage play is not the same as a movie. A lecture capture video is a recorded video of a live lecturer, with all of its flaws, interruptions, and technical failures. Edited lectures (like the TED.com lectures) are better but are typically time-consuming and expensive to create. An enhanced podcast is something you can produce on your own computer and is designed specifically for a computer or a mobile device.

An enhanced podcast is better because you can be *deliberately redundant*, using multiple examples that will appeal to different types of learners. Most of us teach to the middle, so if most students can understand a problem after two examples, we do two examples. We would hesitate to help just a few struggling students with more examples in class when the majority of students seem ready to move on. An enhanced podcast allows you to include all of the examples any student might ever watch, and individual students can skip to the example they like best. You can include easier examples for beginning students and more complex examples for those who are more advanced. Research demonstrates that students do indeed use the ability to skip or repeat sections, and they use these podcasts mostly for the topics that give them trouble (Soong, Chan, Cheers, & Hu, 2006; Lane, 2006; Dey, Burn, & Gerdes, 2009).

An enhanced podcast also allows for different types of pedagogies and examples. We all teach with analogies and examples, but analogies work only if both the teacher and the student understand the specifics of the example. If I like soccer examples but you only speak baseball or dance, my soccer analogies are unlikely to help. An enhanced podcast allows you to be deliberately redundant and explain the same content in multiple ways that appeal to multiple audiences. You could include different examples for premed and prelaw, or mix up your sports examples with fashion or music. You can put in every example you have and still have plenty of time left for more next year.

Research shows that students like the flexibility of mobile content, and they use podcasts and video to study for exams (Fernandez, Simo, & Sallan, 2009; Winterbottom, 2007). Many students (even in 2007!) believe that podcasts are more effective tools than their textbooks and more efficient than their own notes in helping them to learn (Evans, 2007; Luna & Cullen, 2011). Students tend to access recorded lectures just after live lectures and before an exam (Copley, 2007). When presented with both podcasts and readings, more students complete all of the podcasts rather than all of the readings (Luna & Cullen, 2011). All of the hype about students not coming to class seems exaggerated at best, and the current research indicates that even regular lecture capture does not negatively affect student attendance (Bongey, Cizadlo, & Kalnbach, 2006; Brotherton & Abowd, 2004; Dale, 2007; Harrity & Ricci, n.d.). A recent meta-analysis of the scholarship on lecture capture and student attendance confirmed this conclusion (Karnad, 2013).

Note that having a video available and showing one in class are very different things. Students rate professor preparation as one of the most important variables in good teaching. Intensive use of homework raises student ratings, and the use of video in class lowers them (Cochran, Hodgin, & Zietz, 2003). Even before the widespread use of computers and phones to watch videos, students disapproved of spending class time just watching. Showing a video in class today is like paying for your groceries with loose change: the experience may be valid and even important, but you will need to make the argument explicit, and beware of the wrath of those behind you in line.

Here are several questions you'll need to answer before you start your creation and recording process:

- What hardware will you need to ensure a reasonable level of quality?
- Which software will enable you to create the files you need?
- Where will you store your files online so that your students can view and listen to them?
- What do you need to do before you begin recording?
- What steps can you take to ensure your media are accessible by everyone?

The details are in the next section, but once you do a little setup, podcasts are easy to make, and you should make at least a few. Students like to hear the sound of your voice, and appearing on a podcast is a fine opportunity to be a role model and offer support, even if you do not deliver most of the content. Good tutorials, such as Apple's GarageBand support site (Mac Apps – GarageBand, 2016), explain exactly how, but your campus technology support people probably can provide you with additional help. If not, ask a student to spend an afternoon with you.

Step-by-Step Guide

Step 1: Select Appropriate Hardware for Recording

Whether you are recording audio for podcasts or audio for screen capture videos, we advise buying hardware beyond your computer's built-in microphone. The built-in mic is designed to pick up sounds some distance from your computer. As a result, it does a good job of picking up your voice—as well as the sound of air conditioning, voices in the hall, and other ambient sounds, and the addition of white noise to an audio track often makes listeners drowsy.

A good USB headset with a microphone can be purchased for as little as $20, a small investment that will make a significant difference in the quality of the audio you capture. As you might imagine, there are much more expensive USB headsets and USB microphones that will improve the quality of your audio, but most people find the cheaper headsets sufficient. For those wishing to shoot video of themselves in their office, the webcam built into their computer is likely all that is needed for such video recording; however, we again recommend a headset or other USB microphone in conjunction with your webcam.

Step 2: Select Appropriate Software for Recording

There are a number of well-established software options for creating and capturing audio and video on your computer. For Mac users, GarageBand is an excellent choice for both simple and enhanced podcasts. Tool options for Windows users are a little more complex. Windows has a built-in sound recorder; however, it doesn't offer tools for editing if you make a mistake. Windows Movie Maker has some basic tools for editing; however, for basic podcasting from a PC, Audacity, a free, open source tool, is likely the best option. Key among its features are the abilities to cut, copy, and mix multiple tracks of audio. In those ways, it resembles some features of GarageBand; however, you are not be able to create an enhanced podcast with Audacity. Using Audacity in conjunction with Microsoft PowerPoint will provide you with that ability; but note that these Mac and Windows strategies produce enhanced podcasts that function differently from one another.

The most powerful feature of an enhanced podcast is the ability to have articulated segments or chapters. There are two easy ways to do this. Both work on Macs; however, only the second one works for PCs:

- GarageBand for Mac allows you to easily define chapters, with titles and pictures. It also allows for a soundtrack and fading in and out of sound clips.

- PowerPoint also works. Here, each slide can become a single example. Saving as a .ppt file instead of exporting into a movie or other format will preserve the slides as titled segments. You can place Audacity-created audio files within each slide of your PowerPoint, and each slide will serve as a "chapter" for your students.

If you are considering video, there are a number of excellent screen capture software options, and each of them will enable you to record and sync audio while you capture video of the activities on your computer. Such an approach makes it possible to create audio-enhanced PowerPoint presentations and to make software tutorials, such as showing statistics students how to use SPSS. Camtasia is likely the most fully featured such tool, and it's available from TechSmith for both Macs and PCs. A much more affordable option, though containing fewer editing features, is Screencast-O-Matic. This tool is free if you will be making videos that are shorter than 15 minutes, and given what we know about human attention spans (see Stuart & Rutherford, 1978), this is likely a best practice. The full version of Screencast-O-Matic offers unlimited-length recordings as well as richer editing tools.

Step 3: Determine How Your Students Will Access Your Audio and Video Files Online

Once you've created podcasts and videos, the next question is where to put them. Cost and access are the two greatest concerns here. For instance, YouTube and Vimeo are free options for serving your audio and video files; however, controlling access may be more challenging. You can upgrade beyond free accounts to gain more storage and more features regarding privacy and other customizations. Alternatively, you could upload your files into your LMS (e.g., Blackboard, Canvas, Desire2Learn); however, check with your university's LMS administrator before doing so. Some schools discourage this practice as it can slow the performance of the LMS. As a result, some institutions have alternative audio and video hosting platforms. Kaltura and Panopto are two such examples, and Gartner, Inc. produces a yearly report summarizing the market for such tools (Andrews & Preset, 2015). Your best bet is to contact your institution's center for teaching and learning or your learning technologies or information technology team for advice. They will certainly have guidance and best practices to share that are specific to your campus.

Step 4: Complete Key Preparatory Tasks Before Recording

Once you have made the technological decisions, you can confidently move forward with recording. You now have several choices to make regarding preparing to record your podcast or video. Will you just wing it, press Record, and begin? Will you work from a basic outline to keep you on track, or will you create a more detailed script and read it word for word as you record?

Winging it often results in uncomfortable spaces and "ums" as you think through your ideas on the fly. While it's certainly the quickest path to recording, we do not recommend it. If you worked with a production team to create a fully produced, high-quality, edited video, they would most certainly require that you have a detailed script of your presentation, and you would also engage in a process of storyboarding prior to shooting your video. These are the high-end, professional standards and expectations for creating video content, but as you record your own content, you can determine a path that works for you and still produces content of reasonable quality. At a minimum, we recommend that you have an outline from which to speak; however, depending on your content, you may see that you need miniscripts embedded within your outline for items you wish to relate with specificity.

Here are some basic steps for scripting and recording your enhanced podcast:

1. As you think though your content, start with the concept that is most difficult for your students. If you can't explain it in 5 minutes, you probably have too long a segment.

2a. If you're using GarageBand, set up a new file with the title of your content; then create a "first slide of chapter."

2b. To begin recording if you are using PowerPoint, go to the Insert menu and select the Audio submenu. There you should see "Audio from File." If you've created audio with Audacity, this option will allow you to insert the audio into your slide. If you think you can get it right in one take, select "Record Audio" from the Audio submenu and start talking.

3. Then create other slides or chapters that explain the same material in many different ways. Label each of them, perhaps by the type of analogy you will be using. For example, you might label the individual slides "golf analogy," "shoe analogy," "fish analogy," "pet example," "emergency room example," and so on. It is important that each be discrete so students can pick and choose.

Step 5: Consider Accessibility

Another reason to consider creating a fully realized script prior to recording is that it can help you as you take steps to ensure your content is fully accessible to those with disabilities. The U.S. Department of Justice's website provides background on the legal expectations for accessibility, but it is also good practice to ensure that all students, regardless of their disability, can access your content.

Most institutions have a disability resource center that will validate if a student requires an accommodation and may also be able to help you with the creation of a transcript of your media for individual students who need such assistance. We recommend that you reach out to this center to see what services your institution offers. Of course, if you've created a script, you can simply provide that script to a student who is deaf. If you do not have a script, there are other options. Beyond our institutions, a number of companies now offer video captioning, transcription, and subtitling services. Automatic Sync Technologies and 3PlayMedia are two such companies, and they don't require you to provide a script.

Examples

Videos + Textbook + Quizzes

Dara Friedman-Wheeler, Goucher College

A perennial challenge for faculty are students who come to class unprepared to engage in that day's activities because they haven't completed the readings or other assignments. This isn't new to homework that includes audio or video. Dara, who teaches psychology courses, has embraced the flipping model where she provides videos and readings as homework for first exposure. To ensure that students come to class prepared to go deeper into her topics, she gives frequent quizzes in class as well as online to encourage student engagement with the homework and preparation for class.

YouTube Channels

Kendall Kennison, Goucher College

YouTube is certainly ubiquitous, and one strategy for making it easy for students to find your content is to create a YouTube channel—essentially a site within YouTube where all of your videos are listed together and each channel has a unique Web address. Kendall created a YouTube channel of his own lecture series as part of his Music Theory: Introduction to Tonal Practice course. He has heard positive feedback not only from his own students but from students around the globe. By shifting some lecture content outside class, Kendall has been able to increase small group work inside class. There is now more time for student to work with small whiteboards with staff lines on them, exploring key concepts in music theory. Students have expressed enthusiasm for this increasingly active approach in their end-of-term evaluations.

CyberLink YouCam

Paul J. Antonellis Jr., Merrimack College

One of the downsides of audio-enhanced PowerPoint is that students are unable to engage with the range of nonverbal cues you provide as you speak in class. CyberLink YouCam places you *inside* your online PowerPoint, which enables your students to see your facial expressions, hand gestures, and other elements that increase your presence in your presentations. This tool is essentially a presentation and video recording tool. Your face will appear in a small box in one of the corners of your PowerPoint. Paul, who teaches Introduction to Business, uses this tool to create videos that he then posts to a private YouTube channel. Students gain access to the videos through a link in Blackboard. Paul lives in Massachusetts, and when the winter of 2015 brought an unusual number of snow days, he used this approach to keep his course going when class was canceled and then made the most of his time together once class was back in session.

Camtasia

Jack Williams, University of New England

Significant research shows a number of positive effects from frequent quizzing and clear feedback. These range from increased student engagement, to slower forgetting, to better metacognition (Dempster, 1997; Roediger & Karpicke, 2006; Wheeler & Roediger, 1992). The tool Camtasia does more than simple video and screen capturing. It also has assessment tools that can provide built-in quizzing and feedback within the Camtasia video file. Jack, who teaches physiology, has adopted these capabilities. Typically he includes a question or two every few slides within his cardiovascular and respiratory physiology audio-enhanced PowerPoints. These questions reinforce the material just covered and increase student attention throughout the video. Coupling video with assessment and feedback in this way maximizes learning opportunities and increases student preparedness before they come to class.

VoiceThread

Michael Shepard, Goucher College

VoiceThread expands the notion of discussion boards by allowing faculty and students to post their own voice and engage verbally in online discussions. Faculty can post audio, video, and other media types within VoiceThread, and students can then make comments through text, audio, or video. All of these features are built into the app; as long as the students' computers have a microphone, they can engage in VoiceThread discussions. About 15 graduate faculty at Goucher College have adopted VoiceThread. Michael, an anthropologist who teaches for both the master's in cultural sustainability and masters in environmental students programs, has found it to be an enriching way to foster online conversations and ensure students are deeply engaged as they enter his face-to-face classroom.

Crowdsourcing Video

David R. Wessner and Ann M. Fox, Davidson College

You do not have to create or discover all course video content. You can also allow students to create or curate examples. Encouraging students to share their own insights or find relevance is motivating and gives students an important sense of control. You might have students comment on your podcasts or make their own brief videos of how they studied for your exams or found a research topic. Combining those into an indexed podcast of student tips will help your next set of students and also provide valuable feedback for you. Another approach is to have students create two-minute videos explaining complex concepts in their own words. You may find that some are good enough to be incorporated into your course next semester, and over time, you will have a good library.

David (biology) and Ann (English), teach a transdisciplinary course. Students from multiple departments read a range of texts, including scientific articles, plays, and poems, on HIV/AIDS. As a capstone experience within this course, students work in small groups to author a short artist's statement and create a multidisciplinary exhibit based on their vision. These groups then lead the class on a tour of their virtual gallery. Various forms of media are collected, curated, and displayed. David and Ann note that students were not only engaged by such work, they also show true pride in their collections, and many of these materials will find their place in future iterations of the course.

Key Concepts

- There are many tools and options for creating your own online content.

- Enhanced podcasts enable you to be deliberately redundant and share multiple examples to ensure every student has an individual way into your material.

- Invest in a USB headset or USB microphone before you get started to ensure reasonable sound quality.

- Determine where your students will go to access your content online. Your institution likely has a recommendation.

- Create an outline or script prior to recording.

- Keep your podcasts and videos short. Five minutes is a good target, but they should certainly be no more than 15 minutes.

- Find out how your campus supports students with disabilities when it comes to media.

Further Resources

Key Tools

Audacity, www.audacityteam.org

Audacity is free, open source, cross-platform software for recording and editing sounds. Since GarageBand isn't available for the PC, Windows users might find this free tool a great option for recording podcasts.

■ ■ ■

Camtasia, www.techsmith.com

Similar to Screencast-O-Matic, Camtasia performs screen capturing and audio recording tasks. It's editing capabilities are typically considered more robust than Screencast-O-Matic, and it provides some bells and whistles that give its files a higher production value. It's more expensive than its competitor, but it's only a one-time fee (rather than yearly).

■ ■ ■

Cyberlink YouCam, www.cyberlink.com/products/youcam/features_en_US.html

This tool will let you take advantage of your computer's webcam to add a live image of yourself in the corner of a PowerPoint presentation. It will also let you record the resulting feed for placement online later.

■ ■ ■

Garageband, www.apple.com/mac/garageband/

While marketed largely as a music recording and editing tool, Garageband (Mac only) is also a full featured podcast and vodcast creation tool.

■ ■ ■

Screencast-O-Matic, screencast-o-matic.com

This tool enables you to video-record what is taking place on your computer screen in real time with a synced voice-over track. It's available in both a free version and a feature-enhanced pro-version ($15 a year). It's for both Mac and PC.

■ ■ ■

3PlayMedia, 3playmedia.com

This company provides, for a fee, video captioning services that can help make your media more accessible to those with disabilities.

■ ■ ■

VoiceThread, voicethread.com

Extending notions of the traditional discussion board, VoiceThread enables you and students to have an asynchronous online discussion using audio and video files.

Accessibility

Pullin, G. (2009). *Design meets disability*. Cambridge, MA: MIT Press.

Examining a wide range of domains and technologies, this book provides a compelling narrative encouraging design for products made for those with disabilities.

■   ■   ■

U.S. Department of Justice. (2017). *Information and Technical Assistance on the Americans with Disabilities Act*. Retrieved from http://www.ada.gov/

This website provides the background on the legal expectations for accessible media in teaching and learning settings.

References

Andrews, W., & Preset, A. (2015). *Magic quadrant for enterprise video content management*. Retrieved from https://www.gartner.com/doc/3173019/magic-quadrant-enterprise-video-content

Bongey, S. B., Cizadlo, G., & Kalnbach, L. (2006). Explorations in course-casting: Podcasts in higher education. *Campus-Wide Information Systems, 23*(5), 350–367.

Brotherton, J. A., & Abowd, G. D. (2004). Lessons learned from eClass: Assessing automated capture and access in the classroom. *Transactions on Computer-Human Interaction, 11*(2), 121–155.

Cochran, H. H., Hodgin, G. L., & Zietz, J. (2003). Student evaluations of teaching. Does pedagogy matter? *Journal of Economic Educators, 4*(1) 6–18.

Copley, J. (2007). Audio and video podcasts of lectures for campus-based students: Production and evaluation of student use. *Innovations in Education and Teaching International, 44*(4), 387–399.

Dale, C. (2007). Strategies for using podcasting to support student learning. *Journal of Hospitality, Leisure, Sport and Tourism Education, 6*(1), 49–57.

Dempster, F. N. (1997). Distributing and managing the conditions of encoding and practice. In E. L. Bjork & R. A. Bjork (Eds.), *Human memory* (pp. 197–236). San Diego, CA: Academic Press.

Dey, E. L., Burn, H. E., & Gerdes, D. (2009). Bringing the classroom to the web: Effects of using new technologies to capture and deliver lectures. *Research in Higher Education, 50*(4), 377–393.

Evans, C. (2007). The effectiveness of m-learning in the form of podcast revision lectures in higher education. *Computers and Education, 50*, 491–498.

Fernandez, V., Simo, P., & Sallan, J. M. (2009). Podcasting: A new technological tool to facilitate good practice in higher education. *Computers and Education, 53*, 385–392.

Harrity, M. B., & Ricci, A. (n.d.). *How course lecture capture can enhance student learning*. Retrieved from http://www.wpi.edu/Academics/ATC/Collaboratory/News/NERCOMPHandout.pdf

Karnad, A. (2013). *Student use of recorded lectures: A report reviewing recent research into the use of lecture capture technology in higher education and its impact on teaching and learning methods and attendance*. Retrieved from http://eprints.lse.ac.uk/50929/1/Karnad_Student_use_recorded_2013_author.pdf

Lane, C. (2006). *Podcasting at the UW: An evaluation of current use*. Retrieved from https://www.washington.edu/itconnect/wp-content/uploads/2013/12/podcasting_report.pdf

Luna, G., & Cullen, D. (2011). Podcasting and complement to graduate teaching: Does it accommodate adult learning theories? *International Journal of Teaching and Learning in Higher Education, 23*(1), 40–47. Retrieved from http://www.isetl.org/ijtlhe/pdf/ijtlhe854.pdf

Mac Apps – GarageBand. (2016). *Mac apps support. Garageband*. Retrieved from https://www.apple.com/support/mac-apps/garageband/

Roediger, H. L. III., & Karpicke, J. D. (2006). The power of testing memory: Basic research and implications for educational practice. *Psychological Science, 1*, 181–210.

Soong, S.K.A., Chan, L. K., Cheers, C., & Hu, C. (2006). Impact of video recorded lectures among students. In L. Markauskaite, P. Goodyear, & P. Reimann (Eds.), *Who's learning? Whose technology?* (pp. 789–794). Sydney, Australia: Sydney University Press.

Stuart, J., & Rutherford, R.J.D. (1978). Medical student concentration during lectures. *Lancet, 2*, 514–516.

Wheeler, M. A., & Roediger, H. L. III. (1992). Disparate effects of repeated testing: Reconciling Ballard's (1913) and Bartlett's (1932) results. *Psychological Science, 3*, 240–245.

Winderbottom, S. (2007). Virtual lecturing: Delivering lectures using screencasting and podcasting technology. *Planet, 18*, 6-8.

Chapter 4

Instructions and Entry Point

AS FACULTY, WE typically start our course planning with what matters to us: the subject we want students to learn. But since learning begins with motivation and engagement, we need to start our course *designing* by anticipating and understanding the interests and starting place of our students. In fact, this is the essence of pedagogy: taking what matters to students and leading them to what matters to us.

We all have a fantasy of facing rooms full of eager students who want to absorb our hard-earned wisdom. For centuries, being a college professor has been easier than teaching K-12 since college faculty have generally been able to choose their students (or at least the admissions office has), whereas public school teachers face a broader spectrum of talent, preparation, and skill. Congratulations if you have a room full of highly motivated, anxiety-free, and evenly prepared students, but know that most faculty will succeed under these circumstances. Most of the work at Harvard is done by the admissions office. As access to information and free online courses proliferates, knowing more than your students will continue to go down in value.

As phones get smarter, we faculty will need to get smarter too. Online videos that profess content will become more common, but they will remain generic. Knowing your students and their fears and anxieties will increase in value. Teaching starts with understanding your students and knowing what interests and motivates them.

William James argued for the importance of relevance over a century ago. He encouraged those who teach to be aware of students' native interests and to connect those interests to students' existing knowledge (Pajares, 2003). Gagné's (1985) Nine Events of Instruction starts by focusing and connecting with students. So before introducing your students to new content and ideas, use what you know about your students and their interests to create customized entrée into your content that is personally relevant to them and begin to provide scaffolding for their learning

(Hogan & Pressley, 1997; Wilson & Sperber, 2004). You will see increases in their motivation, engagement, and their learning as a result.

Imagine for a moment that you have been asked to teach a required seminar on racial bias to a group of police officers. You are an expert on the subject, and its importance and relevance are obvious to you. You have spectacular credentials and are perhaps the author of countless articles and books on the subject, but will your audience care? You will easily be able to give information to these students, but your real goal is to get them to integrate these new insights into better policing. Your challenge is finding a way to frame what you know in a way that will interest them.

Is there, perhaps, some other place in the lives of these police officers where bias is at work and matters deeply to them? Is there another discussion where they might engage their passions, but also in a safer context than their livelihood or race? In fact, race is almost certainly *the wrong place to start*. Few people want to admit they have a racial bias, and almost no one wants to lose his or her job. Their anxiety and emotion are probably already high given your topic, and they were probably not given a choice about attending this seminar. These hard cases are where pedagogy and design matter most.

Recognizing that engagement precedes learning (Brown, Roediger & McDaniel, 2014), you need to find a safe topic that involves bias where police officers might be willing to have an engaging discussion: perhaps sports teams, footwear, or cars. Does anyone in the room have a preference for either Ford or Chevy trucks? Why? A lively discussion here might provide both the engagement needed and an opening for how bias works in many parts of our lives.

Similarly, a first class on Wagner's *Ring* begins not by writing *Gesamtkunskwerk* on the board, but perhaps with a discussion about who enjoys music with lyrics. Is the relationship between lyrics and music always the same?

Getting students engaged is the first order of business. Then wait. This is the hardest part. In this case, it means waiting for someone to argue that the lyrics and music might not be perfectly aligned, that there might be tension between the two (or in the previous example, that I drive only Fords because my father did). Waiting until the students have reached a place where they need and want to know about your subject is key. Now you can introduce the idea that lyrics use words, which appeal mostly to the head, whereas the music appeals more directly to the heart. If you can do this without any references to Nietzsche or Wagner (which are most likely to kill the conversation and make it seem as if the conversation is about who can top your cultural references), then you might continue to have passionate exchange of views. If you can keep students engaged, then at the end of class, you might suggest that there are some dead Europeans who might provide another framework to continue the discussion. You might even suggest that the students read these authors to see if they can find evidence to bolster or dispute their own argument.

The entry point is therefore the starting place for your students. It is what happens *before* their first encounter with your subject. Students bring lots of assumptions about what they are about to learn, and this is another area to exploit. We know that students learn more when that learning is personal and relevant. Your ability to leverage your knowledge of students is directly relevant to their success. David Ausubel, one of the most important American cognitive scientists, recognized this and highlighted the value of this notion in the following way: "The most important single factor influencing learning is what the learner already knows. Ascertain this and teach him accordingly" (Ausubel, 1968, p. vi). While the ascertaining takes careful thought, it does not generally add significant time to your preparation, and there is a lot of bang for the buck.

One way to do this is through presemester surveying: an online exercise you send to your students before you have even met them. Asking questions about content or attitudes will give you a better understanding of what students already know (or think they know) as they enter your class. This serves as a pretest of sorts. Learning students' prior knowledge influences how you will frame key concepts early in the term and might even have an impact on the starting point for the semester.

You can also ask questions about students' understanding of the software and tools that will be integral to learning during the semester. If students have little experience with them, you might need to locate or develop training materials. If most students have experience, then a buddy system might be used to ensure that the handful of students lacking knowledge have a support structure.

Finally, a presemester survey might include attitudinal questions regarding the course and its content. Knowing if students are collectively anxious about the course or are entering the semester with surprisingly low self-efficacy in the topic area offers information that might influence your pedagogical choices and even faculty-student interactions. Are students worried about how much writing or math might be required in your course? Conversely, a highly motivated and engaged group of students offers other exciting opportunities for instruction. These attitudinal questions also ask how the students imagine using the course's content in the future. How do they see the content as personally relevant? What do they hope to do with the content? Knowing the answers to these questions provides a menu from which aspects of entry points might be constructed that are truly relevant to the students.

Providing Better Instructions

Providing better instructions works at even the most microscopic level: instructions themselves are a pedagogical tool. The way we frame homework or a problem is a vital part of how students are motivated and even for what and how they will learn.

Simply asking students to look for something personal increases motivation and retention. Instead of asking students to "read pages 10 to 20," ask them to find something personally interesting in pages 10 to 20. The more relevant the question is to your subject, the better; for example, you might ask them to identify a relative of who has the psychological characteristics of a person in the chapter. This works in every field:

- Think of an area of global health where this formula might be useful.

- Look at the painting from as many different perspectives as you can.

- Practice your scales in as many different ways as you can imagine.

All of these increase interest, competence, and even basic retention.

We also know that conditional instructions matter. If you teach students that the first step in CPR is that the patient must be lying down, what happens when they confront a patient in a chair? If instead you make a point of saying "usually," "in general," or "normally," your students are less likely to get stuck with a rigid set of rules. Again, this may seem obvious to you as an experienced practitioner, but the research demonstrates that adding this conditional language even to textbooks improves students' ability to better contextualize information later (Langer, 1989).

While the Internet offers almost limitless online content, none of it is specific to your students. Only you know (or can discover) the right entry point that will stimulate them. Use e-mail or other forms of e-communication (see Chapter 10) to offer short motivational introductions to readings, study questions, encouragement, connections, additional thoughts, and further explanations.

Teaching with uncertainty also seems to create more room for a personal contribution. Ken Bain (2004) discovered that teachers who taught the uncertainty of the discipline were more memorable and inspiring: students felt that if the prevailing theory had changed before, it might change again, and they might be the ones to do it. Teachers who insist that these are the facts their students must learn first remove that possible agency.

Asking students if it is possible to develop a nasal contraceptive will not spawn much creative inquiry. Students will assume there is a right answer and maybe even feel some anxiety before answering, but a question that asks *how* they could create a nasal contraceptive, or what would be required for a nasal contraceptive to work, offers space for everyone to explore.

Questions that avoid simple answers have been found to foster greater critical thinking as well as gains in learning. Shim and Walczak (2012), for instance, found that asking challenging, complex questions resulted in student self-reported gains as well as measurable improvements in student critical thinking. In addition, the frequency with which faculty asked challenging questions in class has a positive impact on students' perceptions of their critical thinking improvements. Similarly, Mills (1998) employed a questioning technique termed *provocation*. Here, the teacher's approach is to provoke students to think by making connections to their personal lives. This approach resulted in greater student engagement and learning, which also has the potential to promote abstract thinking.

Assignments are, of course, learning events, so these same notions should be applied to crafting assignments and their instructions. (See Chapter 6.) Assignments that demand analysis rather than description or simple recall have been found to promote critical thinking (Tsui, 2002), so assignment instructions that suggest complexity, evoke prior learning, and take into account what you know about your students is a collective best practice. These principles can be employed across numerous types of assignments, including traditional reading assignments.

Creating a safe space for students to think about something that matters to them, a playful opening gambit, or even simply conditional or motivational instructions are all entry points. The goal is to generate interest, excitement, and engagement that can then be directed.

Step-by-Step Guide

Step 1: Understand What Matters to Your Students

Get to know your students. If you work in a face-to-face environment, you and the infrastructure that supports you are expensive, but it also affords you the ability to understand what motivates or frightens your students.

This information is unavailable to the cheap (or free) talking head online. It is an advantage you must leverage.

E-mail, text, Twitter, wikis, discussion boards, Facebook, or any of the ever-developing forms of social media also provide you with a meaningful way to personalize and localize content for your students. Ask them which social media platform is current and make a determined effort to try to learn this way of thinking (See Chapter 10 for more). It will give you insight into how they process (more entry points!), increase your credibility, and demonstrate that you are open to learning new things (something you are trying to model for them). It is said that "Facebook is for old people," but it is probably something with which you should be familiar. Learning one platform will also help you with the next one. If you decide Instagram is better than Facebook, you will have some basis for comparison. And despite what students say, most students still peek at Facebook more than they like to admit. Find a student or an even younger relative to help you.

Step 2: Create an Entry Point

Create an exercise or question that is focused on something that will matter to your students. A dramatic story can work, especially if you can take something they assume to be true and then turn it around. Here are two examples:

- *Freshman Writing or Linguistics 101.* Write "Shut the #@&* up" on the board. You will now have full engagement in your class, and students will stop looking at Facebook for a few moments. Quickly, then, ask them how the word "#@&*" functions in this sentence. Encourage everyone to participate and propose a theory. This discussion should provide you with a basis to explain why your class will be essential and fun.

- *Wittgenstein's Family Resemblance and Fuzzy Concepts.* Begin in this way: "Here is picture of my family [or a picture of any other family]. Can you find the common relationships between my children and my other relatives?" Note that any two members of the group might share only one characteristic. Some share the shape or color of eyes and others the shape of their nose. Let this go on for a while and let students come to the conclusion that there is not a single defining feature. Prod them further: "Can you see how this might be a useful concept? Where else might this be applied?" Once they have articulated some potential usefulness and applications, ask them to read Wittgenstein's Philosphical Investigations for the next class and write a short paragraph on how this idea might be used to define a set of things that are related in this way—for example, "How might you define the category of games using this tool?" Then once students are preparing to leave at the end of class, you might add, "By the way, all of my children are adopted." Leave them to ponder this contradiction. It may prove an additional motivation to do the reading carefully.

Step 3: Turn What Matters to Them into What Matters to You

This is the hard step. It often requires waiting for the right opening and not being too eager to get to your content. Engagement is fundamentally more rewarding for learners if they find what is being discussed as personally relevant.

Step 4: Make Instructions Personal, Conditional, and Motivating

If your instructions simply are directions with the assignment or pages to read for each class, you are missing an easy opportunity to spark the motivation and learning of your students. Here are some simple modifications:

- "Find something interesting to you."
- "Look for different perspectives."
- "Stop, linger, and imagine."
- "This could be the best solution" versus "This is the best solution."
- "How could you design clothing that dissolves only if you are in love?" versus "Could you design clothing that dissolves only if you are in love?"
- "Usually you want the patient lying down" versus "First, get the patient to lie down."
- "The current theory is . . ." versus "This is . . ."

Step 5: Design Reading Assignments

If you want students to read more carefully or fully when you assign readings, consider the following strategies:

- Analyze the opening in class before you assign the reading.
- Tell students in advance why they are reading, and share why the ending is important.

- Ask students to look for a point of view, mistake, bias, or favorite passage as they read.

- E-mail students between classes about specific passages.

- Encourage students along the way using Twitter or e-mail.

- Require students to reflect on the entire reading in writing before class.

- Give a reading quiz before every class.

- Structure class activities or assessments to reward those who did all of the reading.

Step 6: Consider Reading Summary Sites

Consider how you might leverage reading summary sites (such as SparkNotes, WikiSummaries, CliffsNotes, PinkMonkey, GradeSaver, enotes, Bibliomania, and many others) in your courses. Your students are aware that the Internet contains summaries of most things, and they will find their own ways to use these shortcuts. Here are ideas for how to guide them in using summaries in meaningful ways and to craft assignments where the answers won't be easily found in these summaries:

- Ask students to discuss a famous book that is also a movie. (Harry Potter should be in your repertoire.)

- Convince students to read a few chapters first without using summary sites. Ask them to focus on the author's tone, texture, style, sentence structure, or position, which are less likely to be discussed on summary sites.

- Ask students to internalize the experience in a specific way: "Do you imagine how the characters look?" "Do you take notes?"

- Ask students to read the summary first and discuss how knowing the summary changes the experience of reading the book.

- Ask students to compare the summary sites for a single work.

- Create an assignment that is more about style or character than plot.

- Ask an unusual question that cannot be answered by the summary.

Examples

Google Forms

Gina Riggio, Delaware Technical Community College

Surveys can be used to learn more about your students, and Google Forms provides a free way to administer surveys even before the semester begins. Gina, a general biology instructor, does just that. At the beginning of the semester, she gives her students preclass surveys to learn about their interests and their confidence in their ability to do science. As the semester progresses, she uses Google Forms again, now to collect information from students regarding their perceptions of test readiness. She uses that information to form and schedule small group help sessions as the semester progresses.

Google Drive

Andrew Mills, Otterbein University

Many online tools, when used creatively, have the potential to make students' thinking transparent, and Google Drive is one such tool. Andrew teaches Greek and Roman philosophy. He is fortunate in that all of his course texts are in the public domain. He loads those texts into Google Drive and asks students to annotate, interpret, and provide commentary. All students can see all of the annotations, and sidebar conversations are generated within Google Drive as students debate the meaning of various textual elements. The students evoke other Web resources (e.g., wikis, videos) as part of this process. Andrew can view these discussions prior to class and see which passages are highly debated and which have general consensus. He can form lesson plans for the upcoming class based on student interest as well as their misconceptions.

Entry Points for Deep Learning

Nicolas W. Proctor, Simpson College

Well-designed discovery activities can serve as entry points for deep learning, but the rub lies in the structure and in meaningful activities. Nicolas, who teaches history, has designed a "making history" entry point that has both of these characteristics.

Nicolas found that students struggle with how historical facts and historical interpretation interact, and he designed an entry point into those challenges where students explore "historical facts" about a romantic relationship and its eventual breakup. Each "fact" is printed on an individual index card, and five or six fact cards are given to small groups of students, with each group receiving different facts. The students discuss what they would like to know about the breakup and then, based on the facts they have, share ideas and develop a hypothesis. Students soon make their first realization: a handful of facts is not enough to verify their hypothesis. As the activity progresses, students learn that each fact is time-stamped and recognize that chronology is important because it may reveal casual relationships.

Nicolas soon reveals that the facts are from a variety of sources, including some with clear self-interest. Students see the role that bias might be playing and quickly question the "facts" provided by those sources. As the activity concludes, students recognize that sources can be problematic, that more than five or six facts are needed to verify a hypothesis, and that the range of biases might color the facts as presented. One of these biases are the students' own personal experiences with breakups, and they come to understand the influence those experiences have on their interpretations as well. These are important conclusions that those engaging in historical inquiry must recognize, and the entry point of a student breakup enables Nicolas's students to embrace these foundations as they begin the real work of the course.

Entry Points into Sensitive Subjects

DeDe Wohlfarth, Spalding University

When you teach courses that contain topics that might foster strong responses from students (e.g., biology, political science, women's studies), creativity and sensitivity in your entry points are imperative. DeDe and her colleagues teach human sexuality. Their courses foster critical thinking around several key issues, including how sexual behavior and values are affected by gender, sexual orientation, religion, socioeconomic status, and other factors. Early in 2015, for example, Kentucky's governor argued that the state's ban on gay marriage should be upheld because both gay and straight people are barred from marrying others of the same gender. Therefore, the ban is equal to all and not discriminatory (Wolfson, 2015). Sometimes current events provide an exceptional learning opportunity; however, the entry point requires thought.

The news story about gay marriage appeared several weeks into the semester, and the students had already developed collegial relationships built on the classroom etiquette policy outlined in her syllabus. With that dynamic in place, DeDe began by asking her students to post a response online to two questions. The first was simply a statement of belief: Should Kentucky endorse same-sex marriage? The second was more challenging and spoke to the heart of the focus of the course: How do your demographics and values influence your answer to the first question?

By asking for a post online, students were able to reflect and carefully craft a response for their peers. Responses were personally relevant and provided an opportunity for discussion about the core focus of the course. In addition, DeDe was able to review student perspectives and prepare for class with a full awareness of the landscape of views that would be present in the next class. DeDe also notes that if this had been the first entry point into the topic at the beginning of the semester, she would have had the students e-mail their responses directly to her. Establishing rapport and standards of etiquette for engaging in challenging topics is needed for successful class or online discussions of sensitive issues.

Using Technology for Questioning

Susanna Throop, Ursinus College

Posing open questions can be a difficult task to perform on the fly in the classroom; however, there are technological approaches that enable both you and your students to pose, reflect, and respond to meaningful, challenging questions. Susanna, who teaches history and interdisciplinary courses, asks her students to find items online that relate to her courses a few times during the semester. Students then post the link within a blog and write about its relevance to the course. The class is charged with reading and responding to the posts online. Susanna crafts provocative discussion questions and posts them to these blogs, and when the class meets, students in small groups discuss the most interesting of the posts, using her discussion questions as prompts. The result is an activity that oscillates between course content and real-world examples with discussion that is guided by thoughtful, well-formed questions.

Assignment Instructions

Laura Tejada, Northeastern Illinois University

The best assignments promote more than simple recall by requiring students to grapple with the content in challenging, personal ways. Laura teaches counseling and has standardized "content reflections" for required readings, videos, and other homework assignments. These writing reflections have four prompts, all of which ask the students to reflect on prior knowledge and their personal interests:

- What was new to you in the assignment?
- What were you already familiar with?
- What was of particular interest to you, and why?
- What would you like to learn more about?

These questions require higher-order thinking, such as analysis and synthesis. This reflective approach makes it clear which students are doing the reading, and it also shows Laura what content requires remediation or additional coverage in class.

Key Concepts

- Discover what your students care about and what they already know about your topic. Try a survey before your course begins.
- Use that knowledge to engage your students and then leverage that engagement. Learning, pedagogy, and good teaching start with what matters to students.

- Develop entry points that are personal and specific to your students but then lead to your content. Go as far away as you need to in order to start with engagement.

- Pose questions that allow for exploration rather than limit student responses to brief, factual answers.

- Design instructions that will motivate students to read more deeply or see the value of your assignments.

Further Resources

Cashin, W. E. (1995). Answering and asking questions. *IDEA Center, 31.* Retrieved from http://ideaedu.org/wp-content/uploads/2014/11/Idea_Paper_31.pdf

This brief paper provides specific, practical advice regarding how to ask questions in class to foster rich discussion. The heart of the model is a question–answer–reaction approach that can be used across all disciplines.

■ ■ ■

Dennen, V. P. (2004). Cognitive apprenticeship in educational practice: Research on scaffolding, modeling, mentoring, and coaching as instructional strategies. In D. H. Jonassen (Ed.), *Handbook of research on educational communications and technology* (2nd ed., pp. 813–828). Mahwah, NJ: Erlbaum.

Cognitive apprenticeship is a set of social-constructivist instructional strategies that aim to engage students in authentic learning experiences designed to develop their range of cognitive skills. This chapter provides guidance and direction regarding how to employ this approach.

■ ■ ■

Free Book Notes. (2017). *Free book notes, Cliff Notes, summaries, and study guides.* Retrieved from http://www.freebooknotes.com/

One of many tools your students are using these days. This site provides summaries, study guides, and other resources for over 40,000 books. As the name implies, access to these tools is free.

■ ■ ■

James, W. (2008/1899). *Talks to teachers on psychology: And to students on some of life's ideals*. Rockville, MD: Arc Manor.

Learn from the master. Here, William James provides guidance for faculty and students that is still incredibly relevant today. You'll find that he shares his entry points to connecting with students.

■ ■ ■

Maxwell, M. (2015). *The Socratic Method research portal*. Retrieved from http://www.socraticmethod.net/

This site provides an expansive compendium regarding how to employ the Socratic method. It results from over three decades of research and practice into this domain.

References

Ausubel, D. P. (1968). *Educational psychology: A cognitive view*. New York: Holt, Rinehart, & Winston.

Bain, K. (2004). *What the best college teachers do*. Cambridge, MA: Harvard University Press.

Brown, P. C., Roediger, H. L., III, & McDaniel, M. A. (2014). *Make it stick: The science of successful learning*. Cambridge, MA: Belknap Press of Harvard University Press.

Gagné, R. (1985). *The conditions of learning and theory of instruction* (4th ed.). New York: Holt, Rinehart & Winston.

Hogan, K., & Pressley, M. (Eds.). (1997). *Scaffolding student learning: Instructional approaches and issues*. Cambridge, MA: Brookline Books.

Langer, E. J. (1989). *The power of mindful learning*. Cambridge, MA: Da Capo Press.

Mills, J. (1998). Better teaching through provocation. *College Teaching, 46*(1), 21–25.

Pajares, F. (2003). William James: Our father who begat us. In B. J. Zimmerman & D. H. Schunk (Eds.), *Educational psychology: A century of contributions* (pp. 41–64). Mahwah, NJ: Erlbaum.

Shim, W., & Walczak, K. (2012). The impact of faculty teaching practices on the development of students' critical thinking skills. *International Journal of Teaching and Learning in Higher Education, 24*(1), 16–30. Retrieved from http://www.isetl.org/ijtlhe/pdf/IJTLHE1128.pdf

Tsui, L. (2002). Fostering critical thinking through effective pedagogy: Evidence from four institutional case studies. *Journal of Higher Education, 73*(6), 740–763.

Wilson, D., & Sperber, D. (2004). Relevance theory. In L. R. Horn & G. Ward (Eds.), *The handbook of pragmatics* (pp. 607–632). Oxford: Blackwell.

Wolfson, A. (2015, March 31). Kentucky. No one can marry same sex, ban not biased. *Louisville Courier-Journal*. Retrieved from http://www.courier-journal.com/story/news/politics/2015/03/30/kentucky-one-can-marry-gays-gay-marriage-ban-biased/70684832/

Chapter 5

Online Exams to Improve Student Preparation for Class

IF YOU HAVE the recurring dream of teaching naked (literally), perhaps you also have the very sweet dream of your students all arriving for class early, having eagerly read the material, and prepared for discussion. Go back to sleep. That is a fantasy. It is, however, possible to create conditions that will encourage your students to be more prepared for class.

Chapter 4 discussed the importance of creating a motivational entry point for your students. If you can truly convince students that the material is relevant to them, they are more likely to prepare. Chapter 6 will provide suggestions for creating microassignments that require students to prepare something that can then be used in a class activity. Students are also more likely to prepare for discussion or other classroom activities if they understand the goals (Chapters 1 and 4) and have an explicit assignment (Chapter 6). This will also motivate students to show up to class.

Students, of course, are also motivated by points or grades. This chapter suggests strategies for developing very brief (5 to 10 questions) preclass online quizzes. We know that retrieval improves learning, so low-stakes assessment, early and often, is also a learning tool. Including higher-level learning outcomes in these weekly assessments will provide both you and your students with feedback on the progress toward what really matters. Your learning management system (LMS) makes these easy to create, distribute, and grade. Online exams offer a simple way to provide a little more incentive to prepare for class (a small number of points toward the final grade), a way to judge how much of the material students have understood, and a self-administered retrieval and learning tool. And it might be your dream come true.

Grades, Thinking, and Learning

Students need to develop both intrinsic motivation and tools to create better habits. Ambition or motivation alone will not be enough. Not falling behind, preparing for class, and reviewing material before class are good habits that few students have. A short online test before every class can condition students to all three, but they will need some incentive. You want the exams to be low stakes but still worth doing. Ten percent of the final grade may be enough to prevent anyone from skipping this and losing an entire letter on the final grade. Use points or grades, but focus on how they are cumulative so that missing an individual quiz is not going to hurt any student.

Your grading scheme also needs to signal that these are diagnostic or formative assessments. Give partial credit liberally, and make sure each quiz has some of the easiest and hardest material. These exams should also be a way for students to build confidence through success while also pondering the most complicated thinking in your course.

One way to keep students focused on the big picture is to keep reminding them how the material you are presenting relates to the bigger course goals, and share research showing that quizzing before each class results in better student performance on more heavily weighted tests, like midterms and finals (Geist & Soehren, 1997; Zaromb & Roediger, 2010). In other words, frequent quizzing has the dual benefit of both motivating students and improving their learning. There is more too. Roediger, Putnam, and Smith (2011, p. 1) summarize 10 research-based benefits of frequent, low-stakes testing. Such testing:

- Aids retrieval and retention.

- Identifies gaps in knowledge.

- Causes students to learn more when they study.

- Produces better organization of knowledge.

- Improves transfer of knowledge to new contexts.

- Can facilitate retrieval of material that was not tested.

- Improves metacognitive monitoring.

- Prevents interference from prior material as new material is learned.

- Provides feedback to instructors.

- Encourages students to study.

The only downside to frequent quizzing is the time it takes to create and grade the quizzes themselves. Ultimately, low-stakes, preclass quizzes are a safe way for students to try out the implications of what they are learning. Applying material to new contexts provides an opportunity for recall and motivates students to stay engaged with preclass assignments. This enables class time to be as meaningful as possible.

Here is an example of a question about contracts for artists. Motivating artists to prepare for a class on legal and tax issues is a challenge. This question both reviews the basic material and provides some motivation to come to class.

Application Level Question

The following are all true statements. Which are the best reasons for you to issue, negotiate, and sign a contract (or letter of agreement) before you agree to sell work or services? Check all that apply. Partial credit is available.

NOTE: *"Yes" and "no" indicate what I think are the best answers along with the percent of students who have agreed with me. These are all, of course, my judgments, and like all other judgments, there are arguments for and against each.*

A. A contract helps all parties understand what is expected. (Yes = 50%)

B. Without a contract, you can be sued for damages. A contract allows you to limit your liability. (Yes = 96%)

C. You can break a contract if both parties agree. (No = 80%)

D. You can always amend a contract later if you change your mind. (No = 62%)

E. A "tech rider" specifies what technical requirements you might need. (No = 63%)

F. A contract will help you think about all of the extra charges (e.g., shipping, transportation, parking) for which you might want the client to pay. (Yes = 88%)

G. A contract will help ensure you will get paid. (Yes = 92%)

H. Contracts are often long and boring. (No = 80%)

This question signals several things. Labeling questions with Bloom (1956) levels helps students understand that there are higher levels of thinking and that we want to move to these higher levels. This question will require more than just recall; it also requires judgment. Some students (especially those still in the binary thinking stage common in the first year) will call this "subjective," but in fact, this is the first step in moving toward a more relative view of knowledge and the world (Perry, 1970). "It depends" is the right answer for most questions. Asking students to select "best" answers pushes them to think more about their own thinking.

These sorts of questions are hard to write. While not as difficult for students as having to create their own arguments in writing, these questions can help students break down problems; immediate feedback may further stimulate student critical thinking. They can be graded automatically and that gives you time for other things. These questions are mostly diagnostic, so it is most important that they get at crucial issues and guide student thinking. If students want to argue about the answers in class, that is fantastic. Let them. Think about the class discussion that might follow this new approach. Furthermore, asking students to select from a series of true statements (instead of finding the true information mixed in with the false) also makes it harder to cheat. Siri and Google are good at seeking out facts, but they have no ability to sort answers based on context and judgment.

Just-in-Time Teaching

This approach can be seen as an extension of just-in-time teaching (JiTT) developed in the Physics Department at Indiana University-Purdue University Indianapolis to prepare students for more active classroom participation (Novak, Gavrin, Christian, & Patterson, 1999). Initially students responded to online assignments that were due "just in time" before class. Making all online exams due an hour before the next class will give you time to adjust class to meet the students' needs.

This is also why we are less concerned about the answers where students disagree with what we see as the correct responses. In the example above, the JiTT feedback gives us the opportunity to emphasize in class that a contract is useful for clarifying expectations (something that few students seem to have understood from the reading).

JiTT assignments are designed to motivate students in accordance with desired learning objectives. Some prefer warm-up questions over exams. Initially JiTT students were sent three questions before each class, two on key principles and a third that was open ended. Responses were due two hours before class.

Why Multiple Choice?

If you have plenty of time and only a few students, short written answers will better stimulate your students and increase their critical thinking skills. For most of us, however, time is still a limited commodity. Multiple-choice tests are easy to make, reusable, and scalable for large classes, and the LMS allows many options for feedback, format, question randomization, and further support. Since they can be graded automatically, these tests provide instant feedback and encouragement. This may seem a minor positive, but it allows you to deploy these tests 24 hours a day, which means that even while you are sleeping, your students can be receiving positive feedback. Using multiple-choice exams before every class encourages better preparation for class and provides you and your students with constant feedback.

Timed tests can add stress, of course, but used thoughtfully, they can also demonstrate the speed of recall that is required in many fields like medicine, foreign languages, and music. Timed tests make it hard for students to look up everything on the Internet. Consider some moderate time pressure for information where you really do want memorization.

Consider the opposite strategy too. Students also vary greatly in their ability to use the Internet to find reliable information. This is an essential life skill, and a multiple-choice quiz that allows, or even requires, a little searching, can be good practice using Google paired with recall.

Students are generally confused about what you want them to memorize and why. (You're SO mean!) These exams can help you make it clear what needs to be readily available (or memorized) and what can be searched for in between clients or patients. Most of us take this distinction for granted. We know that if we are giving a conference paper or testifying in a case on a particular subject, we should know a few other names and dates just in case we get a question, but we don't need to memorize the rest of the Internet. How do we decide? If you can clearly articulate this difference and explain it to your students ("This example is rare. You can look it up if you forget, but you will need this other example every day"), they will be much more likely to memorize the material you want them to. Think about how courtroom laptops have changed the work of lawyers; precedent is still vital, but it is very difficult to prepare for every situation, and the ability to find precedent from a database has become a more important skill in the computer age. The types of questions you ask, the conditions of the testing, and how you label the questions can help train your students in all of this.

The real world is open book. Try to design exams that mimic the combination of searching and analyzing that most jobs now demand. Even multiple-choice tests can help your students prepare for a world where the Internet will always be at hand if you design questions that make use of or analyze something that might be found there.

Testing on content sends an implicit message that knowing content is sufficient, that knowledge comes in discrete units, and that the important (or at least measurable) things are black and white. If you want to emphasize that knowledge is a starting point and that argument, insight, and persuasion are where the added value is, write multiple-choice questions that emphasize the message that the important things in life (like intellectual arguments) are messy.

Asking questions that have debatable answers sounds like a recipe for trouble, but there are two ways to manage the resulting controversy: by asking lots of questions and awarding partial credit, you decrease the stakes for each question, and students will soon realize that no single answer will affect their grade. José also tells students they can argue about every question in class, and if he is convinced, he will change the graded answers for the following year.

Feedback

Feedback is integral to the learning process (Chickering & Gamson, 1987), and most LMSs also allow you to give feedback on individual questions. In this way, student mistakes become learning opportunities (see Chapter 9). With most online testing tools, feedback and subsequent questions can be linked, so it is possible that the answer to one question can determine the next question. A student who is doing poorly can get the same type of question again. (This is, of course, how computer games respond.) The point is that feedback is part of the learning cycle and also needs to be a part of the assessment strategy.

Allowing students to write their own feedback to questions can increase engagement and also help clarify their thinking. A discussion board post on a question might start with your feedback and invite argument or simply ask the students why each answer is relevant.

There are, of course, other ways to reach the same goal. Ask students to post strategies for solving problems on the course website, make their own video summary, or post on the course discussion board. Technology provides new ways for both you and students to prepare for class.

Step-by-Step Guide

Step 1: Stimulate Harder Thinking

As you begin to craft your low-stakes, preclass quizzes, keep in mind that they are intended to be diagnostic and formative assessments that foster additional grappling with course content prior to the in-class experience.

Your quizzes are part of the learning process, not a summative measurement of it. While you want your questions to be fair and defensible, you should also build in appropriate challenge and even ambiguity. These questions can then serve as starting points for in-class discussions and activities. Your goal is not to create trick questions, but you are trying to stimulate your students to think harder.

Step 2: Select Controversial Content

It will be easier to write good questions if you start by picking a reading or content area where there is some contradictory evidence or at least some evidence that is more important. Another way to start is to look back to your entry point or instructions for this material and make some connection. Does your entry point provide a particular lens that you might use to evaluate the usefulness of the content? If you asked students to look for a bias or particular argument, which evidence best supports their discovered bias?

Step 3: Use a Bloom Format

Here is a basic format for multiple-choice questions:

- Question (Bloom level). Labeling with a Bloom level helps students know they need to do more than just recall.

- "The following are all true statements." This will prevent students from simply looking for true statements on Google.

- "What would be the best way to improve X?" (Application). Asking for the "best" way requires judgment. Students will initially think this is just another version of "figure out what the professor wants," but if you do it often, discuss in class, and are clear about how these judgments are made, you will be teaching students to think.

- "Check all that apply. Partial credit is available." This is an easy way to lower the stakes and demonstrate that there are often multiple good answers.

Paired questions are especially good for getting students to have to evaluate which evidence supports which argument. Here is a sample:

Analysis Level Question 1

Which of the following statements, all of them true, are most likely to be used by Democrats to support government policy? Check all that apply. Partial credit is available.

A. Government spending creates jobs.

B. Tax cuts stimulate job creation.

C. Uncertainty is bad for business

D. A large debt can hurt the economy.

E. Government spending cuts can hurt the economy.

Analysis Level Question 2

Which of the following statements, all of them true, are most likely to be used by Republicans to support government policy?

Check all that apply. Partial credit is available.

A. Government spending creates jobs.

B. Tax cuts stimulate job creation.

C. Uncertainty is bad for business

D. A large debt can hurt the economy.

E. Government spending cuts can hurt the economy.

You will need to pick an appropriate Bloom level. Here are sample questions by Bloom level:

Knowledge Questions (recall and recognition)

- Which of the following are important theories of X?

- Identify which of the following are symptoms of X.

Comprehension Questions (understanding examples, meaning, and extrapolating)

- Which of the following is an example of X?

- Which of these are summaries of X?

Applications Questions (organize or solve with new situations or terms)

- Which of the following Y might be most useful to X?

- What would be the best way to improve X?

Analysis Questions (breaking apart, compare and contrast, generalizing)

- Which of the following statements from article X are fact, and which are opinion?

- Which of the following facts (all true) are most relevant for the argument X?

Synthesis Questions (combining elements into a new patterns)

- Which of the following statements about X (all true) would be best evidence in SUPPORTING argument Y?

- Which of the following are restatements of the thesis in article X from a person who disagrees?

- Which of the following develop the thesis of X further?

Evaluation Questions (presenting and defending judgments)
- Which of the following statements about X (all true) would be the best evidence in REFUTING argument Y? (Use the same set of answers to choose from as were used in the SUPPORTING question.)

- Which of the following represents the strongest argument for why . . .?

- Which critique of X is most compelling?

Step 4: Write the Answers

This is the hardest part. Writing good answers is usually fairly easy, so you will need practice to write answers that are true but not good. For each question, write three or four answers that are not as good as the best one. You will have to write more answers than you need, and then abandon some. Remember your goal is to stimulate harder thinking and to get some feedback about how your students are processing your content. You will probably want to start with answers that are distinctly good and bad: in other words easier cognitively for your students. In each quiz, however, you will want some questions with answers that are more obvious and others where the answers are more controversial. These harder and perhaps arguable answers will challenge your students, give you more insight into their thinking, and probably give you a starting point for class discussion. Part of critical thinking is understanding that the answer to many questions begins with, "it depends."

It also helps to remind yourself and your students that these problems are both formative and diagnostic. The motivation is not to assign grades or label students (the points you award end up being mostly for completion), but to stimulate their thinking and give you better ways of refining that thought in class.

One way to make writing the answers easier is to use quotes from the reading. Instead of making all of the answers true statements, you can have all of the answers be a quote from the reading—for example:

- "Which of the following statements in the reading is good evidence for the thesis?"

- "Which of the following quotes from the novel provide the best insight into the mind of the main character?"

Examples

Online Quizzing Before Class

Sarah Lovern, Concordia University Wisconsin

Leveraging your institution's LMS can make the process of administering quizzes much easier, and there are a number of ways to use online quizzing to ensure students engage with homework in meaningful ways before class. Sarah, who teaches anatomy and physiology, often leads lab sections that require students to come to class prepared for hands-on activities. Sarah assigns prelab quizzes that are not timed and are open notes with the goals of ensuring students are well acquainted with key concepts and material as they begin lab activities. Before assigning these quizzes, it was clear that the majority of the students had not completed the prelab readings. Now, as students work through labs or identify anatomical components, she often hears students reference the preclass work: "Oh, that was on the prelab." Everything is graded by the LMS, so very little additional work is required with each passing semester, and students are far more prepared for hands-on work than before.

Feedback Through the LMS

Jason Cherubini, Goucher College

While preclass quizzes within your university's LMS are a great way to ensure students complete various types of homework, your LMS also has features that capitalize on teachable moments as students take these quizzes. Jason, who teaches accounting, uses LMS quizzing; however, he also uses the feedback capabilities within the LMS quizzing tools to explain why correct answers are correct and why incorrect answers are incorrect. This immediate feedback helps explain and clarify as students are in the act of recalling and processing.

Using Bloom in Quizzing

Marcia L. Cordts, University of Iowa

Being cognizant of Bloom's levels as you craft quiz questions can ensure that you ask questions that move beyond facts and figures and inspire critical thinking and synthesis. Marcia, who teaches microbiology, crafts quiz questions that are aimed at Bloom's level 3 and above. She recognizes that most students are conditioned through past experiences to see quizzes as tests of recall, and she finds that her students struggle with the critical thinking she hopes to develop. Recognizing this, she has developed a "no-stress quizzes" approach that gives students two opportunities to succeed on each quiz. Her strategy requires her students to take an in-class multiple-choice quiz with six questions. After they take the quiz, they are provided with a summary of which questions they answered correctly and which ones they missed. Students then have an additional week to respond to their graded quiz. For questions they answered correctly, they must describe why the right answer was right. For questions they missed, they must explain why their answer was wrong and justify the correct choice. During this second phase, students are allowed to discuss their answers with other students, but the ultimate response has to be in their own words. Through her no-stress approach, student engagement with higher-order Bloom questions is maximized, and Marcia's students can still earn a perfect quiz score for their efforts.

Just-in-Time Teaching

Robert Talbert, Grand Valley State University

The key notion in just-in-time teaching (JiTT) is that students' work before class has an effect on what takes place when they are in class with their professor. Math faculty at Grand Valley State University have adopted this approach as central to their flipped strategy.

As an example, Robert teaches calculus. He and colleagues have developed their own textbook (http://scholarworks.gvsu.edu/books/10/) and their own YouTube Channel (http://bit.ly/GVSUCalculus) that provides brief lectures (all under 15 minutes) on various topics. Students work through structured preparatory activities prior to class (for an example, go to http://goo.gl/Z8SXnO). Google Forms are then used to collect student responses to activities, and this work is due one hour prior to class. This leaves just enough time for Robert to review student answers and determine misconceptions prior to class.

Robert begins class by addressing these misconceptions and other questions the students bring forth from the preparatory activities. Class time is then spent working collaboratively on applications of the material.

As this suggests, the overarching point of JiTT is for students to go beyond simply reading the material to working with it before class. In the sciences at Indiana University Purdue University Indianapolis, they refer to this approach as warm-ups. They often ask students to "estimate," "explain in [their] own words," or ponder "what might happen if . . ." (see Further Resources below). Creating pointed but not overly open-ended questions leads to student engagement before and during class, when a student-raised controversy can become the center of discussion.

Just-in-Time Teaching and Process-Oriented Guided Inquiry Learning

Jeffery Schwehm, Concordia University, Ann Arbor Campus

Process-oriented guided inquiry learning (POGIL) emerged from the sciences in the 1990s. Jeffrey, who teaches chemistry, has developed a model that merges characteristics of POGIL and JiTT. In his classes, students work in groups on chemistry activities that provide a proposed model. Students work with the model to generate content that then feeds into other exercises. Prior to class, students take an online quiz that asks three open-ended questions: What is the main point of the activity? What part of the activity is easy to understand? What part is difficult to understand? Students receive full credit only if they are specific in their answers. Jeffery reviews the answers prior to class. In class, he then emphasizes overarching themes and corrects misconceptions he found in the student responses.

Immediate Feedback Assessment Technique for Feedback

Sarah Leupen, University of Maryland Baltimore County

Immediate feedback assessment technique (IF-AT) is a form of multiple-choice testing where the students receive a card with all of the responses covered. To answer questions, students use a coin or the edge of a pen to scratch off the covered answer. It works the same way as lottery scratch tickets. IF-AT cards are generically printed, with A, B, C, and D along the top and numbering down the left-hand side. A single star is present on each numbered row under one of the four letters. Faculty are provided the answer key for the card. As they construct their multiple-choice quiz, they must make sure that the correct answer for each question matches the location of the covered star on the IF-AT (see Further Resources for additional description).

Sarah, who teaches comparative animal physiology, uses IF-AT to encourage preclass work, provide feedback, and foster discussion. In her courses, students have various assignments to complete before class, including readings, animations, and videos. Before class begins for each unit, Sarah provides a 20-question readiness assessment test that students take alone. Then, in groups of five or six, students compare answers and decide collectively on the right answer to scratch off on their group's IF-AT card. Students can immediately see if their answer is correct. If they were wrong, they can then collectively scratch a second answer and receive partial credit. Because guesses are scratched off, it is clear how many tries it took to find the correct answer. This game like quizzing process encourages preclass preparation, fosters active engagement in class, and provides immediate feedback and opportunities for additional discussion as the activity unfolds and concludes.

Key Concepts

- Preclass quizzes or quizzes given at the beginning of class can help foster student engagement with readings and other forms of homework.

- Frequent quizzing has been shown to have significant benefits, including increased student learning and increased test performance on midterms and finals.

- Making quizzes due an hour or two before class provides you with data that can influence what you talk about in class that day (just-in-time teaching).

- Feedback is integral to the learning process, and using online quizzing offers a great opportunity to provide immediate, built-in feedback.

- Using quizzing to encourage homework completion before class requires a unique approach. It is okay for questions to be diagnostic and formative in nature (i.e., they may foster debate regarding the correct answer).

- Keep Bloom's levels in mind as you craft quiz questions. They will help keep you honest regarding the challenge you are building into your questions.

Further Resources

Epstein Educational Enterprises. (2017). *What is the IF-AT?* Retrieved from http://www.epsteineducation.com/home/about/

This site provides information on the immediate feedback assessment technique and is also a place where you can order IF-AT cards.

■ ■ ■

Marrs, K. (2006*). Just-in-time teaching workshop: Warm up 5*. Retrieved from http://jittdl.physics.iupui.edu/jitt/sampler/biology/bio_archive/warmup5.html

This page provides examples of the types of questions you might use to elicit information from your students for just-in-time teaching approaches.

■ ■ ■

Novak, G. (2006). *Just-in-time teaching*. Retrieved from http://jittdl.physics.iupui.edu/jitt/

This rich resource provides examples and research findings that highlight how best to implement just-in-time teaching.

■ ■ ■

POGIL Project. (2017). *Process-oriented guided inquiry learning*. Retrieved from http://pogil.org/

Originating in chemistry, POGIL uses guided inquiry with students in small groups. It's an approach that seeks to foster process skills in team environments. This site provides best practices and case studies for those who are interested in trying POGIL in a range of disciplines.

■ ■ ■

Quizlet. (2017). *Simple free learning tools for students and teachers*. Retrieved from http://quizlet.com/

This free tool and app make it easy for students to quiz themselves while on the bus or between classes. Students can collectively contribute multiple-choice questions to a common question pool and then use Quizlet to take these quizzes as an additional test preparation strategy.

■ ■ ■

Roediger, H. L., III (2012, February). *Cognitive enhancement of education: From the lab to the classroom*. Paper presented at the Harvard Initiative for Learning and Teaching Symposium, Cambridge, MA. Retrieved from https://www.youtube.com/watch?v=7me7PCROc7Y

Hear Henry Roedigger share many of the key findings from "Make It Stick: The Science of Successful Learning," a lecture he delivered in 2012 at Harvard.

References

Bloom, B. S. (Ed.). (1956). *Taxonomy of educational objectives, handbook I: The cognitive domain*. New York: McKay.

Chickering, A., & Gamson, Z. (1987). Seven principles for good practice in undergraduate education. *AAHE Bulletin, 39*, 3–7.

Geist, J. R., & Soehren, S. E. (1997). The effect of frequent quizzes on short- and long-term academic performance. *Journal of Dental Education, 61*(4), 339–345.

Novak, G., Gavrin, A., Christian, W., & Patterson, E. (1999). *Just-in-time teaching: Blending active learning with web technology*. Upper Saddle River, NJ: Prentice Hall.

Perry, W. G., Jr. (1970). *Forms of intellectual and ethical development in the college years: A scheme*. New York, NY: Holt, Rinehart, and Winston.

Roediger, H. L., III, Putnam, A. L., & Smith, M. A. (2011). Ten benefits of testing and their applications to educational practice. In J. P. Mestre & B. H. Ross (Eds.), *Psychology of learning and motivation* (vol. 55, pp. 1–36). San Diego, CA: Elsevier Academic Press.

Zaromb, F. M., & Roediger, H. L., III (2010). The testing effect in free recall is associated with enhanced organizational processes. *Memory and Cognition, 38*(8), 995–1008.

Chapter 6
Preclass Assignments

HOMEWORK IS AN essential part of learning, especially if the goal is to create self-regulated learners (Ramdass & Zimmerman, 2011). As students, we faculty were (at some point) largely self-motivated about homework, grasped its importance in our learning, and were probably successful in getting help when we needed it. None of this is obvious to most students, so we need to design assignments in ways to help them succeed. Convincing students that they will learn more in class when they are prepared is not a trivial task.

The first step is transparency. We know that our methods may seem odd to most students, so simply identifying why we have made assignments, how they improve learning, and how these tasks relate to the brain and learning will improve motivation and learning (Winkelmes, 2013). This is especially true for first-generation students, but you will be amazed at how much you take for granted about assignments. Some students really do wonder why some professors assign only the odd- or even-numbered problems. José was once asked this and made up something about reducing the number of problems or the answers to some being in the back of the book. The student looked cautiously over her shoulder and then whispered, "Please, won't you tell me what is really going on?"

In addition to transparency, there are three key questions to ask about homework assignments:

1. Are there better ways to interrogate this material? What are the questions with which I really want students to wrestle?

2. What are the things with which I want students to struggle on their own, and for what issues or problems might I want to be present as a guide?

3. How can this homework be preparation for a more meaningful class session?

Another way to think of this is to ask about where you want the failure to occur. We often think of education with a "light bulb" analogy: When will the light bulb turn on? But we may forget that the light bulb can only turn on after it has been off—and that failure precedes most learning. For most faculty perseverance through the failure led to light bulb moments, but for most students, the failure is the beginning of the end.

Alternatively, is there a way for complexity to reach its peak in the classroom on a regular basis? Homework, then, would be a place for students to have their first contact with material and gain some regulated familiarity. Pedagogy is about sequence. Teachers routinely simplify for their students, but *we* understand the context. Often we do not think about the paradoxes we create for students as they struggle to integrate partial knowledge into their own contexts. We should always acknowledge the necessary simplifications we foist on our students and explain (1) that we are going to simplify and (2) why we are going to limit our initial trials to these simple examples so that they can become comfortable, build good habits, or have initial success. But we should also make sure we return and acknowledge the complexity we have hidden. Often referred to as *scaffolding*, this is a concept we should explain to students so that they understand that these are deliberate choices we are making in our teaching that are based on what we know about how students learn. At the same time, we need to create conditions that support failure, which precedes most light bulb moments. We need to design our sequences so that both complexity and failure happen more often in the classroom than at home.

The goal of homework assignments, then, is to give students both (1) some controlled and limited experience on their own and (2) the motivation to come to class to deal with more complex material under our guidance. Motivation is generally built on success rather than failure: most of us pursue activities where we are having some success, and motivation is closely tied to notions of self-efficacy. Positive self-efficacy—an individual believes she or he can indeed "successfully execute the behavior required to produce the [desired] outcomes" (Bandura, 1977, p. 79)—results from four principal sources:

1. Mastery experiences (trying something and getting it right)

2. Vicarious experiences (watching others get it right)

3. Verbal persuasion (encouragement from others that you can indeed get it right)

4. An individual's affective states (e.g., feeling up to the task due to mood, diet, sleep) (Bandura, 1997, p. 79)

Of these four, mastery experiences (as good video games are designed to provide) have the greatest positive impact on self-efficacy and motivation, and conversely, failure has a significant negative impact on self-efficacy and motivation. A students tend to enjoy school more than C or D students partly because they enjoy higher self-efficacy due to their continued success. It is not surprising, then, that first-year grades are one of the best predictors of graduation rates (Hiss & Franks, 2014). Homework completion is highly influenced by students' self-regulatory strategies and their levels of motivation (Bembenutty, 2009), and this is why appropriately gauging the level of complexity for homework is so important. Exceptionally difficult homework reduces students' self-efficacy due to continuing struggles and failure, and self-efficacy is a significant contributor to motivation. Homework that provides opportunities for success and preparation for greater challenges in class has multiple benefits.

This chapter deals mostly with the creation of meaningful assignments, and Chapter 7 focuses on classroom activities. The best assignments can become the basis for classroom work, so anticipate that connection. How can the homework be used later for an in-class activity, and what classroom complication or "surprise" can you reserve to complicate the material? Since you reveal this "surprise" in class, students have to attend class both to understand the complexity you have withheld and to apply and practice their new knowledge in a real-world context.

Step-by-Step Guide

Step 1: Identify Learning Goals and Tasks

Start with your learning goals, and ask what types of tasks are useful or appropriate to reach that goal. Is this assignment discovery, practice, analyzing, or making? Bloom levels revised and their verbs can help you think about the types of activities students might do.

- *Remembering* (know, define, repeat, describe, identify, recall, list, tell, locate match)

- *Understanding* (comprehend, classify, convert, explain, summarize, predict, discuss, compare)

- *Applying* (demonstrate, modify, arrange, solve, relate, apply, examine, classify, illustrate)

- *Analyzing* (infer, estimate, order, separate, subdivide, distinguish, contrast, categorize)

- *Evaluating* (critique, justify, discriminate, support, conclude, judge, verify, assess, argue)

- *Creating* (synthesize, design, formulate, revise, construct, compose, invent, imagine, propose) (Anderson & Krathwohl, 2001)

All of these skills require practice, and that is a common motivation for homework. The ability to recall or distinguish requires both information and repetition. Making these connections as transparent as possible will help motivate students to persevere. Problem sets and musical scales, for example, can feel like busywork and drudgery (a motivation killer) unless students clearly understand the benefits they bring. Students who understand the learning goal and how the assignment will get them there have a massive advantage.

For higher-level learning, students will need to be clarifying, analyzing, judging, and inventing. One place to start is reading or video content that is used for first exposure (see Chapter 2). Articulate the bias of the writer, argue for an alternative view, support the same position using different evidence, or propose an implication. All of these will most often be done in writing (see below), but they can also be done as video or other presentations.

Step 2: Use Motivating Instructions

Including Bloom learning goals with each assignment can improve motivation, but you may need to do more to set up your students for success. Your attitude about homework matters. Let students know some of it will be hard and they may fail. (You can tell them that F.A.I.L. stands for "first attempt in learning.") Make it clear that you want them to try again and that you will support them. Will they lose points if they try and fail?

Your instructions are also key. Instructions can be both motivating and the first step in better retention (see Chapter 4).

Step 3: Create Microassignments and Index Cards for Attendance

If you need to take attendance, try to make that process a learning opportunity. Asking students to bring their assignment to class on an index card provides an easy way to take attendance and also limits the scope of the assignment. These "microassignments" are useful because they are short enough that everyone will have time to do them before every class and you do not have to grade them. (If you need to grade them and have a large class, you can grade a random 10% of them every day or grade only with a check or check+.)

For most students, this will be an incentive to do good work because they know that you will have other students read their work. Begin class by asking students to pass their card to the person behind/forward/left/right and ask him or her to write a rebuttal/extension/revision to what they have written. Or find a credible source on the Internet that disproves what was written on the card. Another option is to have peers grade each other's work as you go over better answers together in class. Remember that writing IS thinking (Menary, 2007). It is not simply communication of thought: the manipulation of sentences forces us to process how our thoughts integrate or contradict, so even if you cannot grade these microassignments or do not like this peer review process, you are providing an incentive to write and think.

Step 4: Prepare Students for Class

Think about what students will most need to succeed in class. This can be a skill or some content, but it might also be a list or a collection of examples. You might ask them to bring in a list of television characters who display the characteristics of various psychological conditions, traffic patterns that might be improved using a particular theory, or samples of music in their collection or plants in their yard to use to explain a phenomenon.

Have students prepare something they will then use for an activity in class. If you want students to learn about market resistance in class by trying to sell things, you might assign them to make a price list for products; in class, they then use the listed products in a trading activity. Having to produce materials in advance that are required for class is extra motivation. It is also good practice for the workplace where preparation is key. Telling students that this preparation cycle is a professional skill is another example of how transparency can be compelling.

Step 5: Ask Students to Create Analogies

Having students create analogies is a great assignment. We all learn new things by comparing them to things we already know. When we are confronted with something truly foreign or different, it means nothing. We have no context for understanding. Have you ever said, "This tastes like chicken," to describe some unfamiliar food? Why don't you say, "This tastes a bit like snake?" Because you know that if you don't already know what snake tastes like, this information has no meaning. We all use analogies to explain things as we teach, but students often have a different context. If you use legal analogies, your engineering students may be baffled. And do not ever appeal to popular music or pop culture references from your own adolescence unless you first clarify how many of your students know this particular "oldie."

After introducing students to Billie Holiday, Ella Fitzgerald, and Sarah Vaughan, José asks them to compare the three singers and explain the differences to a friend using an analogy that that person will understand. He learns new things as this tells him about their world, but it also reveals if they listened carefully. Some favorites include:

- If Fitzgerald is like hardwood floors and Vaughan is like shag carpet, then Holiday is stained concrete.

- If Fitzgerald is like champagne and Vaughan is like cabernet, then Holiday is whiskey.

Ask students to explain the contents of the reading to their roommate, a Martian, or their mother. This works on an index card or as a video assignment.

Step 6: Offer Case Studies

Case studies do not have to be complicated. They are simply a real-world scenario where students can apply recently acquired information. Typically cases aren't cut-and-dried. There's some uncertainty to them, and they may lack the structure found in other types of homework or classroom assignments. This is one of the benefits of case studies because the real world is filled with unstructured problems. You may find that assigning targeted word problems in advance of in-class case discussions provides students with opportunities to reflect on aspects of the upcoming case and develop some degree of competency with the ideas prior to the start of class. Sharing elements of a complex case with questions or guidance that focus students' attention rather than providing the entire case from the start ensures more opportunities for meaningful success prior to class by scaffolding the way you reveal complexity.

Finding small ways for students to apply what they have just learned is good repetition, but it also provides application and increases motivation (higher on Bloom!). Connecting everything students learn to their goals improves their learning and retention. Students can also do this themselves. Another good index card assignment is to ask students to find a practical application of an idea and identify how they might use this information with patients, clients, or students.

Step 7: Require Homework Logs

Knowing that students often do not come to us with exceptional self-regulatory strategies, homework logs are a useful approach to assist them as they develop these behaviors. Homework logs enable students to track how and when they complete homework assignments and can reveal poor homework choices, such as studying in areas full of distraction. They also provide opportunities for you to suggest alternatives to the way they are approaching homework. Key outcomes are often that students learn how to manage their time better and choose calmer and quieter environments within which to complete homework (Ramdass & Zimmerman, 2011). Homework logs make students more aware of their choices, which help them delay more tempting activities as they prioritize homework and manage their time. A better understanding of how they study and where their time goes will ultimately improve their self-regulation abilities (see Chapter 8).

Step 8: Consider Sequence and Failure

The hardest part of all of this is determining what work you want students to do before class and what you want them to do in class. Moving what you anticipate will be the most likely failure into class time means that you will be present to help students. Of course, that means you will need to make sure you can detect failure in your classroom so that it does not become even more isolating.

If you assign problem sets, have students do the most straightforward problems first. Remember, success is motivating. Perhaps warn students which are the hardest problems and that you will go over those in class. Try starting class with an easy problem, but complicate it somehow with a new condition or different data (in Chapter 7, we call this the "surprise"). Confusion is useful, but you want to be there to guide what happens next. Trying to anticipate when the confusion will happen and how to help is the hardest part of teaching and course design (see Chapter 10).

Your students will try to understand your assignment in the context of your course, so the other pieces all matter. Here are some questions to consider:

- Does the assignment line up with your learning goals? Can you make this explicit?

- Is the assignment part of the entry point or first encounter, or will they be doing something while they read or watch?

- How might you structure an advance organizer (see Chapter 1) to help students see how the pieces fit together?

Again, think about sequence: Do you want students to do the reading looking for the answer to a particular question, or do you want them to do the reading looking for one thing and then go back and do something else?

Step 9: Use Flash Cards, Polling, and Simple Quiz Tools

An increasing number of websites and applications allow you to create flash cards or simple quiz games. Quizlet is one of these flash card tools. As the teacher, you can create a study set of multiple-choice questions. Students can then take your quiz on their phone or online to ensure they have an understanding of key concepts before class. They can also create their own set of flash cards to study for tests, and groups of students can work together and contribute questions to a shared question pool. On the Quizlet website, students can gain access to thousands of quizzes created by other faculty and students, and the quizzes are searchable. In Quizlet's "study sets" section, a search for biology reveals over 500 flash card sets. There are a number of ways Quizlet can be used in conjunction with readings, homework, and test preparation.

Turning a quiz into a game lowers the stakes and can provide additional motivation. As an example, Kahoot! allows you to ask questions and students can compete for points in or out of the classroom. There are also polling websites and student response system applications, such as Socrative, Top Hat, and REEF Polling (and even Facebook allows simple polls). Some are better designed for out-of-class quizzing, while others are clearly designed specifically to increase engagement in face-to-face settings. It's likely that your institution's learning technologies team or center for teaching and learning has already selected and supports one of these systems, so check with them as a first step in deciding which system to adopt.

Using polling or quiz applications or clickers technology, in or out of class, encourages all students to participate (Klein, 2009), provides instant feedback (Briggs & Keyek-Franssen, 2010), increases engagement and satisfaction in class (Fredericksen & Ames, 2009), and fosters more honest feedback and more difficult discussions (Bruff, 2010). Polling before class can be a great preparation for class for both you and your students, and it can serve as a tool to support just-in-time teaching strategies (see Chapter 5). There are many questions you do not want to ask in open discussion like, "Who thinks this classroom is not a safe place to suggest minority views?" But you could surely use that information from polling to prepare for your next class session.

Imagine how you might use the following questions as preparation for discussion (see also Chapter 7):

- Are you worried about expressing your views in this course?
- Do you think this course will be useful in life or a profession?
- Do you think members of the other political party are irrational?
- Do immigrants contribute to U.S. society?

Step 10: Develop Concept Maps

Concept maps have a range of applications within the higher education classroom (Figure 6.1 shows the key features of a concept map). Some faculty provide a large concept map for the entire course on the first day of class and reference it often as the semester progresses. Here, concept maps function as a meta-advance organizer. Concept maps also make an excellent preclass assignment. After watching a video or finishing a reading, ask students to depict visually the various concepts discussed:

- How do they relate to one other?

- Is there a hierarchy?

- Was there a system of ideas that had inputs and outputs?

- Maybe the reading presented ideas that are linearly connected to one another. Depict those in visual form.

Better yet, ask students to incorporate ideas from earlier in the semester or from other courses they are taking with what they learned through your preclass assignment. This requires recall of prior knowledge and the

FIGURE 6.1

A Concept Map

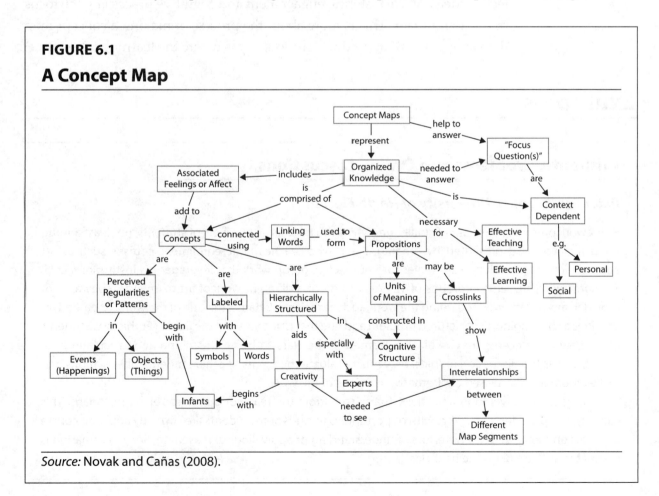

Source: Novak and Cañas (2008).

integration of new knowledge into preexisting mental models. On the last day of class, regardless of the topic, Eddie has his students work in teams to create a concept map of the course. Once they finish, the teams trade their concept maps and revise the maps they've now inherited. In this second stage, they include concepts the first team neglected and reorganize what is there to accommodate the new ideas. Recall and synthesis are the key activities of these semester-ending activity.

Regardless of how you might choose to use concept maps, since most students haven't created them before, it's a good idea to teach a few basic norms of the genre and provide examples. This will help ensure they struggle less with the mechanics of building concept maps and can focus on the learning you are intending for them. We should also note that grading can be challenging for these assignments, and students may argue that their map reflects their understanding and is therefore correct. That's a good argument, so an excellent part 2 to a preclass concept map assignment is to have students bring their concept maps to class. There, they can then work in groups to synthesize their various structures into a new map that embraces their collective ideas. Make fostering engagement and cognitive processing the focus of the assignment. This is more about the process of making a concept map than simply the final product. The journey is where the learning takes place.

Examples

Authentic Problems and Online Discussions

Peter Scott Brown, University of North Florida

Homework presents a number of challenges when you have large numbers of students, not least among them the workload presented by grading. Peter, who teaches large-enrollment courses such as art appreciation, has developed strategies for before-class group work that leverages his institution's LMS. For homework, students in groups of 10 are each given a different work of art to analyze. They are not provided any information regarding the work, such as the artist's name, the title of the work, or dates. This provides a challenging, ill-structured problem and one that is authentic to the field of art history. Students must draw on concepts they've already learned in the class to begin describing and articulating the object, and as the discussion unfolds, they must evaluate the merits of other students' observations and make arguments for revised or alternative readings of the work.

This is a high-level Bloom's activity that also mirrors the real-world practice of art historians. This strategy also provides instructors with opportunities to see where students are correctly applying course concepts and where they have errors of understanding or apply illogical reasoning. Such information is invaluable as Peter plans the next class.

Daily Lesson Plans

Richard Pennington, Georgia Gwinnett College

Sometimes homework seems to be an end unto itself rather than preparation for the class that is to come. To combat this perception, Richard provides his chemistry students with daily lesson plans at the beginning of the semester. This document covers the entirety of the course in exceptional detail. The content is broken down day by day, along with descriptions of the class activities that will occur, and this information is mapped to specific goals as well as the homework assignments that will precede class. This information creates transparency for the students regarding how the course fits together, and as they complete homework, they understand the dependencies the next class has on their success with those assignments.

Concept Maps and Reflective Writing

Becky Ericson, George Mason University

Most of us learn through visual analogy (hence the phrase "I see" for "I understand"). A concept map is a great way to get students to sort and visualize information. Designing homework that includes concept mapping tools such as FreeMind and Cmap can reveal gaps in student understanding of complex concepts. Becky teaches astronomy, and as a pretest of sorts, she has her students create a concept map regarding a specific topic, such as stars, prior to instruction. It becomes visually clear where students lack understanding or possess misunderstanding, and this provides important information about where emphasis should be placed in class. Becky also leverages these maps in important ways. After a unit concludes, she again has her students build a concept map of the topic and then asks them to compare the two maps. Students write a reflection where they consider the evolution of their maps and discuss their growth of understanding. These narratives are placed in the student's class portfolio. Such a process makes students acutely aware of how far they have come in their learning.

Writing Toward Outcomes

Oana Godeanu-Kenworth, Miami University

Almost all college courses have readings that are an integral part of homework assignments. The challenge isn't simply to have the students complete the reading; rather, it is to have them possess some level of understanding regarding what they've read when they come to class. Oana, who teaches an American studies course entitled America: Global and Intercultural Perspectives, has developed a series of targeted short assignments that use course readings as precursors to writing assignments, and these writing assignments are themselves precursors to in-class activities. Each part of the sequence is carefully designed to address a specific learning outcome, such as critical thinking or making a persuasive argument.

These homework assignments require students to apply the strategies and information found in the readings to content that students find either online or in the readings. Students therefore come to class with initial experience practicing the concepts and strategies under consideration. Class time provides opportunities for more challenging practice, deep discussions of the more difficult ideas, and making connections between the current class and past conversations.

Digital Storytelling

Brooke Hessler, California College of the Arts

Well-structured homework assignments have the potential to foster deep engagement in unexpected ways. An example can be found in Brooke's first-year composition courses. At the end of each unit, students must create a two- to three-minute short video, often with voice-over narration, still images, music, and/or video, that explains something interesting or unexpected they have learned. This assignment includes questions that help foster the development of student metacognition, such as, "How did you come to learn this?" and, "How does this idea relate to course goals?"

As students engage in fieldwork or as interesting events occur in the community or on campus, they often take photographs and are actively engaged in the development of a homework assignment that isn't due for days or weeks, and these activities can inform class discussion and activities. Homework assignments that help students integrate knowledge and concepts learned in class with what is taking place in the real world in real time result in deep learning and the instantiation of skills they will use beyond the course.

Games and Other Tools

Arthur Roberts, University of Georgia

In the past, developing online games meant that faculty required a team of instructional technologists to achieve their game design goals; however, Kahoot! Quizlet, Anki, and other new tools make such development far easier. Arthur teaches in the Pharm.D. program in the university's College of Pharmacy. He has built digital flash cards and flash-based quizzes to assist students as they prepare for tests. The cards and quizzes aren't graded, and students can use them as many times as they like; however, participation is incentivized: students must print out a certificate of completion that is available at the end of the game. This certificate can then be turned in to validate participation. When this simple gaming strategy was implemented, student grades on exams were far higher than before.

Key Concepts

- Revisit Bloom's taxonomy to ensure you are providing homework that speaks to the learning outcomes you hope your students will achieve prior to class.

- Be transparent about your assignments. Let students know why you are making certain pedagogical choices.

- Craft homework assignments with appropriate challenge that offers opportunities for students to succeed but requires effort and engagement. This will increase their self-efficacy and motivation in your course.

- Consider microassignments as a way of stimulating thinking about content and an easy way of taking attendance.

- Use homework as preparation for a more complex classroom activity. Excellent options for preclass assignments include writing analogies, case studies, flash cards, and concept maps.

- Ask students to log how and when they complete homework. This will help them better understand where their time goes and make better choices regarding when and where to do their homework.

- Learning design is largely about sequence: think carefully about when students might fail and when you introduce complexity.

Further Resources

Tools

Anki, ankisrs.net

Designed for repetition in the service of memorization, Anki provides a way to create flash cards that works on multiple platforms, is open source, supports a range of media, and is available free of charge.

■ ■ ■

Cmap, cmap.ihmc.us

This is a free concept mapping tool resulting from work at the Florida Institute for Human and Machine Cognition. With Cmap, students can create concept maps that are typically easier to read than those created by hand because revision is easy. These maps can also be shared online and printed. There's even a version created specifically for the iPad.

■ ■ ■

FreeMind, freemind.sourceforge.net

FreeMind is a free, open source tool for creating mind maps, a variation of concept maps. Mind maps typically radiate out from a central concept placed in the middle of the page, and FreeMind's tool set is designed to support the norms of this form of concept maps.

■ ■ ■

Kahoot! getkahoot.com

This tool enables you to create games built on multiple-choice questions. It supports a range of media, including video, and is an effective way to foster discussion and increase engagement during class.

■ ■ ■

Quizlet, quizlet.com

Quizlet might be seen largely as a study aid tool. It's a way to create a virtual flash card deck to review content. Students can create question pools and quiz themselves in the days before a test, and groups of students can work together to create and share question pools.

Additional Readings

Anderson, A. D., Hunt, A. N., Powell, R. E., & Dollar, C. B. (2013). Student perceptions of teaching transparency. *Journal of Effective Teaching, 13*(2), 38–47. Retrieved from http://uncw.edu/cte/et/articles/Vol13_2/Hunt.pdf

This study looks at the relationship between faculty making their pedagogical choices transparent to students and the success of the associated active learning strategies. Also considered is how student feedback on teaching practice can have a positive impact on teaching improvement.

■ ■ ■

Bandura, A. (1986). *Social foundations of thought and action: A social cognitive theory.* Englewood Cliffs, NJ: Prentice Hall.

If you're interested in self-efficacy and student motivation, this is an excellent Bandura title to explore. A number of interrelated concepts, such as self-regulation, cognition, motivation, and self-efficacy, are examined and explained in depth.

■ ■ ■

Bembenutty, H. (2011). The last word: An interview with Harris Cooper: Research, policies, tips, and current perspectives on homework. *Journal of Advanced Academics, 22*, 342–351.

This article provides an engaging discussion of various perspectives on homework.

■ ■ ■

Goldstein, D. S. (2013). What are they thinking? Best practices for classroom response systems ("clickers"). *National Teaching and Learning Forum*

Newsletter, 22(3). Retrieved from http://cgi.stanford.edu/~dept-ctl/cgi-bin/tomprof/posting.php?ID=1270

This is an excellent overview of the various types and uses of classroom response systems. There are now Web and mobile applications that do this more easily than the infrared technology of clickers, but the science and pedagogy remain the same.

■ ■ ■

Wilkemes, M. A. (2017). *Transparency in teaching and learning in higher education*. Las Vegas, NV: UNLV Office of Faculty, Policy, and Research. Retrieved from https://www.unlv.edu/provost/teachingandlearning

The University of Nevada, Las Vegas has developed and implemented a transparent teaching framework that functions in the service of college students' success. This site describes how their model works, along with evidence regarding its effectiveness.

References

Bandura, A. (1977). *Social learning theory*. Englewood Cliffs, NJ: Prentice Hall.

Bandura, A. (1997). *Self-efficacy: The exercise of control*. New York, NY: Freeman.

Bembenutty, H. (2009). Self-regulation of homework completion. *Psychology Journal, 6*, 138–153.

Bloom, B. S. (Ed.). (1956). *Taxonomy of educational objectives, handbook I: The cognitive domain*. New York, NY: McKay.

Briggs, C., & Keyek-Franssen, D. (2010). *CATs with clickers: Using learner response systems for formative assessments in the classroom*. Paper presented at the Educause Learning Initiative 2010 Annual Meeting, Austin, TX. Retrieved from http://www.educause.edu/Resources/CATswith Clickers UsingLearnerRe/196503

Bruff, D. (2010). Multiple-choice questions you wouldn't put on a test: Promoting deep learning using clickers. *Essays on Teaching Excellence, 21*(3), 1–6.

Fredericksen, E. E., & Ames, M. (2009). *Can a $30 piece of plastic improve learning? An evaluation of personal response systems in large classroom settings*. Retrieved from http://net.educause.edu/ir/library/pdf/csd2690.pdf

Hiss, W. C., & Franks, V. W. (2014). *Defining promise: Optional standardized testing policies in American college and university admissions*. Arlington, VA: National Association for College Admission Counseling.

Klein, K. (2009). Promoting collaborative social learning communities with student response systems. *Journal of Online Teaching and Learning, 5*(4). Retrieved from http://jolt.merlot.org/vol5no4/klein_1209.htm

Menary, R. (2007). Writing as thinking. *Language Sciences, 29*(5), 621–632. doi:10.1016/j.langsci.2007.01.005

Novak, J. D., & Cañas, A. J. (2008). *The theory underlying concept maps and how to construct and use them.* Pensacola, FL: Institute for Human and Machine Cognition.

Ramdass, D., & Zimmerman, B. J. (2011). Developing self-regulation skills: The important role of homework. *Journal of Advanced Academics, 22*(2), 194–218.

Winkelmes, M. A. (2013). Transparency in teaching: Faculty share data and improve students' learning. *Liberal Education, 99*(2). Retrieved from https://www.aacu.org/publications-research/periodicals/transparency-teaching-faculty-share-data-and-improve-students

Chapter 7

Massively Better Classrooms and the Classroom Surprise

COMING TO CLASS needs to be worth the effort for students. As faculty, we feel comfortable in classrooms and may even look forward to class sessions. That is not normal. In truth, when you look at almost every characteristic of faculty, we are indeed not normal. As an example, according to 2014 U.S. Census data, approximately 1.77% of Americans over the age of 25 have a Ph.D. (U.S. Census Bureau, 2014). When you consider education level, most of us are more than two standard deviations away from the mean. A great many of our students are indeed far more normal than we are. It's probably best that we don't design our courses for the undergraduate that we once were because there really aren't very many of us. We need to think about who students are, consider the options available to them, and design our courses for those who are actually in our classrooms.

Some students wonder why they should go to class at all, and you should take the time to be transparent about what will happen in the physical classroom and why this learning is better than the learning that can happen on their own or on their phone. The world is now full of learning alternatives. You can learn much from web pages, videos, or the many courses offered online by the best brand-name institutions. Your belief that something special happens in the classroom will not be enough to get students to attend. Classroom time is much more expensive and inconvenient than online, so you will need to be explicit and demonstrate repeatedly that what happens in your classroom is not reproducible elsewhere.

We know that emotions are a part of learning (Robinson, Watkins, & Harmon-Jones, 2013). Content that comes within more emotional or multisensory experiences (Calandra, Barron, & Thompson-Sellers, 2008; Clark & Mayer, 2003; Pavio, 1991) is more likely to stick. Doyle and Zakrajsek (2013) give the example of the difference between telling your students how many grams of fat are contained in a burger and measuring lard into a cup and then eating a spoonful of it in front of students. You could show a video of this, but your doing it in front of students will have more impact. Classrooms are great places for visceral and emotional experiences.

It's also important to note that faculty often enjoy following a complex argument for an hour or longer, but again, we are odd. This is not an essential life skill or one that most students possess. Sermons work typically because they are not primarily about content: we mostly know how it all ends. A good sermon may contain some fresh insight, but sermons are mostly about emotion and enthusiasm. They are also about community and connection: people attend religious services because of how the experience makes them feel. If you must lecture, do it in small segments interspersed with more active learning (Velegol, Zappe, & Mahoney, 2015). What we know about attention spans suggests this is an important strategy (Stuart, 1978). It's clear why TED Talks are typically limited to 18 minutes. Even minimal active strategies, such as the pause procedure (allowing students a 2-minute break during class to revise their notes every 20 minutes or so) has been shown to have a positive impact on learning and retention (Ruhl, Hughes, & Schloss, 1987).

Classrooms are also places for building community and encountering difference. Learning from each other and sharing in the creation of learning and teaching are both highly motivating and useful in their own right. Most workplaces today are collaborative. Employees say that the skill they most highly prize is the ability to solve complex, unstructured problems with others who are not like you (Association of American Colleges and Universities, 2015). This is a skill that can best be developed face-to-face and with supervision.

Student-faculty interaction has surfaced repeatedly as the most important part of college—for students, finding someone who excites them about learning (Gallup-Purdue, 2014). That is the most effective face-to-face teaching practice: to understand what matters to your students and demonstrate you care about their learning. Remember too that class time is a good time to be a role model. Only you can demonstrate to students what really makes you (and them) smart: it is not how much you know but rather the ability to change your mind. If what you are really teaching them is how to think critically, then your best teaching will come when you demonstrate how you yourself are open to new ideas and model how new perspectives can alter your thinking. You are already an intellectual superhero for your students (see Chapter 13): they have mostly come to watch you think.

Step-by-Step Guide

Step 1: Connect with Preclass Assignments

Massively better classrooms work in tandem with preclass assignments (Chapter 6) and student preparation (Chapters 4 and 5). If your students are better prepared, there is much more you can do with your class time, and there is a connection between the two processes (Gross, Pietri, Anderson, Moyano-Camihort, & Graham, 2015).

Start your design with the content students will need to learn, but also determine the most important cognitive skill you want your students to master. If you can create the motivation for your students to do some of the first exposure before class, then you can do more analysis and thinking in class. The reverse is also true: dealing with bigger questions in class will increase their motivation to be prepared.

Instead of "covering" topic A on Monday and topic B on Wednesday try asking students to prepare for a discussion on Monday of how A and B are different; then on Wednesday, ask them to explain why this might be. Pick a discovery, problem, or controversy and provide students with reading or other material that prepares them to argue for or against something. You don't need to give them both sides initially. On a macro and more sophisticated level, this is how the Reacting to the Past games work (Carnes, 2014; see below). The key is that the more sophisticated the assignment and the more interesting the in-class activity are, the more students will need and want to prepare. It is easy to complain about the problem of students being underprepared, but that is the essential design problem of teaching: designing a learning path where the excitement about engaging in class becomes part of the motivation to prepare. The more you can connect the preparation directly with the class activity, the more successful you will be and the more likely students are to prepare well for the next class.

Step 2: Avoid Punitive Measures

There will be times, of course, when you will have prepared everything carefully and students will not be prepared. Avoid taking your frustration out by cancelling class or giving a diatribe on the disrespect of not being prepared. This is a bit like lecturing the students who have arrived on time about why they should not be late. Avoid summarizing the work they did not do and trying to carry on, which only reinforces the message that you will "cover" the material that was assigned in advance anyway. This demonstrates that doing the homework is actually inefficient. Instead, explain to students the value of discussion and learning to connect different points of view, and then sit silently in front of them (perhaps after posing a question related to the reading). If you have to sit for the entire hour (provided you can stay silent), students will be more prepared for the next session.

If you have prepared an activity that requires advance work, you can ask the unprepared students to sit and watch—and without their devices. You could also put them to one side and ask them to finish the materials they need, but with some small penalty for entering the game or activity late.

Step 3: Create Prompts for Writing and Discussion

Writing is a key skill for any job and a great way to help students process. A very short essay (on an index card or one page of paper) before every class is an important way to get students writing and thinking. These essays are also important preparation for discussion.

One of the criticisms faculty often have of resources available through discovery online is that they may contain errors or out-of-date information. Rather than avoid such content, embrace it as a learning opportunity. Ask your students to view a video, but share that you know that there are at least three inaccuracies in what is presented (this will not be a challenge). Make the preclass writing assignment to bring a list of the three inaccuracies to class. This shifts the viewing of the video from passive to active. Students are then required to examine each element of the video critically and will have processed its content far more closely than if the video was simply presented as an expert's presentation. Reading or watching with intention increases basic retention (Brown, Roediger, & McDaniel, 2014); it also increases critical thinking and skepticism about all sources, another key skill.

Too often students think discussion is about sharing opinions, so they question the validity of listening and talking with others. Writing in advance can help students clarify their thoughts on their own before they make them up in real time.

Writing can be a preclass assignment, but it can also be useful during class. Before an activity or discussion, have students make a list, summarize material, create an analogy, or clarify their argument. Ultimately such approaches provide opportunities for students to evoke the appropriate prior knowledge in preparation for the forthcoming dialogue. This not only enables the students to be better prepared for class activities; it also adds a moment for recall and reflection, which further aids in the learning process.

Your prompt is key. Christensen, Garvin, and Sweet (1992) divide the roles of discussion into questioning, listening, and response. Start by preparing a few good questions in advance (but not organized sequentially since discussions are never linear). Different types of questions lead to different types of discussions, and one of the first tasks of the professor is to assess student needs and interests and connect them with his or her goals. Since you want students to think carefully about the sort of answer that would be appropriate, give them time to write a response to one key question—for example:

- What does the text say?
- How do you and others interpret this text?
- What problem might there be with this method [or theory]?
- What is the main argument the text is making?
- What is the most important evidence for this argument?
- What is the author's main bias or assumption?
- How do you understand this text?
- How does this text do a good or poor job of conveying its message?
- Why is this passage important?
- Why is this passage disturbing?

Again, connect to your learning goals for the discussion. What do you most want students to discover? Give students a chance to process on their own, and then start the discussion.

Step 4: Lead Better Discussions

Discussion will always be a classroom staple, but it is hard to do effectively. The patience and experience to understand when and how to intervene take practice. Stephen Brookfield has written several great books on how to improve your skills as a discussion leader and also has a website (Brookfield, 2016) that offers templates along with brief and helpful tips. You are not looking for opinion, however much students think you are, so you will need to clearly differentiate fact, opinion, and judgment.

Start by clarifying for yourself and your students what your learning goals are for the period of discussion. If you plan to spend more than 20 minutes in discussion, you might want to have learning goals for different parts of the discussion. Learning goals might include these:

- Find the right entry point.
- Enhance intellectual curiosity.

- Confront contradictions.
- Practice listening or empathy.
- Increase tolerance for ambiguity.
- Increase the ability to think critically in real time.
- Recognize assumptions.
- Challenge beliefs.
- Deepen investment in the material.
- Reflect on the significance of material.
- Connect ideas across disciplines.
- Demonstrate the human dimension of learning.

Once you are clear about your goals, you can prepare prompts for either a preclass assignment or an in-class discussion. Consider a brief thinking moment before your discussion where all students respond in writing (or at least in their heads) before you start sharing thoughts.

Before your first discussions, you will need to clarify good student discussion behaviors, which are rarely obvious to students. Harnish (2008), for example, suggests focusing students on comments that introduce substantive points and deepen the discussion. Clarify that discussion is a group exploration and students (like faculty!) should weigh the individual importance of what they want to say against how it will help the group progress.

Inventive grading can also reward the discussion behaviors you seek. Grading participation will encourage students to talk, but a system that rewards quality over quantity will improve the substance and depth of your discussions. Pause after 15 minutes and ask students what they thought were the best or most useful contributions in the past few minutes for discovering new insights, opening a new line of inquiry, or including new members in the discussion. Who asked the question that most demonstrated an interest in what someone else had to say? Award a few bonus points to the person who made the comment the group most likes.

Managing good discussion takes practice. Structuring discussion as part of a broader class plan is the best way to get a little practice at a time and avoid disaster. If you have prepared yourself and your students, asked good questions, defined good behaviors, and created a positive reward system, you may still run into choppy waters. Just acknowledge that discussion is hard and unpredictable, but is a useful pedagogy precisely because those are the characteristics of both thought and life.

Step 5: Design Classroom Activities

There are many good sources of ways to build more active learning into your classroom (See the Further Resources section later in this chapter). As you begin to prepare for a more active classroom, note that these activities are likely to take more class time than you anticipate. That is not a bad thing, since you will inevitably overprepare (again, you are not like the typical student!). Allow enough class time to reap the benefit of the time you have spent preparing a really good activity.

Discovery

Think about the key content. What could students discover on their own rather than have you tell them? This is a much more powerful experience. Try for example, to give students some of the "facts" or information, and let them discover the key theory or main point. This can be accomplished individually or in groups by asking questions—for example:

- Can you anticipate or find the controversy?
- Can you explain the data?
- Do you understand how this works?
- Now that you have the how, can you guess why?

The Internet has also made many more primary sources available. Is there something students can discover themselves from looking directly at Beethoven manuscripts or the human genome?

Clickers and Polling

Polling is also covered in Chapter 6 largely because the technology to do this has evolved from infrared in-class clickers to Web-based platforms that work with any phone; hence, they work equally well outside class.

Clickers can be used in meaningful ways or in ways that have little impact on learning. For instance, requiring students to purchase a clicker or software license for the purposes of taking attendance is probably not the best collective expenditure for your students, and if you use clickers to reset students' attention spans in class, take note of what you learn as a result of the polling that you do. For instance, if you lecture for half an hour, and only a third of your students can correctly discern the difference between, say, an ANOVA and a t-test, do you continue to move forward with your lesson as planned, or do you improvise and try to address what you just learned about your students' current level of understanding? Probably the latter is the better bet. If that many are lost at this point in class, moving forward would be pointless. Polling is an easy way to get immediate feedback about what is clear or confusing.

An even more effective use of clickers is exemplified by Eric Mazur's approach at Harvard ("Eric Mazur Shows Interactive Teaching," 2012). Here, the goal is to pose thorny questions where students in the class are somewhat split between two of the multiple-choice answers for each question. Once that conflict is revealed to the class, students are then asked to discuss the rationale for their answer with someone near them. The point is to convince the other student that your answer is correct and theirs is not. After this debate, Mazur then polls his students again, and typically, the response distribution has shifted, often in favor of the correct answer; however, sometimes, even greater disagreement has developed. His students are highly engaged by this process and motivated to learn the correct answer and why that is the case. The best examples of clickers foster such levels of engagement and interaction.

Peer Review Writing

Simply telling students that other students will read their writing motivates them to edit more carefully. Using class time for writing and editing may help students understand the benefits of focused time. The experience of reading the work of others and having others read one's own work can help students see both the value of audience and the universal importance of clarity.

Tell students in advance that other students will read their work. Then dedicate some time in class for students to edit and respond to each other's writing. Start with short samples and provide students with a simple rubric. A good preassignment is to have students fill in a rubric; provide some sample descriptions, and have students fill in some remaining open spaces. Then ask students to edit each other's papers for one criterion at a time. For example, ask students to edit each other's papers for clarity or to identify the main point of each paragraph.

Ask students to find an example of something positive to share: an apt metaphor, a vivid visual example, or a punchy paragraph ending. Having students share the best work of others will provide good examples and positive support to everyone.

Hafer (2014) offers an additional strategy that uses a writing group workshop process beginning with students in small groups reading their essays aloud. The other group members write brief descriptions, without critique or criticism, of what they heard. The "writer" in the group gains a picture of what the others heard and then is asked to develop a path for revision to clear up misconceptions and polish the essay.

Confronting Contradiction and Motivating Change

If one of the goals of higher education is the ability to change your mind, especially after you have reconsidered something you thought you knew in light of new information, then the classroom has to be more than content delivery. Classrooms are an ideal place to confront and try to resolve contradiction. While Socratic questioning with the faculty member can accomplish this, setting up student-to-student dialogue is the more scalable proposition, and it can often be more effective.

When students encounter contradictions at home or on the Internet, they can skip over them. Ask students to find the contradictions or key new insights in homework readings and bring them to class. Then in class, ask students to articulate these (starting with an in-class summary of the contradiction is also a good way to hold students accountable for coming prepared). This can serve as a basis for many group activities: students can work in pairs to identify the key point of difficulty, try to resolve the problem, or determine how this new information changes the previous assumption or working theory.

Change is hard, especially change that makes us confront something uncomfortable. You will need to model this and provide students many opportunities to practice.

Reflection

A related strategy is to give students a chance at the end of class to reflect. Cognitive wrappers (a brief but structured reflection that is not graded) work for this (Chapter 8), but it may be as simple as asking students to discuss or write about how this new knowledge or insight might change their thinking or process in the future. In addition to writing, another key strategy to make sure students are using focused time to reflect is to take time in class to do that.

Problem Solving

The traditional class in science, technology, engineering, and mathematics has long been structured to focus on theory and sample problems, followed by problem sets to be done at home. Mazur has completely flipped this approach: problem sets become the focus of class time. Through his model of peer instruction, students explain solutions to each other and argue over the best solutions (Rosenberg, Lorenzo, & Mazur, 2006). Since practice is an important part of problem solving, it is reasonable to ask students to do some practice outside class, but consider saving a few of the harder problems for in-class work.

Group projects are also often left to time outside class, but class time is often the only common times groups have. Try using class time for the group to divide up tasks before the next meeting, and note that meetings that result in "action items" are a key workplace practice.

Studios and Labs

To set up your classroom as a laboratory or studio, think of the rules, practices, and feedback that lead to the key collaborative discoveries and creative solutions of your discipline. Just calling your classroom a lab or studio will signal that you want your students to be more collaborative, self-directed, self-motivated, and intellectually ambitious. Studio work tends to be project based and might be done individually or in teams; painters work individually, but dancers, scientists, actors, engineers, designers, and programmers often work in groups. In a studio, students have a goal (often a project, performance, or a design) and must try different approaches to get there. Students in a studio know they must arrive prepared; directors, conductors, and choreographers are constantly reminding students that they have an obligation to each other (and not simply to the teacher) to know their part and be ready to work when they arrive. Studios too are places where knowledge is constantly being discovered and shared.

Think of what discovery and research look like in your discipline, and try to mirror that experience for your introductory students. Students who have taken only one class in a discipline often have wildly inaccurate visions of what professionals in those fields do: art historians appear to sit in the dark looking at slides and doctors memorize parts of the body. Finding a safe way for students to mimic the actual process of the discipline will also help students make better career choices. Students who think of themselves as scholars with something to contribute also become deeper learners.

Role Playing, Games, and Simulations

Many fields have relevant role-playing games that have a history of practice that makes them easy to implement. The Reacting to the Past games developed by Mark Carnes (Professor of History at Barnard College) are the best developed, and they are the model for what a flipped classroom might be. Instead of coming to class and taking notes on information you provide, students are given a role to play in some historical drama or controversy. They may be underprepared the first day, but they quickly realize that each student has a piece of the puzzle, and the solution to it (or winning) requires collaboration and their individual knowledge, which is power. This becomes the motivation for preparing better for the next speech or activity. Reacting games come with a large support group of faculty, and you can even attend a conference to play a game yourself (Carnes, 2014).

Games and simulations can take many forms. You can start with a short situation game. Ask students to interview each other in a short game of 20 questions. One of the students could be an enzyme, a type of star, a historical figure, or a character in a book. Equally brief can be the mock argument, where one student presents three arguments for a proposition and the other offers the counterarguments. Have everyone do this simultaneously in pairs, and then ask one group to "perform" for the entire class.

If you want to get everyone up, assemble your entire class on one wall and ask them to walk to the other wall (one at a time) as a political candidate, physical property, emotional state, or mathematical formula while the other students try to guess what is being demonstrated. Physical movement reengages the attention span, so instead of asking a question with a clicker, ask your students to position themselves as a human Likert scale. Those who agree most passionately with the proposition stand near one wall, those who disagree equally vehemently stand near the other, and those who are uncertain stand somewhere in the middle. Then ask the different groups to explain their positions to each other.

Some of this will appear silly to you and some of your students, but note that learning is messy and complicated. Most of our brain was developed for movement, and we were designed to learn while moving. You may have been good at learning while sitting still, but that is unusual. If nothing else, your students will get to laugh and relax a bit, and they will have activated another part of their brains (interleaving) and be ready for the next bit of learning. Engagement precedes learning.

Collaborative Learning

The workplace is now highly collaborative. New companies often have shared "hot" desks that anyone can use or cubicles with acres of whiteboards and shared spaces for teams. By training, all professors have at least some comfort with more solo and isolated work, and we tend to privilege that. Students too come to college because they were successful working individually in high school. Learning that we all have much to teach each other may seem contradictory to our assumptions about school, but it has many benefits.

All of the techniques in this section, even writing, have some element of collaboration; very few of us, for example, publish any writing without some degree of collaboration. Your reviewers, editor, coauthors, publicist, or legal expert probably have some say, and today virtually every memo, report, or white paper is written by a committee. This is so common that even passing around a file seems like old technology. Try an assignment that uses Google Docs, a collaborative online tool designed precisely to allow multiple people to edit one document simultaneously. Elizabeth Barkley, Claire Major, and Patricia Cross's revised handbook on collaborative learning techniques (2014) provides plenty of specific ideas, but start by looking for something where students can help, support, or teach each other.

Students often object to the grading of group projects on the grounds that it is unfair. There are ways around this—mostly clarity in advance (also see Barkley et al., 2014, for this)—but don't shy away from good teaching just because it is hard to grade. Frankly, one reason collaborative work is more common in the workplace is that there are no grades (or at least not individual grades). Good managers learn who really does the work by being engaged in the work and observing carefully. This is good practice in teaching also.

Step 6: Reveal Your Surprise

We have highlighted the close link between student preparation and its extension and application inside the classroom. Students should come to class knowing that their preparation is going to matter, and perhaps even that they will not be able to learn in class without it. One way to create intrinsic motivation is for the homework to be the basis for what happens in class. Giving students simple and clear tasks to do in advance allows class assignments to build on this foundation. Class time should come with application, complication, extension, and a surprise—some form of additional difficulty, new ambiguity, or real-world complication. Yes, students will start to try and anticipate the surprise, and this is a great thing. When you start a job or buy a house for the first time, you might not know what surprises lie in store for you, but when you know there will be surprises, you can try to anticipate and then seek further information or advice in advance.

Ask students to prepare something for class: a pitch for a meeting in New York City, an experimental design, a hypothesis based on simplified data, a plan for a new transportation system, or an outline for an opera production. Some potential in-class surprises might include these:

- Alter the conditions
  - The venue has changed, or the meeting has been moved from New York City to Tokyo.
  - The client has changed the request.
  - The marketing person is sick: you're on!
- Change of data
  - A recent test unexpectedly failed.
  - The data you used were flawed.
  - Here is new [or additional] information.
- Extend conditions
  - The panel you are presenting to now includes someone who hates something you planned [or has a new agenda].
  - Can you find a way to appeal to multiple groups?
  - Add another condition.
- Complicate
  - Your competition has just released a better technology [or product or plan].
  - There is an interesting new side effect to consider.
- Reframe the problem
  - How might you have prepared differently?
  - Suppose you were allowed to change one of the conditions?

Once you have unleashed your surprise, give students some time to think and adjust. This is a good time to allow open laptops for them to do additional research. Then ask the students to do something collectively, typically an activity or a discussion. Students might have to revise materials and still make the presentation or write a group essay about what now needs to change.

Surprises can also be used to prepare materials for a simulation or game. For arts entrepreneurship, José asks students to prepare a list at home of 10 products or services they could sell. Then in class, he asks them how much they should charge. For a double surprise, he sometimes alters the conditions: "Instead of portraits, suppose you are now going to sell dog portraits." Then he gives students 10 minutes to figure out how to price their services (using the Internet and searching for the services as if they wanted to buy them themselves). The culmination is a game where students now try to sell products to each other for 10 minutes. He says the object of the game is to sell the most. In debriefing the game, he asks not only who made the most money, but who had 100% of customers accept their price. What does that mean? Pretty soon students are asking if they charged too little and why it might be useful to keep track of rejections. At the end, José lets them know there is a name for this concept: *market resistance*. This is the real objective of the game. Since artists are often suspicious of business terms, *market resistance* would make a terrible entry point for this course, and if it appears on the syllabus, many students might not even come to class.

Such activities do more than make for meaningful and memorable classes. They also help students achieve the most challenging outcomes of the college classroom: synthesis and transfer of concepts to new contexts.

Examples

Preclass Assignments

Linda Wanless, Michigan Technological University

The best preclass activities not only prepare students for the material that will be covered in class; they are a part of the class itself and are integral to course activities each day. Linda teaches a technology computer applications course where preclass activities seamlessly transition students into each class. Like many who flip their course, Linda's preclass activities variously include readings, articles, videos, and tutorials.

She begins class with a brief overview of key concepts before providing students with an in-class assessment that focuses on the preclass work. As they complete the assessment, usually leveraging interactive software, she circulates around the room to clarify specific misconceptions and points of confusion that appear. This just-in-time teaching evokes a mastery learning strategy designed to ensure that most students have an accurate, foundational understanding of the material provided in the preclass assignments. Students are then placed into groups and are provided problems based on the content from the preclass assignments. An integrative approach that connects and joins preclass and classroom activities ensures that students see the connections between the two and understand how they build on one another. Not only does this approach establish that the students are prepared for the group activities; it also aids students' understanding of the connections between the two.

Preclass Preparation for Discussion

Katherine Moore, Arcadia University

Brief preclass writing assignments can be used to prepare and organize class for discussion. Katherine teaches a senior capstone course in psychology. Most of the preclass assignments are readings of primary literature articles. Students are required to submit two discussion questions using Blackboard, the class LMS; however, online discussion tools are not used. Rather, for each class, a different designated student discussion leader must review the questions, determine the main themes, and then design and deliver a lesson, typically including an activity or video example, based on these discussion questions. All students are held accountable for completing the preclass reading, and the class builds on the threads the students themselves have identified.

Preclass Assignments and Incentives

Denise Thorsen, University of Alaska Fairbanks

An alternative is to build a culture of rewards that incentivize students to engage and participate. Denise teaches an introduction to electrical and computing engineering course that implements the typical flipped model of preclass assignments followed by preclass assessments. In this lab-based course, the assessments and homework are graded automatically, and students can submit as often as they would like up until the due date; therefore, pursuing perfect scores on the preclass activities is incentivized through multiple opportunities. In addition, students are given 1 point each day for attendance, 5 points for the preclass assignments, and 50 points for homework. As a result, students have greater control over their performance in the class, and their greater effort results in a higher grade.

Purposeful Games

Janine Bowen, Goucher College

While gaming can be a highly motivating instructional strategy, one of the challenges with this approach is finding or developing a meaningful game scenario that furthers the learning goals of the class. Janine, who teaches organizational behavior, has found a strategy that helps students understand the challenges that manager's today face. For this unit in her course, she uses Barnga, a card game that places students in situations that highlight the differences between individuals and ultimately cultures.

Students are placed in groups of four and are provided rules to a card game that is similar to euchre or hearts. They are not permitted to speak; however, they are allowed to gesture. As a winner emerges at each table, the winners rotate to other tables to begin new games. As play continues, clear disagreement emerges at the tables, but it is expressed only through gestures. Reactions range from amusement to frustration and even anger. At the conclusion of play, it is revealed that each table was initially provided with slightly different rules. The class then explores the behaviors that were exhibited during the points of confusion regarding the norms of the game. Discussion leads to the attributes that tend to make someone behave inappropriately, along with strategies to avoid similar challenges in real-world settings. Having the students engage in such activities leads to a lived, firsthand understanding of the issues at "play" during the class.

Lead Them to the Answer

Gretchen Kreahling McKay, McDaniel College

In her medieval art class, Gretchen covers the change from the Western-style basilica church plan (a long hallway that leads to the altar) to the domed church plan, first built in Byzantium by sixth-century emperor Justinian. Gretchen posits that the shift to a dome was influenced by theological ideas of the time and not a change in liturgical practice. Rather than tell the students in a lecture that Justinian changed the focus of his church plan from the horizontal basilica to a vertically accented dome, she has them plan a new church, based on theological texts to present to Justinian. She assigns the students to groups of four or five. They are given a handout that explains that they are architects tasked by Justinian to develop a new church plan corresponding to new theological ideas. On this same sheet is a short excerpt from contemporary Byzantine theologians who stress the ideas of hierarchy and the celestial sphere. Students must first grapple with the texts themselves to understand the themes and how they might translate into a church plan. (This reading can also be done as a preclass assignment.) Individual groups then create a floor plan and present it to the class.

The first time Gretchen used this exercise, the students all created plans that had actually been built by early Christian and Byzantine architects. Students were excited by this and begged her to show them the "real" church that corresponded to "their" plan. When they actually saw Hagia Sophia, in Istanbul, the reactions ranged from, "Oh, yes! That really does explain the ideas!" to "Aw! Our church plan was better!" This is an example of how an entry point that creates engagement and a preclass assignment that adds motivation can result in a classroom session where students more deeply understand—in this case, the reasons for a shift to a dome.

Key Concepts

- Be explicit about the benefits of attending class.
- Limit the length of lectures, and break them up using active learning strategies. Even brief strategies, such as the pause procedure, have been shown to be effective in terms of student learning.
- Leverage class time for emotional connection, community, and relationships.

- Meaningful preclass activities are essential to the success of active learning classes.

- Avoid punitive responses to students who don't come to class prepared.

- Brief writing assignments are a high-engagement strategy that can be effectively used for preclass assignments, as well as in-class activities.

- Leading effective classroom discussions is a skill that takes practice to develop and improve.

- The world of active learning strategies is immense. Among the many options available are group learning, problem solving, case-based approaches, games, simulations, and labs.

- The "surprise" is integral to taking the class to the next level. Consider how you might problematize or complicate an earlier solution in class. Class time is an opportunity to reveal real-world complexities and messiness.

Further Resources

Barnard College. (2016). *Reacting to the past*. Retrieved from http://reacting. barnard.edu

Learn more about the range of opportunities represented by Reacting to the Past. It's a collection of role-playing and simulation games for a range of disciplines. You may even want to write one yourself.

■ ■ ■

Bean, J. C. (2011). *Engaging ideas: The professor's guide to integrative writing, critical thinking, and active learning in the classroom* (2nd ed.). San Francisco, CA: Jossey-Bass.

This book offers a number of creative strategies regarding how to incorporate writing into your course in ways that will have a strong impact.

■ ■ ■

Centre for Teaching Excellence. (2016). *Nine alternatives to lecturing*. Waterloo, ON: University of Waterloo. Retrieved from https://uwaterloo.ca/centre-for-teaching-excellence/teaching-resources/teaching-tips/alternatives-lecturing/active-learning/varying-your-teaching-activities

As the name suggests, this website provides details of nine strategies you can use in class in place of lectures. Brief writing assignments, pro and con grid, guided analysis, and others are all described in detail, including procedures.

■ ■ ■

Duke Center for Instructional Technology. (2009). *Active learning with Dr. Richard Felder*. Retrieved from https://www.youtube.com/watch?v= 1J1URbdisYE

Felder, a chemical engineering professor at North Carolina State, shares his thoughts on active learning. This video includes excerpts from his own classroom; you can see how this one professor does it.

■ ■ ■

Faust, J. L., & Paulson, D. R. (1998). Active learning in the college classroom. *Journal on Excellence in College Teaching, 9*(2), 3–24.

This article provides a catalogue of active learning strategies and their descriptions. The authors also explain how some of these strategies have worked for them.

■ ■ ■

Freeman, S., Eddy, S. L., McDonough, M., Smith, M. K., Okoroafor, N., Jordt, H., & Wenderoth, M. P. (2014). Active learning increases student performance in science, engineering, and mathematics. *Proceedings of the National Academy of Sciences, 111*(23), 8410–8415.

This article provides a meta-analysis of studies investigating the merits of active learning. If you're looking for evidence regarding its effectiveness, this is one place to look.

■ ■ ■

Hake, R. R. (1998). Interactive-engagement vs. traditional methods: A six-thousand-student survey of mechanics test data for introductory physics courses. *American Journal of Physics, 66*, 64–74.

Looking at students from various types of institutions, this study provides compelling evidence for active learning. It's not that students don't learn from lectures; they do. But they clearly learn more when active engagement techniques are employed.

■ ■ ■

Mazur, E. (2016). *Mazur Group*. Retrieved from http://mazur.harvard.edu/

Mazur is one of the evangelists for active learning. His website contains strategies, articles, and evidence to consider and adopt.

■ ■ ■

Meyers, C., & Jones, T. B. (1993). *Promoting active learning: Strategies for the college classroom*. San Francisco, CA: Jossey-Bass.

Although this is an older book, the strategies described here are still relevant and effective.

■ ■ ■

Paulson, D. R., & Faust, J. L. (2016). *Active learning in the college classroom*. Retrieved from http://www.calstatela.edu/dept/chem/chem2/Active/main. htm

This site provides another catalogue of active learning strategies. This one is freely available online.

■ ■ ■

Reacting to the Past. (2017). *Reacting to the past*. New York, NY: Barnard College. Retrieved from https://reacting.barnard.edu/

Truly a pedagogy of deep engagement, Reacting to the Past is a set of elaborate games typically played over several class periods. In some cases, play takes several weeks. It ensures that all students in a class engage in rich, intellectual discussion, as well as preparatory research. Students truly feel transformed after participating in courses that leverage Reacting to the Past.

References

Association of American Colleges and Universities. (2015). *Step up and lead for equity: What higher education can do to reverse our deepening divides*. Washington, DC: AAC&U.

Barkley, E. F., Major, C. H., & Cross, K. P. (2014). *Collaborative learning techniques: A handbook for college faculty* (2nd ed.). San Francisco, CA: Jossey-Bass.

Brookfield, S. D. (2016). *Dr. Stephen D. Brookfield*. Retrieved from http://www .stephenbrookfield.com/

Brown, P. C., Roediger, H. L. III, & McDaniel, M. A. (2014). *Make it stick: The science of successful learning*. Cambridge, MA: Belknap Press of Harvard University Press.

Calandra, B., Barron, A. E., & Thompson-Sellers, I. (2008). Audio use in e-learning: What, why, when, and how? *International Journal on E-Learning, 7*(4), 589–601.

Carnes, M. C. (2014). *Minds on fire: How role-immersion games transform college.* Cambridge, MA: Harvard University Press.

Christensen, C., Garvin, D., & Sweet, A. (Eds.). (1992). *Education for judgment: The artistry of discussion leadership.* Boston, MA: Harvard Business Review Press.

Clark, R. C., & Mayer, R. E. (2003). *E-Learning and the science of instruction: Proven guidelines for consumers and designers of multimedia learning.* San Francisco, CA: Jossey-Bass.

Doyle, T., & Zakrajsek, T. (2013). *The new science of learning: How to learn in harmony with your brain.* Sterling, VA: Stylus.

Eric Mazur shows interactive teaching. (2012). *Harvard Magazine.* Retrieved from https://www.youtube.com/watch?v=wont2v_LZ1E

Gallup-Purdue. (2014). *Great jobs great lives: The 2014 Gallup-Purdue index report.* Washington, DC: Gallup.

Gross, D., Pietri, E. S., Anderson, G., Moyano-Camihort, K., & Graham, M. J. (2015). Increased preclass preparation underlies student outcome improvement in the flipped classroom. *CBE-Life Sciences Education, 14,* 1–8.

Hafer, G. R. (2014). *Embracing writing: Ways to teach reluctant writers in any college course.* San Francisco, CA: Jossey-Bass.

Harnish, J. (2008, February). *What's in a seminar? Seminar process to encourage participation and listening. Identifying good seminar behaviors.* Paper presented at the Collaborative Learning Conference II, Everett Community College, Everett, WA.

Pavio, A. (1991). Dual coding theory: Retrospect and current status. *Canadian Journal of Psychology, 45,* 255–287.

Robinson, M. D., Watkins, E. R., & Harmon-Jones, E. (Eds.). (2013). *Handbook of cognition and emotion.* New York, NY: Guilford Press.

Rosenberg, J. L., Lorenzo, M., & Mazur, E. (2006). Peer instruction: Making science engaging. In J. J. Mintzes & W. H. Leornard (Eds.), *Handbook of college science teaching* (pp. 77–85). Arlington, VA: NSTA Press.

Ruhl, K., Hughes, C., & Schloss, P. (1987). Using the pause procedure to enhance lecture recall. *Teacher Education and Special Education, 10,* 14–18.

Stuart, J. (1978). Medical student concentration during lectures. *Lancet, 312*(8088), 514–516.

U.S. Census Bureau. (2014). *Educational attainment.* Retrieved from https://www.census.gov/hhes/socdemo/education/data/cps/2014/tables.html

Velegol, S. B., Zappe, S. E., & Mahoney, E. (2015). The evolution of the flipped classroom: Evidence-based recommendations. *Advances in Engineering Education, 4*(3), 1–37. Retrieved from http://advances.asee.org/wp-content/uploads/vol04/issue03/papers/AEE-15-Velegol.pdf

Chapter 8

Critical Thinking, Metacognition, and Cognitive Wrappers

CRITICAL THINKING IS a process that culminates in the ability to change your mind. It starts with skepticism and testing assumptions, but also requires curiosity, exploring new information, formulating hypotheses, and, most important, self-reflection. We need not only to understand that our own assumptions and framework might require revision, but practice in making these alterations and observing the process of changing the way we think.

Producing students who agree with us is all too common. Critical thinking does not mean thinking like the professor, a common misconception students have. The hardest part of teaching is helping students find their own voice and learning how to disagree with us appropriately. Music teachers are perhaps particularly prone to the "imitate me" problem. The temptation to pick up an instrument and demonstrate the "proper" way to play ("Try it like this") can be overwhelming. It is much harder to create paths where students find their own best solutions. Self-reflection helps students practice a key component of critical thinking and opens the door to individual discovery and thinking.

A third reason to devote course design and class time to reflection is that it helps with learning. As examples of the range of benefits, systematic reflection has been shown to increase learning following positive and negative experiences (Ellis, Carette, Anseel, & Lievens, 2014), and even students with math anxiety who write about it before the exam perform better than those who do not (Ramirez & Beilock, 2011). Reflection is also seen as a key lifelong learning strategy that is integral to career development and success (Brookfield, 1995; Schön, 1984). As our knowledge of intelligence, learning, and the brain has exploded in the past 30 years, we have discovered that metacognition, or thinking about your thinking, is key not only to students' ability to adjust and improve their own mental processing but for learning to happen at all (McGuire, 2015). Furthermore, mindsets matter: if you have a fixed mind-set and believe that talent, intelligence, and personality are fixed, then failure only confirms that you lack something you need to succeed (Dweck, 2007).

A teacher who can alter this to a growth mind-set, where talent and other abilities can be developed with practice and hard work, transforms a student's ability to learn everywhere. Here again, faculty are at a disadvantage: we were probably good at learning (at some stage), and we clearly believed that we could transform ourselves through study and hard work. Helping students understand that failure is an opportunity and that learning is largely about work and not talent, is a prerequisite for critical thinking. We often skip this step and are still discovering the implications of this insight.

The emerging field of affective neuroscience is giving us more specific information about how emotions and motivation guide learning. Mary Helen Immordino-Yang (2015) has discovered that we use the most fundamental survival part of our brains when we try to think about meaning or integrate new learning: we actually "think with our gut" in a way. Passion does indeed precede learning: we remember only what matters to us. We also have to learn to feel inspiration, awe, and potential, and these complex notions are developed through reflection. Call it downtime or processing space, but integrative and complex thinking can be developed only through repeated exposure to inspiring stories, ideas and models, and some sort of contemplative practice. Cognitive wrappers—brief non-graded exercises that are designed to match specific assignments—then, are designed to give students space to reflect on their own power to transform themselves.

Two studies, one led by Mary-Ann Winkelmes (2013) and the other by Marsha Lovett (2013), demonstrate how metacognition and reflection can be used to improve study habits and exam performance. Winkelmes (2013) demonstrated that the following activities significantly improved student learning:

- Discussing the rational of assignments
- Connecting "how people learn" data with activities
- Debriefing grades, tests, and assignments in class

The benefits of this transparency, including more learning and higher retention, were magnified for underrepresented groups, transfer students, and nontraditional students. Simply being more transparent in class about why we assign what we do and connecting it to stated learning goals is especially beneficial for students with less family experience of college.

At the same time, Lovett (2013) and her colleagues at Carnegie Mellon were experimenting with exam wrappers: a very short reflective survey (online or a single sheet of paper) given to students with an assignment or exam feedback. They demonstrated that math and science exam wrappers provide a quick and easy way to improve student learning and connect learning and thinking habits across disciplines.

From Socrates' "self-examination" to William James's "introspective observation" and Jean Piaget's "directed thought," reflection has been the foundation of critical thinking. In *How We Think* (1910), John Dewey describes it as "active, persistent and careful consideration of any belief or supposed form of knowledge in light of the grounds that support it and the further considerations to which it tends" (p. 6). For Dewey, our job is to find problems and "forked-road situations." The critical thinker will be able "to maintain the state of doubt and to carry on systematic and protracted inquiry" (p. 13). As noted in Chapter 7, employers highly desire this tolerance for ambiguity. The ability to hold two opposing ideas at once without making up your mind about either would make an excellent graduation requirement.

We like to call these *cognitive wrappers* since they help students become critical thinkers by helping them learn to self-regulate. A significant line of research shows a complex interdependence between the two concepts (Phan, 2010). Ultimately, only students themselves can decide to adopt a more complex mental model, but we have to provide the situations that generate "optimal conflict" (again Piaget, but also James Mark Baldwin, Heinz Werner, and Lawrence Kohlberg) in what Kegan and Lahey (2009) summarize in this way:

The *persistent* experience of some frustration, dilemma, life puzzle, quandary, or personal problem that is . . .
   Perfectly designed to cause us to *feel the limits* of our current way of knowing . . .
   In some sphere of our living that we *care about*, with . . .
   Sufficient supports so that we are neither overwhelmed by the conflict nor able to escape or diffuse it (p. 54).

We find it significant that neurologists, developmental psychologists, organizational business gurus, residential life professionals, therapists, and educational theorists have all come to the same conclusion: change is hard, and it requires motivation, persistence, design, and support. Kegan and Lahey are writing about organizational change, but their formulation seems remarkably like Dee Fink's (2013) version of how we craft significant learning experiences or William Perry writing about Harvard students in 1970. It is not enough just to care, or just to have high standards, or even just to provide provocative situations for students. Pedagogy and learning design are essential for moving students to more advanced models of thought.

Note that metacognition is a complex set of skills. Like critical thinking, the process begins with self-awareness, noticing and knowing your strengths and weaknesses. Helping students develop metacognition equally begins with transparency and giving them clarity about learning goals and why we study the way we do. Cognitive wrappers can then help students move to more active monitoring, evaluating, reflecting, and adjusting. They can make students more metacognitively aware.

Like critical thinking, much of this seems discipline specific. Just as generic study skills courses have not proven effective, metacognition happens more efficiently within subject content. Repeated exposure to self-reflection, labeled as part of critical thinking, in different contexts, greatly helps students develop transferable thinking skills. Wrappers too work best when they are discipline specific, but used simultaneously in different contexts in different classes. How is studying for an art history exam different from practicing for a music lesson or doing calculus homework? How is my preparation for sociology and history papers different? What counts as appropriate skepticism in philosophy, anthropology, or biology? Note too that we assume these sorts of questions are the obvious by-product of a liberal arts education (perhaps obvious to students who became faculty), but students often do not have a way to make these connections if we do not provide a structure for this. Students need to understand both that self-regulation is a part of improving each of these activities and that the adjustments will be different for each type of learning.

The best way to avoid the production of "mini me" students is to focus on increasing the metacognition and reflective capabilities of each individual. Since reflection requires space and time without devices (something students have a hard time doing), these are exercises best done in class. Our real goal as teachers is to help students learn how to learn. Cognitive wrappers provide a quick and easy way to improve study habits, connect learning and thinking habits across disciplines, increase self-awareness and reflection, and ultimately provide a key building block of critical thinking: learning to change your mind requires some level of self-reflection. Cognitive wrappers are a design structure that will help you produce the voracious self-regulated learners that lead to career success, what employers want, and the 21st-century demands.

Step-by-Step Guide

Cognitive wrappers should be brief, easy, flexible, and specific to both the discipline and the specific task at hand. They should be structured to help students understand that they need to understand their own strengths and weaknesses, assess their own performance, identify strategies that work for them, and make adjustments.

Step 1: Make it Brief

Wrappers are a very short survey given to students with assignment or exam feedback. They can be done online, but a single piece of paper with a few simple questions and space for writing is often all you need.

Step 2: Do Not Grade Them

This is an exercise for students to help themselves. They need to be low stakes and intrinsically motivated. You do not need to collect them. Some faculty collect them and then hand them back before the next similar assignment. You can ask students if they want you to read them or if they want to discuss them, but they work best when students are honest and clearly understand no grade is involved.

Step 3: Provide a Structure for Reflection and Action

Most wrappers consist of four parts, each designed to guide students during the process of reflection:

- *Rationale.* "This is only to help you improve."
- *Reflection.* "How did you prepare for this exam/assignment/ discussion?"
- *Comparison.* "What kinds of mistakes did you make?"
- *Adjustment.* "How will you prepare differently next time?"

Step 4: Imagine New Moments for Reflection

Think of all the places, circumstances, and times when you want your students to pause and think about how they learn and how they might self-regulate more. Wrappers began as a way to force students to stop and review their exam performance, but this idea can be extended to many situations. Music schools are using wrappers to help students evaluate their preparation for lessons, rehearsals, and performances. Engineering students are reflecting on how they work in teams. Wrappers can also help students understand that preparation for class discussion is essential and how they prepare can make a difference. Wrappers at the beginning of a new problem set or other assignment can also provide a rationale for that assignment.

Wrappers are especially useful with papers. Students often believe that paper grades are about "pleasing the professor." A student may read your comments about grammar and think you are just nit-picking. Try an exam wrapper that asks, "What percent of your preparation time did you spend on each of these activities?" and then provides a list: thinking, researching, drafting, and editing. Students may be surprised by this set of choices. A student with feedback for poor grammar may notice that she allocated 0% of her work time to editing and make an adjustment on her next paper. A student who sees that you thought his thesis was underwhelming may now connect this comment with the possibility that thinking is an activity that requires more time in working on the next paper.

Step 5: Offer Them Before Grades Are Revealed

Wrappers are an excellent way to get students to read your comments. Many faculty wait until the end of class to hand out papers and are then dismayed when students turn to the back page, glance at the grade, groan or smile, and then stuff the paper into a backpack. If you want students to read your comments, hide the grade online, and allow class time for students to read your comments. Then ask students to complete the wrapper without knowing their grade (see Chapter 9).

Step 6: Customize Wrappers for Your Discipline and Work

Wrappers need to be discipline specific and customized for your particular assignment or situation. The template in the next section offers far too many choices for any wrapper. Your choices are an essential guide for students. If you want students to spend some time thinking or editing as part of the paper-writing process, include those choices. If you want students to work in groups when they do your problem sets, make that a choice on the wrapper. Students will learn gradually that your suggestion to "explain the chapter to a friend or relative using an analogy they will understand" is a good way to help them extend their understanding of the material. A wrapper is a way to reinforce your class suggestions for study and get students to connect these study habits with real outcomes.

Theater students audition a lot, but their tendency is to think that directors cast only people they like, a safe assumption for them. When asked, "Why do you think you did not get the part?" a student might respond, "Because they hate me." An audition wrapper can be used to get students to reflect, but the preparation choices have to be customized. Asking students if they memorized their lines, rehearsed with a friend, studied other versions of the role, did research on the play, and tried the part with different accents might itself give students insight into other ways to prepare (perhaps it never occurred to them that the character might have an accent or that research might have given them insight). If you then ask a student where he thinks he lost points in the audition, he might now admit he forgot a line and realize that might be an action item for the next audition. It also has the fringe benefit of removing the director's like or dislike of him from the equation.

Step 7: Repeat Sparingly

Like anything else, wrappers and reflection exercises can become a chore, and when they do, they lose their meaning and power. They are also easy to spoof, and if you do this weekly, students will grow weary of them. Try giving them similar wrappers spread across the semester every time there is a paper, for example, or once a month after a discussion session.

Wrappers work best when students can see how taking their own advice to modify how they study improved the quality of their work. To facilitate this, try using wrappers for the same type of assignment: if you do three wrappers for three different types of situations, you may be asking students to compare three different types of study patterns. The opportunities for students to modify their own behavior are greatest if your repeat the exercise at the same moment for the same type of assignment.

Wrappers work best when used sparingly in each class but in multiple classes at once, and even across different activities (e.g., sports, student life situations). Coordination of the focus helps.

Step 8: Modify This Template

What follows are questions for multiple situations. This exercise needs to be short, so select only one or two of each type of question (i.e., only one or two letters from each of the four categories) and tailor them to your situation. Wrappers should be no longer than a single sheet of paper.

Items in the Reflection list with an asterisk tend to be time-consuming and not very effective. Rereading or highlighting, for example, creates fluency (the material feels more familiar), but the material does not stick in long-term memory. It is much better to switch to items with a dash, as elaborating on the material is faster and more effective. For example, try thinking of new examples, making analogies (How would you explain this concept in baseball or fashion terms?), or looking for a larger context and restating ideas in your own words. Trying to remember the exact phrase or syntax of an idea is actually counterproductive: come up with your own rule, phrase, or language.

Cognitive Wrapper Template
(Here are many many options for each category.)

Rationale

a. This assignment/activity/exam and this feedback were designed to help you/give you practice/ improve your . . . [achieve what learning outcome?]. Do the activities and feedback really support the goal?

b. This form will help you evaluate your own preparation and performance for this assignment/exam/ lesson/activity/class session and allow you to adjust your study/practice habits in the future. Your responses will have no effect on your grade and are solely to help you improve. Being brutally honest with yourself here is a useful and important part of self-examination.

c. Ask in advance (i.e., give the wrapper with the homework): "The goal of this assignment/homework/ reading/exam is to give you practice with X [or to help you analyze your Z]. Before you begin, rate your awareness of Y [or think about Z]."

d. This form is designed to help you prepare more fully for class. Did you participate fully in class today?

Reflection

a. How much total time did you spend preparing [or writing/reading/reviewing]?

   When? How did you spread out your preparation?

b. How did you prepare for this exam/lesson/activity/class session?

c. How much time did you spend reviewing X [or Y or Z]?

d. What percent of your preparation was done alone/groups?

e. What percent of your preparation time was spent on each of these activities?

Reading textbook section(s) for the first time ___

*Rereading or highlighting textbook section(s) ___

*Rereading your class notes ___

Reading/studying other materials ___

(What other materials did you use? _____)

—Rewriting key concepts into your own words ___

—Rephrasing ideas ___

—Creating personal examples or analogies ___

—Self-testing (or working on extra problems) ___

—Relating new material to things you already know ___

Finding online content ___

Thinking ___

Preparing ___

Researching ___

Drafting ___

Editing ___

Listening ___

Finding inspiration ___

Analyzing posture ___

Working on problems ___

*Focusing on one thing at a time ___

—Interleaving (varying your studying) ___

Playing through pieces ___

Resting ___

Memorizing ___

*Repeating concepts by rote ___

—Flash cards ___

Playing for fun ___

Brainstorming or conceptualizing ___

Experimenting ___

Sharing ideas with others ___

Practicing technique ___

Working on new material ___

Focusing ideas ___

*Reviewing homework solutions ___

*Reviewing your own notes ___

*Reviewing concepts and ideas ___

—Contextualizing concepts in new ways ___

—Solving new harder problems for practice ___

(*continued*)

(*continued*)

Reviewing other materials (which?) ___

Other: Please specify: _____

Comparison

Now that you have listened to my feedback and the feedback of your classmates, looked over your graded exam, and read my response to your paper, address these points:

a. What kinds of mistakes did you make?

b. Estimate the points you lost due to:

- Trouble understanding a concept (or list specific concepts) ___
- Trouble remembering lines/formulas/structures ___
- Trouble with definitions ___
- Trouble with technique ___
- Not concentrating/focused enough ___
- Careless mistakes ___
- Lack of preparation ___
- Not being able to formulate an approach to the problem ___
- Arithmetic/grammatical errors ___
- Unclear expectations ___
- Reviewed the wrong material ___
- Not practicing enough ___
- Anxiety (and specifically over what?) ___
- Other ___

c. After having completed this assignment, rate each of the following statements in terms of how true it is for you on a scale from 1 to 5 [insert a list similar to that in part b).

Adjustment

Name at least three things you will do differently next time in preparing. Be specific. For example, will you spend more time, start your preparation earlier, change a specific study habit, try a new one (if so, try to name it), sharpen some other skill (if so, name it), or participate in more review opportunities or something else?

a. What study/practice strategy worked best/worst for you?

b. Students sometimes have difficulty drawing appropriate force-body diagrams and applying Newton's second law appropriately. Was either of these a difficulty for you (check question 2 on the exam)? If so, try to self-assess your understanding: Identify what aspects of these skills are causing you difficulty and what you can do to improve your ability to solve problems using these skills.

c. What aspect(s) of your preparation for this exam/session seemed different from your exam/session 1 preparation? Did these changes have any effect?

Examples

Affinity Research Group Model

Graciela Perera, Northeastern Illinois University

Student engagement, both inside and outside the classroom, is a prerequisite to critical thinking, and Graciela has adapted the affinity research group (ARG) model to foster deep student engagement in her computer networking and cybersecurity courses. ARG is a team-based learning strategy for undergraduate research that develops scholarly inquiry skills in students through an intentionally inclusive, cooperative approach. Graciela has adapted the model to ensure her students are active in the research settings she constructs within her courses. Because the approach is overtly supportive and reassuring, students can be challenged and engaged with minimal distractors that are often present in competitive research environments. Her students are more comfortable to freely engage in the critical thinking activities that are foundational to performing research.

Semantic Networks as Active Learning Strategy

Ajay Sharma, University of Georgia

Key attributes of all active learning strategies are that students are forced to think about, reflect on, grapple with, explain, synthesize, support, and/or defend aspects of the content of the course. In other words, they must actively process what is being delivered. As has been said many times, what we process, we learn.

Ajay teaches a diagnostic imaging course in veterinary medicine that employs an inventive case-based approach. In it, he uses a variation of concept maps that he describes as semantic networks, a notion popularized by Nicole Woods at the University of Toronto. At the beginning of the semester, he introduces a complex case and asks his students to pretend they are graduate veterinarians who must interpret the data he presents. Then they are asked to build a semantic network of nodes and connectors based on the case. As the semester progresses, he returns to the same case each week and adds a new layer of complexity. Students must then reevaluate their semantic network and add, adjust, revise, and delete nodes and connectors to appropriately accommodate the new information. This strategy requires students to revisit content early in the semester and synthesize it with new information. Processing of course content is a hallmark of this approach.

Assessing Others to Foster Metacognition

Barbara Juncosa, Citrus College

Evaluating and explaining errors in others' works can increase awareness of metacognitive strengths and weaknesses, and Barbara has students reflect on the work of others as a strategy to foster metacognition in her microbiology courses. She provides students with a sample essay question that might be found on her exams, along with a student response that she wrote. The response contains common errors that she often finds in student writing and in answers to that particular question. Students are asked to grade the response and describe the flaws and accuracies they find in the answer. A discussion then follows that includes modeling of how she approaches such questions and things she expects in quality essay responses. Students become aware of Barbara's expectations and learn successful strategies for approaching such writing assignments that tend to lead to good grades.

Adapting Cognitive Wrappers

Sarah Lovern, Concordia University Wisconsin

Deep engagement with cognitive wrapper activities could be a critical strategy for increasing students' success for those who are struggling within our institution's most challenging courses. Sarah, also highlighted in Chapter 5, has adapted cognitive wrappers as an intervention strategy in her anatomy and physiology courses. If students score below 70% on her first exam, they must meet with her briefly. Typically that's about 30% of her students. While all students are encouraged to complete a cognitive wrapper following the exam, those meeting with her must bring their responses to the wrapper with them. Reviewing their answers is the focus of the discussion. Not surprisingly, many of these students already know what they did "wrong" in terms of preparing for the test; however, Sarah now has the opportunity to provide specific, contextual advice to each student and to affirm their thoughts regarding how they might perform better on the next test. This approach assists students in developing practical approaches, as well as metacognitive skills, that will serve them well on future exams.

Wrappers for Writing

Brenda Hardin Abbott and Lisa Ruch, Bay Path University

In addition to assessing exam performance, cognitive wrappers can be used to assist students as they review their performance on writing projects. Brenda and Lisa use this approach in the freshman writing sequence at their university. In the two-semester set of courses, they employ three cognitive wrappers in each course. In the first semester, students assess their writing performance as they begin their first semester of college, midway through their first semester, and at the end of that semester. In the second course, the process is problematized further by asking students to reflect on their skills as researchers and with writing research papers. The professors as well as the students are able to chart the development of their metacognitive skills throughout the first year. Students can also see their improvement as writers and researchers by intentionally and transparently examining their roles within the writing process.

Learning Projects as Cognitive Wrappers

Robin Black Wilson, Goucher College

There are a number of creative ways to structure cognitive wrappers within a course. Robin teaches mathematics and problem solving and has developed a fully realized flipped model for her courses. In addition to out-of-class content and actively engaged classes, she is also using a variant of cognitive wrappers that she calls "learning projects." Four times during the semester (the first day of class, after the first exam, after the second exam, and the last day of class), her students complete brief online surveys that are intended to gauge their efficacy with math content and with notions of their future careers as math teachers. Part of this process includes questions about study habits as well as the students' perceptions of the course at these key points in the semester. While these learning projects explore a number of topics, metacognitive questions are among the issues students reflect on during this process. By combining these elements, students see metacognition as important and coupled with expectations regarding their success in the course and their future careers.

Key Concepts

- Self-reflection enables students to practice a foundational component of critical thinking and opens the door for individual discovery.

- Opportunities for reflection have been shown to result in a range of benefits in terms of learning and human development.

- Reflection is essential to metacognitive development.

- Cognitive wrappers are a form of reflection that require critical thinking that leads to metacognitive development.

- Cognitive wrappers should be brief, ungraded, and customized prompts that provide a structure for students' metacognitive reflection.

- Cognitive wrappers should also lead to clear action steps that students can take to ensure greater academic success.

- Consider opportunities you may have to shift students away from a fixed mind-set toward a growth mind-set.

Further Resources

Eberly Center at Carnegie Mellon University. (2016). *Exam wrappers*. Retrieved from http://www.cmu.edu/teaching/designteach/teach/examwrappers/

Exam wrappers are a form of cognitive wrappers that are used as students turn in their exams. Here, they are asked to reflect on various aspects of their preparation for the exam. In addition to a description of the exam wrapper process, this resource provides several examples of exam wrappers as PDFs.

■ ■ ■

Flavell, J. H. (1979). Metacognition and cognitive monitoring. A new area of cognitive-development inquiry. *American Psychologist, 34*(10), 906–911.

This article shares some of the foundational concepts underscoring our beliefs about metacognition.

■ ■ ■

Jenson, J. D. (2011). Promoting self-regulation and critical reflection through writing students' use of electronic portfolios. *International Journal of ePortfolio, 1*(1), 49-60.

This article provides practices and research regarding how e-portfolios and writing can be collectively leveraged. The emphasis here is on reflection and promoting self-regulation.

■ ■ ■

Kephart, K., Villa, E., Gates, A. Q., & Roach, S. (2008). The Affinity Research Group Model: Creating and maintaining dynamic, productive, and inclusive research groups. *Council on Undergraduate Research Quarterly, 28*(4), 13-24. Retrieved from http://cahsi.cs.utep.edu/cahsifiles/Files/Resources/The AffinityResearchGroupModel.pdf

This article describes a specific model for undergraduate research that is designed to create and maintain "dynamic, productive, and inclusive research groups."

■ ■ ■

Livingston, J. A. (1997). *Metacognition: An overview.* Retrieved from http://gse.buffalo.edu/fas/shuell/cep564/metacog.htm

This brief introduction to metacognition provides several seminal references for those who would like to explore further.

■ ■ ■

Mezirow, J. (1990). *Fostering critical reflection in adulthood: A guide to transformative and emancipatory learning.* San Francisco, CA: Jossey-Bass.

Focusing on lifelong learning, this book describes techniques and strategies used to help adult learners leverage their life experiences in the service of learning.

■ ■ ■

Project for Education Research that Scales. (2016). *Mindset kit*. Retrieved from https://www.mindsetkit.org/

If you're interested in trying to shift your students' beliefs about how they learn (their mind-sets), you will find this set of resources and online lessons of exceptional interest.

■ ■ ■

Schön, D. A. (1990). *Educating the reflective practitioner: Toward a new design for teaching and learning in the professions*. San Francisco, CA: Jossey-Bass.

Focusing his ideas from *The Reflective Practitioner* (1983) into educational settings, this book advocates reflective practice as an essential component of higher education, especially for students in professional schools.

■ ■ ■

Silver, N. (2013). Reflective pedagogies and the metacognitive turn in college teaching. In M. Kaplan, N. Silver, D. LaVaque-Manty, & D. Meizlish (Eds.), *Using reflection and metacognition to improve student learning* (pp. 1-17). Sterling, VA: Stylus.

This chapter serves as an introduction to the book. It provides a history and definitions of reflection and metacognition that many will find enlightening.

References

Brookfield, S. D. (1995). *Becoming a critically reflective teacher*. San Francisco, CA: Jossey-Bass.

Dewey, J. (1910). *How we think*. Boston, MA: Heath.

Dweck, C. (2007). *Mindset: The new psychology of success*. New York, NY: Ballantine Books.

Ellis, S., Carette, B., Anseel, F., & Lievens, F. (2014). Systematic reflection: Implications for learning from failures and successes. *Current Directions in Psychological Science, 23*(1), 67–72.

Fink, D. (2013). *Creating significant learning experiences: An integrated approach to designing college courses* (2nd ed.). San Francisco, CA: Jossey-Bass.

Immordino-Yang, M. H. (2015). *Emotions, learning, and the brain: Embodied brains, social minds, and the art of learning.* New York, NY: Norton.

Kegan, R., & Lahey, L. L. (2009). *Immunity to change: How to overcome it and unlock the potential in yourself and your organization.* Boston, MA: Harvard Business Review Press.

Lovett, M. C. (2013). Make exams worth more than the grade: Using exam wrappers to promote metacognition. In M. Kaplan, N. Silver, D. LaVague-Manty, & D. Meizlish (Eds.), *Using reflection and metacognition to improve student learning: Across the disciplines, across the academy* (pp. 18–52). Sterling, VA: Stylus.

McGuire, S. (2015). *Teach students how to learn: Strategies you can incorporate into any course to improve student metacognition, study skills, and motivation.* Sterling, VA: Stylus.

Perry, W. G., Jr. (1970). *Forms of intellectual and ethical development in the college years: A scheme.* New York, NY: Holt, Rinehart, and Winston.

Phan, H. P. (2010). Critical thinking as a self-regulatory process component of teaching and learning. *Psicothema, 22*(2), 284–292.

Ramirez, G., & Beilock, S. L. (2011). Writing about testing worries boosts exam performance in the classroom. *Science, 331*(6014), 211–213.

Schön, D. A. (1984). *The reflective practitioner: How professionals think in action.* New York, NY: Basic Books.

Winkelmes, M. A. (2013). Transparency in teaching: Faculty share data and improve students' learning. *Liberal Education, 99*(2). Retrieved from https://www.aacu.org/publications-research/periodicals/transparency-teaching-faculty-share-data-and-improve-students

Chapter 9

Grading and Feedback

FEEDBACK IS ESSENTIAL for learning. Grades are not.

Well-timed and thoughtful feedback (including short videos) can increase student engagement, improve learning, and reduce grade complaints. Too often we focus on grading as a necessary evil. Grades are only "symbols of relative achievement in a class section" (Barkley & Major, 2016, p. 25) where feedback or assessment aims to be a more precise attempt to guide or determine what was learned. We know students won't read most of our feedback, and yet we spend an enormous amount of time writing it. Can we not help ourselves? Given that most of us are required to do grades, can we instead spend as little time as possible calculating grades that are not going to boost learning and create a better feedback process that will enhance learning but can eventually be turned into grades?

The design challenge starts with making sure our learning goals (Chapter 1) and assignments (Chapters 6, 7, and 8) are connected with our feedback: students learn best when the goals, activities, and feedback are clear and aligned (Chapter 11; Fink, 2013). Good assignments should produce learning products that will allow you to provide feedback related to your goals and a way to assess each student's progress toward those goals. We therefore need a strategy for assessment.

First, we need to clarify our vocabulary. The word *assessment* means two very different things depending on with whom you are speaking and in what context in higher education. Our due diligence to find best practices around grading and feedback by consulting the literature, the Web, and other sources (Allen & Field, 2005; Richlin, 2001) may be compromised by these two different meanings of *assessment*. In this chapter, we are speaking of assessment as grading of student work. In other places on your campus, *assessment* refers to programmatic assessment. A key part of that process is student learning outcomes assessment, which looks at your students' performance toward meeting larger programmatic learning goals (Walvoord, 2010). As a result of regional accreditation processes, most programs at most institutions throughout the United States have now articulated program-level student learning outcomes; however, course-level grading and feedback are typically only marginally associated with that other notion of assessment. Sometimes even the titles of very different books on assessment use similar language (see Barkley & Major, 2016; Walvoord, 2010). There is some overlap, of course, but here we focus on the feedback and grading you do in your classes.

Given this often confusing context, Barkley and Major (2016) have combined their work on assessment, engagement, and collaborative learning into a series of learning assessment techniques (LATs) that provide the kind of instructional alignment Fink (2013) described. This alignment includes (1) significant learning goals, (2) effective learning activities, and (3) learning artifacts that can then be used to ensure success with grading and feedback. The learning cycles described by Fink (see Figure 1.1), Barkley and Major, and here in *Teaching Naked Techniques* use different terms, frameworks, and processes, but all attempt to connect learning goals, student work, and assessment into a continuous feedback loop (Figure 9.1).

This kind of assessment alignment is well established and is sometimes referred to as criterion-referenced assessment. In other words, students are being graded based on their performance in meeting a specific learning goal, not on how well they did compared to other students in the class (norm-referenced assessment) (Biggs & Tang, 2011).

Instructional alignment is key (see Chapter 11), and Fink provides a worksheet packet online that can walk you through the process of ensuring

FIGURE 9.1

The Interconnected Nature of Goals, Learning Design, and Assessment

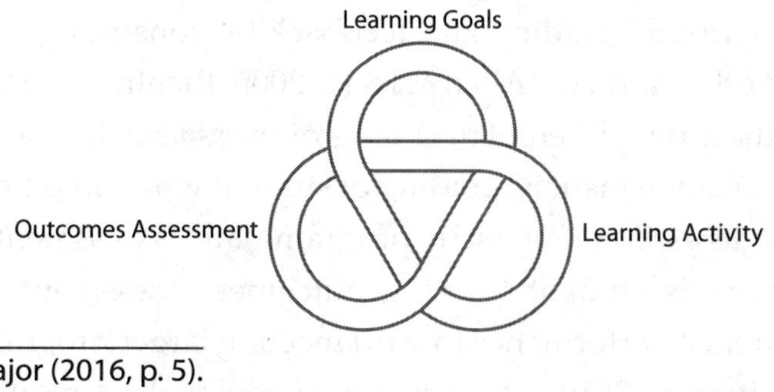

Learning Goals

Outcomes Assessment

Learning Activity

Source: Barkley and Major (2016, p. 5).

alignment of goals, activities, and assessment (Fink, 2005), but here's an additional way to think about the specific issue of grading. Once you have learning goals and assignments, try thinking about the question of feedback instead of the problem with grades. What mistakes do you most want to correct? What mistakes are most likely? To where do you want to guide students?

Start in an ideal world. You will almost certainly not be able to reach all of these ideals as time, workload, student preparation, and experience may intervene—still, better that than abandoning your ideals at the gates of grading requirements. You may also find that once you have articulated your ideals to yourself and perhaps your students, everyone may be willing to focus on the goal a bit more. If you complain to students about the insanity of grading without providing them a glimpse of what you really are hoping to accomplish, they will not understand why you became a professor.

Fink (2013) uses the acronym *FIDeLity* to summarize best practices for feedback. All of these are design issues—although loving feedback is probably easier if you truly care about your students:

- *Frequent*. The more often you can provide feedback, the better. Feedback can also just be encouragement.

- *Immediate*. Students are very sensitive to how long it takes you to return work. While most of us are used to waiting months for feedback, students will notice if you can get work back in days, not weeks.

- *Discriminating*. The more specific, focused, and clear your feedback is, the more likely it is to move students toward your learning objectives.

- *Loving*. The way you provide feedback matters. In all, critique, trust and context matter. If students understand the goal and why it matters, believe you want them to succeed, and are genuinely trying to help them improve, they will receive your feedback more readily.

Start by thinking in advance about the types of feedback you can and will provide. Are you capable of ignoring grammatical errors and reading for content? Are you willing to see past calculation errors or an incorrect setup of the numbers to see that a student's strategy was inspired? Will you have time to read everything as carefully as you wish? This is partly alignment with course goals, but it is also knowing yourself. If you know you are going to downgrade any paper without a bibliography, then make sure that including a bibliography in the paper is included in the assignment description and in your rubric as a key item.

Rubrics make grading easier (see Chapter 1), but there may be the temptation only to check the boxes of the rubric (literally). For large classes where detailed feedback is impossible, this is a reasonable strategy that will allow more frequent and immediate feedback. Spend time on a detailed rubric table (criteria on one axis and standards on the other) that can also be an assignment guide, and then check the boxes that correspond to what students achieved in each area. Take the time to write a few encouraging words and perhaps *one* additional point you would like the student to try and fix the next time; add this at the bottom of the rubric, staple the rubric to the assignment, and hand it all back. (There is software, like iRubric, rubrix.com, or rubistar, that will do this for you, and most learning management systems, such as Canvas and Brightspace by Desire2Learn, make it easy to create rubrics within courses). For a large class, this is more discriminating (giving students a first focus) and makes the feedback appear more personal or even loving. This may be the most efficient and best feedback you can offer.

If your rubric is this clear, then the grade will be obvious, but still do NOT do the calculations on the page. A final grade will draw most of the attention, due in part to the primacy effect where our brains privilege information that appears to be discreet or quantitative evidence: college applications that include SAT scores, for example, are read differently from those without them (Sternberg, 2010). If students can see grades, they will read feedback differently. When given a choice, we assume that the number of stars on Yelp is more important than the actual reviews. A grade is a label, and it sets off a chain of emotions that inhibit the learning your feedback is hoping to spark.

The way you return assignments is also critical. If you want students to ignore the hours of work you spent writing detailed comments on papers, problem sets, or exams, then hand back assignments at the end of class and include the grade on the hard copy. Students will find the grade, get emotional, stuff the assignment into a backpack, and never look at the work again (thanks to that primacy effect again). Technology has given you a better way and allows you to reveal the grade later—only after the feedback has been processed (see below).

In addition to making a rubric, you can grade papers or exams with your laptop handy and type your comments into a file. This can also be beneficial for exams and problem sets that are heavily mathematical. Our routine is often to correct only the equations and numbers, but that often does not help the student who may not understand the corrections. The narrative explanation might be as simple as, "You made an error in your calculations," but these comments provide another type of feedback.

Rather than write, "You made an error in your calculations" 300 times, just put a number 1 next to the problem and then refer students to your feedback guide.

It is almost certain that multiple students will make similar mistakes, and as you start articulating the common mistakes, you will also start remembering your numbering system; you will recognize a number 5 error, for example. This also allows you to put much more information into the notes. You might circle the grammatical error, "Bob and myself went to the movies," but now you can refer students to your easy trick for remembering when to use nominative pronouns and also refer them to a grammar website. You can also post these online; future classes will then be able to see common mistakes of previous years and work to avoid them before you have even started grading.

It is true that students may see this as less personal (it is, although they probably can't read your handwriting anyway!), but in a large class, you may have little choice. Since you are going to distribute this guide to lots of students, you can counteract this effect by being careful to write more detailed, clear, supportive, and kind feedback than you might in the margins. A feedback guide can immediately improve the quality and reception of your feedback, and it saves you time, making your feedback more immediate.

Another way to provide feedback is to ask students to do a self-assessment or provide feedback for each other. Self-assessments are standard practice in the business world, and self-reflection is an essential part of critical thinking, so there are multiple desirable benefits. Many of the reflective techniques explored in Chapter 8 can be adopted here as well.

Peer review, and cooperative learning in general, are useful in part because students are motivated differently when they interact with each other (Millis, 2002). It may even appear that they care more about what their peers think than what you think. A rubric here is essential to help standardize the process and guide students in knowing what they are looking for and how to evaluate it when they find it. This, of course, also helps them think about their own work (again, metacognition!). You will also need to calibrate peer review in some way; this is often called *norming*. If you have a lot of students, then the online Calibrated Peer Review (CPR) from UCLA is an excellent way to both figure out who is a good grader and also to generate usable scores that can be used as grades. In short, the system calibrates other student graders against your model and then assigns grades in proportion to the quality of the grader.

Most of us do written feedback for a variety of reasons. We are used to it, and it seems faster than meeting with every student, but we are also often a bit conflict avoidant. We'd rather hand back an "F" than look a student in the eye and say, "I don't understand what you were trying to do here." Verbal feedback, however, has the distinct advantage of starting a conversation; we may learn why the student is under stress or confused. Verbal feedback is also subject to misinterpretation, and a written record seems safer, but in the arts, it is common. In a studio art or music class, nearly all of the feedback might be verbal. While short student conferences are common in the humanities, they should be adopted in the sciences as well. Students learn better when they think you care, and feedback, especially verbal feedback, is an opportunity to understand students better and help them see that you care.

Video feedback is another option. Video is personal and direct, but also fast: most of us talk faster than we can write individual comments. This enables us to give more detailed feedback than we could possibly provide through writing. Students seem to like this method, and there is evidence that video results in strong comprehension of feedback (Borup, West, Thomas, & Graham, 2014; McCarthy, 2015; Robinson, Loch, & Croft, 2015). Another attractive attribute of using video is that there is also a shared record of the feedback.

With clearer expectations and multiple channels to encourage students to read, watch, or reflect on your feedback, what do you want to say? Teaching Naked is designed to move more failure and critical work into the classroom. This requires a redesign of assignments and class time, but it is also an opportunity for rethinking how your assessment and feedback might help students move toward your learning goals. What types of feedback promote more critical thinking? If your assessment and feedback seem authentic and aligned with your learning goals, students will pay more attention.

Step-by-Step Guide

Step 1: Provide Clear Goals, Rubrics, and Assignments

Feedback begins with clarity about what is required and why. Your rubric should provide transparency about both. It's good practice to share your rubric with your students as you provide the assignment; at the very least, make sure students know what they are trying to learn and how the assignment relates to that learning. Inexperienced graders sometimes think they need to examine a few sample assignments first to understand the mistakes and problems, but that is letting the students determine the goal. (If you need to know more about where your students are, do a pre-semester survey or just get to know them better (See Chapter 6). Provide clarity in advance and accept that your rubrics will become clearer with experience.

Step 2: Consider the Type of Feedback You Will Provide

Clarity up front will allow you to predict better where feedback is needed. If you have transparency about the purpose of the assignment, your feedback should align. You can't correct everything at once, so understanding your focus and what you are able and willing to grade is essential.

Barkley and Major (2016, appendix B or online; see below) have created a learning goals inventory score sheet that makes it easy to assess how your goals and assignments map to Fink's Taxonomy of Significant Learning (2013). Are you more focused on the cognitive or the emotional, foundational knowledge, or learning to learn? This can help clarify the goals you have for your students and help you develop assessments (e.g., projects, assignments) that are in alignment with those goals. Once those have been determined, you can then consider the types of feedback you will provide to students as you grade.

Step 3: Write Less and Sequence Your Feedback

The corollary is that students can't fix everything at once. Even if all of your assignments are of the same type (say, papers or problem sets), you need a sequence of goals and feedback. Your feedback is also a design problem. What is the first thing you want students to learn? That will determine your first set of feedback. Once you have eliminated mathematical or grammatical errors, what will students and your feedback focus on next?

This is also, of course, a major time saver for you. Students tend to ignore the vast majority of our markings and comments, in part because we have not designed and focused our feedback on the most important aspects of the assignment. Most feedback is overwhelming in its complexity and scope. Students need to know what ONE improvement to make for the next time they try this assignment, and you need to ignore some (maybe even most) of their errors as you prioritize during grading.

Step 4: Calculate Grades

At some point, you will probably need to convert some of your feedback into grades. The more alignment you have among your goals, assignments, and feedback, the easier it will be to assign fair and transparent grades—and the more your feedback will directly support what you want students to learn. Again, rubrics can make calculating grades much easier and defensible.

Step 5: Try Video Feedback

Most of the issues noted in Chapter 3 regarding the creation of digital content apply here as well. Hardware, software, and storage location are among the key issues you must address as you begin to develop your strategy for providing video feedback. For example, good hardware (e.g., microphone, headset) and your overall recording environment will be important to the quality of your recorded audio. Your best bet is to chat with your department's IT professional for guidance regarding the technical aspects of recording, as well as the best online location for returning feedback to students. You may find that your institution's learning management system (LMS) can require your students to watch your video feedback prior to releasing the grade to them.

Once you have the technical requirements taken care of, what do you want to say? One of the advantages of video feedback is that you can say more than you might write, and it will also seem more personal. Start with something you liked about the project, and congratulate or thank the student for something. As always, focus on one or two items; do not try to correct everything. Especially if you have been harsh, end with some words of support: mostly that this is hard, and you are always willing to help the student improve.

Step 6: Learn to Use Your Online Grade Book

Do not include grades with feedback! Technology has provided you with an easy way to get students to pay more attention to your comments and feedback, so never put grades on hard copy. Enter grades directly into your LMS, but hide them from students until after the class when you return the work. All LMSs easily allow you to set a common release time for grades on specific assignments.

In class, hand back hard copies (if that is what you do) or allow access to online or video feedback and give students time to read the comments in class. Most students will have headphones with them for listening to your video comments privately. You must save time in class for this. Have students do a cognitive wrapper (see Chapter 8) or provide some other way for them to demonstrate they have read and reflected on your feedback. Asking them to estimate their grade based on the feedback is an easy hurdle to require before revealing the grades online. Many LMSs also allow you to release the grades individually. For example, grades can remain hidden until a student has completed another task or filled in a survey.

Examples

Peer Review of In-Class Performances

Veronica McComb, Lenoir-Rhyne University

We have known for quite a while that performance, followed by feedback, is essential to learning, and immediate feedback, regardless of the source, is a key variable to meaningful learning as well (Chickering & Gamson, 1987). Veronica teaches U.S. history courses from 1865 to the present and has taken this knowledge to heart. As an example, she has an activity that spans three class periods that are aligned to specific learning outcomes, including explaining change over time and analyzing primary sources for historical significance. Students are assigned readings to complete before coming to class; in class, they are asked to create 5- to 7-minute skits across three acts that answer specific questions associated with, in this case, the Great Depression and the New Deal. Students are provided rubrics and are asked to evaluate how well each group achieved various era-specific criteria for the assignment that mapped to the overarching learning outcomes.

Instructional alignment was achieved through this approach and reinforced for the students because they were using the rubric over and over again as they scored their peers. This also enabled them to adjust their performances in each class to meet the expectations of the assignment. In addition, copious feedback was provided to the students in a timely fashion as discussion followed each performance and the performers received the completed rubrics of their peers.

Leveraging Bloom to Align Assessments

Mary Miller, Baton Rouge Community College

Now over 60 years old, Bloom's taxonomy continues to be evoked in important ways in higher education. Mary Miller, who teaches biology and microbiology, uses Bloom as she creates her learning objectives in all of her courses and makes this approach transparent to her students. She begins every semester with a discussion of Bloom's taxonomy and describes how it relates to her assessment choices. She explains how her learning objectives map to activities in the course, which then map to specific questions on quizzes and exams. The first day of class isn't the last time her students hear of Bloom. Bloom and Mary's learning objectives are an integral component of each class activity. She strives to post grades in the LMS within 12 hours after the exam, and students are encouraged to compare the questions on her exams to the course learning objectives to highlight the alignment she has designed into her courses. Students then see that the structure and activities of her course are intentional and purposeful. As a result, her expectations are easier for her students to recognize and meet.

Structured Feedback with Pecha Kucha

Mathew Mitchell, University of San Francisco

Pecha kucha is a short, timed presentation format for showing 20 images or slides, and each of these appears only for 20 seconds. Mathew teaches cognitive psychology and uses this format to manage time in class and ensures that each presenter receives feedback on his or her presentation. Because pecha kucha presentations are exactly 6 minutes 40 seconds in length, student presentations become far more predictable. As a result, in-class feedback following presentations can be anticipated and structured in such a way to ensure all students receive similar amounts of feedback from both the professor and fellow students.

Frequent Performance and Feedback Cycles

Rae Jean B. Goodman, U.S. Naval Academy

It is sometimes challenging to provide multiple opportunities for performance with feedback for all students in a class, but Rae Jean has designed an inventive strategy in her macroeconomic forecasting class that does just that. As the semester begins, her students select a macroeconomic variable that they are interested in forecasting and will be working with throughout the semester. As classes progress, her flipped model incorporates a variety of materials with which her students must engage prior to class. Each class begins with a short, extra-credit quiz on the previous night's assignments. Correct answers with brief explanations and feedback are provided before her active learning activities begin. She often starts with demonstrations of how forecasting can be performed with the statistical package STATA. Students are then provided with a data set and attempt to apply the forecasting techniques themselves in an in-class lab setting. Models and answers are then discussed, and students can compare their findings to what Rae Jean shares.

With this scaffolding in place, students are asked to apply this forecasting technique to the variable they selected at the beginning of the semester. They then present the results of their forecast and explain whether the technique performed well for their variable. Each presentation receives feedback from the students as well as Rae Jean, and each student tracks the performance of the various models on his or her variable. This culminates in a final paper and presentation that compares their variable's performance across each of the techniques. Self-assessment, peer feedback, and professor feedback are hallmarks of this scaffolded, iterative performance approach.

Screencasting Feedback

Bonni Stachowiak, Vanguard University

Written feedback requires a significant amount of effort, and the return (in the form of student engagement with our words) may not equal the work. An alternative approach is to provide screencasts with voice-overs. Bonni teaches introduction to business courses and has adopted this strategy. She has found that screencasting helps with clarity as students can see what is being discussed while it is being discussed, and the novelty of this approach helps engage students in the feedback process. Because feedback is coupled with voice inflections and references to what is currently on the screen, students have a clearer understanding of the intended outcomes of the feedback. Screencasting enables Bonni to pull up a student's essay, as well as the grading rubric, during the feedback discussion she provides. This approach enables her to present as if she is present with the student and give rich feedback that is meaningfully contextualized by the visuals in her video.

Key Concepts

- Learning goals, assignments, and feedback should align. If you think carefully about the sequence of goals and provide feedback for only one area at a time, you will improve learning and save time.

- You don't have to be the source of all feedback for your students. Students can provide meaningful feedback on each other's work.

- Self-assessments should be seen as another means of feedback.

- Feedback should occur frequently and occur as soon as possible after students practice, perform tasks, or hand in assignments.

- Rubrics can be helpful in providing structure for your feedback. They are also a form of instruction and make grades defensible.

- Consider alternative means of delivering feedback, such as audio or video feedback. You can provide much more guidance in less time through such strategies.

- Technology's greatest gift is the ability to separate student reflection on feedback from the moment when they have to see your grades.

Further Resources

Barkley, E. F., & Major, C. H. (2016). *The learning goals inventory*. Retrieved from https://www.aacu.org/sites/default/files/files/gened16/AlabamaLearning Goals.pdf

This is a tool freely available online designed to help college faculty self-assess the quality of the learning goals they have crafted for their courses.

■ ■ ■

Brookhart, S. M. (2013). *How to create and use rubrics for formative assessment and grading*. Alexandria, VA: Association for Supervision and Curriculum Development.

The title says it all. The components of effective rubrics are described, and guidance is provided regarding how to build and use rubrics, even for standards-based grading.

■ ■ ■

Carless, D. (2006). Differing perceptions in the feedback process. *Studies in Higher Education, 31*(2), 219–233.

This article, based on a large-scale study across eight universities, examines the challenges of providing effective written feedback. It concludes with helpful recommendations, including notions of "assessment dialogues."

■ ■ ■

Kolowich, S. (2015, January 26). Could video feedback replace the red pen? *Chronicle of Higher Education.* Retrieved from http://chronicle.com/blogs/ wiredcampus/could-video-feedback-replace-the-red-pen

This article contains interviews with faculty who have traded in traditional written feedback for video feedback strategies. Their experiences and recommendations are provided.

■ ■ ■

PechaKucha20x20. (2017). *Pecha kucha 20x20.* Retrieved from http://www. pechakucha.org/faq

Those new to the pecha kucha concept will welcome the answers provided in this frequently asked questions website. All of the rules associated with the form are provided.

■ ■ ■

Regents of the University of California. (2017). *Calibrated peer review: Web-based writing and peer review.* Retrieved from http://cpr.molsci.ucla. edu/Home.aspx

Growing out of the sciences, Calibrated Peer Review is a web-based tool that enables faculty to frequently assign writing assignments. Students then provide peer reviews of other students' writing, thus reducing the faculty workload typically required of writing assignments. It's an intriguing process that is open to schools outside California as well as within.

■ ■ ■

Sendziuk, P. (2010). Sink or swim? Improving student learning through feedback and self-assessment. *International Journal of Teaching and Learning in*

Higher Education, 22(3), 320–330. Retrieved from http://www.isetl.org/ijtlhe/pdf/ijtlhe800.pdf

This article provides an overview of the principles of learning-oriented assessment as well as a description of the strategies the author employed with his history students.

■ ■ ■

Stevens, D. D., & Levi, A. J. (2012). *Introduction to rubrics: An assessment tool to save grading time, conveys effective feedback, and promote student learning* (2nd ed.). Sterling, VA: Stylus.

Another excellent resource for learning how to create and use rubrics.

■ ■ ■

Thompson, R., & Lee, M. J. (2012). Talking with students through screencasting: Experimentations with video feedback to improve student learning. *Journal of Interactive Technology and Pedagogy, 1*. Retrieved from http://jitp.commons.gc.cuny.edu/talking-with-students-through-screencasting-experimentations-with-video-feedback-to-improve-student-learning/

This article includes embedded examples of video feedback as well as a narrative regarding the practices.

■ ■ ■

University of North Carolina at Charlotte. (2017). *Writing objectives using Bloom's taxonomy.* Retrieved from http://teaching.uncc.edu/learning-resources/articles-books/best-practice/goals-objectives/writing-objectives

Those looking for guidance for writing Bloom-based learning objectives will welcome this website. Three models provide different lenses through which to conceive of this task.

References

Allen, M., & Field, P. (2005). Scholarly teaching and scholarship of teaching: Noting the difference. *International Journal of Nursing Education Scholarship, 2*(1), 1–27.

Barkley, E. F., & Major, C. H. (2016). *Learning assessment techniques: A handbook for college faculty.* San Francisco, CA: Jossey-Bass.

Biggs, J., & Tang, C. (2011). *Teaching for quality learning at university* (4th ed.). New York, NY: McGraw-Hill.

Borup, J., West, R. E., Thomas, R. A., & Graham, C. R. (2014). Examining the impact of video feedback on instructor social presence in blended courses. *International*

Review of Research in Open and Distributed Learning, 15(3). Retrieved from http://www.irrodl.org/index.php/irrodl/article/view/1821/2909

Chickering, A., & Gamson, Z., (1987). Seven principles for good practice in undergraduate education. *AAHE Bulletin, 39,* 3–7.

Fink, L. D. (2005). *A self-directed guide to designing course for significant learning.* Retrieved from https://www.deefinkandassociates.com/GuidetoCourse DesignAug05.pdf

Fink, L. D. (2013). *Creating significant learning experiences: An integrated approach to designing college courses* (2nd ed.). San Francisco, CA: Jossey-Bass.

McCarthy, J. (2015). Evaluating written, audio and video feedback in higher education summative assessment tasks. *Issues in Educational Research, 25*(2), 153–169.

Millis, Barbara J. (2002). *Enhancing learning-and more! through collaborative learning* (IDEA paper 38). Manhattan, KS: IDEA Center. Retrieved from http://ideaedu.org/wp-content/uploads/2014/11/IDEA_Paper_38.pdf

Richlin, L. (2001). Scholarly teaching and the scholarship of teaching. *New Directions for Teaching and Learning, 86,* 57–67.

Robinson, M., Loch, B., & Croft, T. (2015). Student perceptions of screencast feedback on mathematics assessment. *International Journal of Research in Undergraduate Mathematics Education, 1*(3), 363–385.

Sternberg, R. J. (2010). *College admissions for the 21st century.* Cambridge, MA: Harvard University Press.

Walvoord, S. E. (2010). *Assessment clear and simple: A practical guide for institutions, departments, and general education* (2nd ed.). San Francisco, CA: Jossey-Bass.

Chapter 10

E-Communication

IT SHOULD BE obvious by now that student norms around social proximity have changed. Having an e-communication strategy allows you to appear more supportive of student learning and also capable of learning new things. Mostly, it gives you further opportunities to connect with and encourage students outside the classroom. This also provides additional face time in class for the more important things.

Put aside your fear or judgment for a moment. You might as well try to teach your dog that butt sniffing is inappropriate behavior. Generation Z has grown up with a device in hand (a third of current students always use a phone while using the toilet; Chronicle of Higher Education, 2014) and feel a deep sense of security in being able to communicate all the time. One in three Generation Z students report sending roughly 100 text messages a day (Seemiller & Grace, 2016). You can and should encourage reflection without devices, but you need to recognize that e-communication is a comfortable, natural, and automated behavior for most students today.

Start by recognizing that what is online can appear more real and even initially "safer" to this generation of students. A recent graduate pointed out to José that she expects to meet the most important people in her life online first: her first impressions of romantic partners (and eventually a spouse), in-laws, and prospective employers will all occur online. Choosing a college roommate routinely happens online, and dating has been utterly transformed by Tinder, Tinder Plus, Bumble, OkCupid, Hinge, Coffee Meets Bagel, Hitch, PlentyofFish, How About We, Hot or Not, Blendr, and Down. Alexandra Chong, cofounder of the controversial women-only 2013 app Lulu, which allows women to anonymously rate men (think Yelp for dating and sex), claimed that one in four college women used it before Lulu was acquired by global dating giant Badoo in February 2016 (Kosoff, 2016).

Students arrive on campus deeply accustomed to a 24/7 Internet world. Their bank is always open (online), and their balance is easily available on their phone. They investigated your college or university by looking at its web page and college ranking websites. One student told us that "if a professor has no social media, then I rely on RateMyProfesor." Another thought it normal that he "might never meet his best friend" because he lives in another country, and they know each other only from playing video games together online.

Then you arrive with your funny concept of "office hours" where you sit in what appears like an inner circle of hell and wait for social interaction. Even at a residential college, where office hours are desirable and (we hope) attainable, you need to encourage a different first impression. Students expect to meet, date, and live with their friends and partners: they just want to make sure those potential friends are safe first. Having some social media presence makes you appear safer too (and, ironically, also more real and more human).

Social media, or at least some way of communicating online, is also going to improve your teaching and student learning. Students learn more when they perceive you care about their learning, and they often want and need help inbetween classes. This notion is supported by evidence that has emerged from research in the online learning world. There, it is often termed "social presence" because a face-to-face presence is simply not an option. Students' perceptions of their learning, as well as their satisfaction with the instructor, strongly correlate with their overall perception of the teacher's social presence, and as a result, online instructors are exploring a wide range of strategies and tools to increase their social presence in those courses (Dunlap & Lowenthal, 2014; Lowenthal, 2009; Richardson & Swan, 2003).

Faculty social presence is especially helpful for first-generation students, as it is often the little things that can trip them up. What do I do if I get stuck on the first problem of the problem set? What do I do if I don't understand the reading or I have a question about the assignment? Some of this you can surely anticipate and put on your syllabus or your website. However, no one is always motivated and confident enough to behave perfectly. Nudging students in the right direction and providing information at the right time and in the right place can make an enormous difference.

The exact time that students can most usefully use the advice, "If you get stuck on problem 8, just skip it and try the next one," is most likely the night before it is due (and not in the syllabus). A text message is much more likely to be read than an e-mail. Personalized encouragement is also more likely to have an impact if it comes at the moment someone is about to give up, and not at the end of class. "Hi Alex. I am on Facebook right now. If you have any questions about tomorrow's problem set, just ask."

Some of this will require more collaborative teaching. You can't be online all the time, but faculty might rotate the on-call duties (much like a medical practice), and if you have teaching assistants, perhaps you can reorganize your class sessions to offer different face and support time. Try having some online support in addition to a writing or math center or small group sessions. Reevaluate too if putting some of the content delivery and support online would allow you to offer more complex problems or activities in person.

Importantly, note that having a shared group page or chat group will reduce the flow of e-mail and motivate your students to support each other online. Your response to general questions on e-mail should be, "Try posting that to the group page, and I will answer where everyone can benefit." E-communication is now a common part of all learning management system (LMS) tool sets, but there are many options. Whatever platform you choose, pushing students to share questions in an online group forum will eventually encourage them to respond to each other too. As in a face-to-face discussion, your encouragement, while resisting the urge to answer all of their questions yourself, is crucial.

Multitasking and Student Devices in the Classroom

Using social media outside class is one thing, but what are the parameters for social media use within your classroom? Research has provided us with much guidance, but the final decision is, of course, yours. In the early 2000s, one line of thinking theorized that our students, with all of their practice with technology growing up, would be able to multitask like no other generations before them (Aratani, 2007; Carlson, 2005; Oser, 2005; Wallis, 2006). From a teaching and learning perspective, this was very exciting. Even B. F. Skinner predicted that the world would one day produce advanced teaching machines that would double student learning (Seidensticker, 2006). Maybe this was it?

It wasn't. Research is consistently showing that "humans lack the cognitive, behavioral, and cortical structures necessary to multitask effectively" (Watson, Terry, & Doolittle, 2012, p. 303). Ultimately, what we know is that humans are really good at doing one thing at a time. Throw a second task in the mix, unless it's something practiced to the point of automation such as walking or eating, and performance on both tasks plummets. Sit in the back of any large lecture class these days, and you'll see a range of "modern learning" behaviors being practiced.

To better understand this in-class phenomenon, Sana, Weston, and Cepeda (2013) simulated a large lecture setting where half of the student participants were randomly assigned to perform a set of non-lecture-related online tasks; however, they were given the flexibility to choose whenever to engage in those tasks during the class. Not surprisingly, the multitasking group performed significantly lower on comprehension tests of the content covered in the lecture than those who were not multitasking. The difference equated to a little over a full letter grade. These researchers then repeated this study and strategically placed some nonmultitaskers in places where they could see the screens of the multitaskers, and this is where it got interesting: *those in view of their multitasking peers' computers scored significantly lower than other nonmultitaskers*—in fact, almost two letter grades lower. Regardless of your feelings about social media and technology, these findings are troubling. While we were already certain that multitasking had a negative impact on learning and performance, the new idea here is that distraction from others multitasking is even more detrimental to learning than multitasking itself.

Furthermore, recent research from the AAA Foundation for Traffic Safety found a residual, cognitive cost to switching from between two tasks that require performance. (In their study, the tasks were driving and engaging with smartphones.) They found that even when drivers had returned to just driving, there was a lingering distraction from working with smartphones that had a negative impact on reaction time and driving performance. It takes most of us up to 20 seconds for our attention to fully return to driving. It is as if our brains must reset themselves after performing these secondary tasks (Strayer, Cooper, Turrill, Coleman, & Hopman, 2015).

Several important points emerge from these studies. One is that our students aren't capable of multitasking. No surprise there. What we also know is that students who try to multitask in class have a significant negative impact on the learning of the students around them. Furthermore, the notion that students are effective "rapid switchers" is also a myth on par with the notions a few years back of students being multitaskers. So what do we do?

Some have chosen to ban smartphones or other technologies from their classrooms. (If you hang a see-through plastic "shoe-rack" on the back of your door, you can require students to deposit their phones there, but students will anxiously watch them buzz and blink. The research suggests this may be even more distracting (and it is not clear if it violates the Geneva Convention protocols on psychological torture!). Others select to have students sign technology contracts on the first day of class, where students agree to use their devices only for note taking and other class-related behaviors. Some ask students to dim screens as much as possible to keep from distracting others in class. Another strategy is to have everyone interested in using technology sit in one specific area in class. Yet another approach is to allow students to check texts and social media for two minutes during the middle of class with the expectation that phones will be put away for the rest of class (cell phone breaks for checking e-mail have become common practice during long business and conference meetings). While these strategies can prove effective at diminishing off-task technology use, there is a cost to classroom climate and culture if policing technology becomes a daily part of your pedagogical practice.

A better approach to classroom technology use is to have a meaningful, active classroom. When students are engaged in problem solving, discussions, simulations, role playing, and any number of other active learning strategies, multitasking behaviors around technology decrease. If students see the class as meaningful and purposeful, they will stay on task. Ultimately, our classroom practices are the best deterrent to student multitasking.

Step-by-Step Guide

Step 1: Determine Which Platform You Will Use

As you explore and make decisions regarding how to increase your social presence in your courses, a good place to begin is with instructional alignment. You may find that some platforms assist you as you help students achieve specific learning outcomes. For instance, some tools are more text-centric, while others are designed to incorporate visuals and other forms of media. Some, like Instagram, are entirely mobile. Ideally, your choice should contribute to both course goals as well as increasing your opportunities for interaction with students. With that said, your best bet is to pick a common platform to use with your students. The LMS and e-mail are likely givens at your institution, but an additional social media tool or two can provide opportunities for presence that are immediate and don't require your students to log in somewhere to find what you've shared. Each platform has distinct advantages, explored briefly next:

LMS

Your campus surely has an internal learning management system, and they all have some communication functions. If you are using the grade book and post all of your documents here, it can make a lot of sense to also use the chatrooms and group discussion functions. An LMS also provides a host of monitoring functions that let you know which students are logged in, when, and how often, and many LMSs are extending these capabilities into the learning analytics domain. Of course, because they are password protected by your institution, Family Educational Rights and Privacy Act (FERPA) and copyright protections are more easily managed within your LMS.

E-Mail

E-mail is for old people and more formal communication. You are probably most comfortable here, but your students may not check e-mail as often as you do. If you must use e-mail, you can always post on Facebook or send a text that you have sent an important e-mail, but this will seem as inefficient as it is.

Text

Texts come directly to phones and are the most likely communications to be read, and read immediately, but you will need to be brief. This is a good thing. You will almost certainly want a group text system (like WeChat or GroupMe), and if you don't type with your thumbs, you will want the ability to type texts on your computer (Messages on a Mac, for instance). You will need to collect student phone numbers, and this will supply students with your cell phone number. Many colleges are now moving to voice over Internet protocol systems that allow you to use your computer to make and receive phone calls from a variety of numbers. This gives you the ability to have different phone numbers for different classes or purposes—all going through your computer (This will change your life!).

Twitter

Twitter will also ensure brevity and make it easier to connect students with additional material, but not everyone will be used to checking this. You do NOT need to create a special profile for your course or to follow students. You simply need to create a hashtag, like #myclassatCollege, and by "creating a hashtag," we mean to choose one. A hashtag is simply a unique identifier for your course that begins with a hash sign (#). You don't have to sign up for one somewhere. You and your students can then search for messages that include this hashtag and see the stream of messages that students have tagged. It's very simple and easy to manage. The technical hurdles are very low, but you will immediately appear hip and savvy to your students.

Facebook

For many students, Facebook is home for hours a day. A minority of students may resist (they think, "Facebook is for kids and parents"), but it is still how the majority of college students introduce themselves to classmates and find a first-year roommate. It's certainly the most widely used of the social media platforms (Duggan, 2015). Try setting up a group within your college.edu. This way, anyone with the same .edu can join, and you do not have to "administrate" who can join your group. Students do not need to "friend" you. Facebook also has an internal chat function, which is very popular and gives you two channels at once. Students will often send a chat message with a question, and you can then either respond (if it is personal) or request that the question go on the group (where everyone can see the response).

Instagram

This too will make you appear hip, but Instagram is primarily designed as an app for photos on your phone. It is mobile, and not a place to store documents. If your learning objectives focus on visuals or your class involves taking lots of pictures in the field and communicating them quickly, this is for you.

Pinterest

If your class is visual or deals with lots of available media online, Pinterest is designed to "pin" and share images from the Internet. It's essentially a visual bookmarking system that enables you to share your collections of websites with others.

Google

Google has a suite of collaborative tools. You could create a Google Group (a shared e-mailed platform); share documents in Google Docs; and talk, chat, and share video in Google Hangout. Google Education is also constantly introducing new tools that enhance these channels; for example, Cast for Education allows anyone to share screens, and there are autograded quizzes in Google Forms.

Class Website or Blog

You can also start from scratch and create your own website in a neutral space. Many campuses provide storage space, and some textbook publishers are eager to have your traffic. WordPress and other blogging sites might be used to accomplish the same goals and even provide opportunities for your students to contribute to the site.

Step 2: Be Consistent

Don't use more than two channels. It will be more work for you to repost everywhere, and your students will get confused. Pick a single place as the home; this is where you should put all course documents and syllabus. It is also important to have an online grade book. This has pedagogical advantages (see Chapters 8 and 9), and using a secure site that keeps all of your documents and grades private (do not post your spreadsheet with student numbers) will give you peace of mind about FERPA.

If you have access to an LMS with features you like, then you might be done, but remember that you will need to create daily incentives for students to visit this foreign platform. You will need fresh content and messages and will need to remind students that they need to check here daily. A second faster and more modern group communication (like texting or Facebook) makes a great complement and can also be used to direct students back to your LMS or website—for example, "Hi. I've just posted a study guide for this week's reading. Check it out with this link." Including the link will make it easier for students, and they are more likely to use your new resource.

Step 3: Create Your E-Communication Schedule

You need a schedule, and you need to be reliable and on time. If you are online at the same time every day, tell your students this and post at the same time each day. You can also automate when and where you post with Hootsuite or any of a dozen other social media management tools. As the LMS platform is evolving, it too will have similar scheduled messaging tools, as well as reactive tools that send individual messages based on your students' behaviors and tasks. These are often called automated alerts or triggers and, depending on the context, will send messages to individual students or to you for action.

Timing and frequency are important. You should post one tip a day, or maybe two, but do not inundate your students. Think about what encouragement and information students need at specific times. When are they likely to be doing the homework or struggling? That is the moment to remind them you care and want to support their success.

Step 4: Establish Virtual Office Hours

Physical office hours are also vital (see step 7 below) and you may be required to hold them, but virtual office hours are an important complement and may make it easier to give students support in the evening and on weekends when they are more likely to be looking for it. There are many choices for free videoconferencing (e.g., Skype, Google+Hangout, Spreecast, FreeConferenceCall, Join.me, ooVoo, and Goober), and many allow you to share screens or other material with students. This is very useful and efficient for helping a student with a paper, for example, because you can watch students make corrections in real time and provide advice along the way.

Step 5: Distribute an E-Communication Policy

You need to decide about the options outlined in steps 1 to 4 and then include an e-communication policy on your syllabus. Here is a template with several options:

E-Communication Policy Template

- Course documents and all information will be available at _____.

- Course communication will be done on _____. It is optional [mandatory] that you join our Facebook group [or use our Twitter hashtag]. You need to post once a day [week] and check the site daily. I will post here daily.

- The best way to contact me is: _____ [e-mail, Facebook, Google+, LinkedIn].

- I will respond to e-mail [Facebook chat, messages] within _____ hours, except on ____ or between _____ [e.g., 9 p.m. and 9 a.m.].

- I am online on _____ [FB/Skype/Twitter] on ____days and also available for _____ [Screensharing sessions, video conferencing or anything else you want to try].

- If you want an individual [physical/Skype/chat] appointment, _____ me.

- I accept [do not accept] Skype/Facebook/LinkedIn friend requests (until graduation).

You need to decide if you want students to friend you, but it makes no difference to the rest of this. Some students will interpret this as more accessible (and it allows them to send you Facebook chat), but others will find it creepy that you are Facebook friends with them. This communication policy can also be an opportunity for you to articulate your expectations regarding technology use in the classroom.

Step 6: Use E-Communication for Some Basics

Having gone to all of this trouble (for both you and your students), you now need to use this platform daily. Here are some easy things to do on social media or in e-communication. This is partly about content: what you can communicate in social media so you don't have to repeat in class. This is both more secure and creates more class time for more important activities. This is also about timing: think about when students need to get your messages. Here are some suggestions.

Announcements

Save your breath and class time for more important interactions. Most of us want written confirmation of important information (e.g., a deadline extension or change of venue for the midterm), so establish this pattern (a syllabus quiz can do this—see Chapter 5—but so can your answer: "All important dates and deadlines are on the course website"). Then you can concentrate your class time on teaching.

Encouragement

Communication is highly motivating and has a direct impact on students' learning. Students want to know that you care about their learning, and a little timely encouragement ("Chapter 1 seems like just theory, but it is essential for understanding this process. Just keep going!") can go a long way.

Hints, Tips, and Summaries

Students don't sleep with your syllabus, and they will not think to check it daily. They need hints, tips, and encouragement even to start the reading or to continue trying problems: "These problems are hard, but make sure you try all of them and then start over." This is not a place for deep content, but the need for brevity provides both you and your students an opportunity to focus.

Introductions and Questions

You can put long lists of study questions or introductions to readings on your website or in the LMS, but short texts are an opportunity to provide a single item for consideration.

Make Connections

Social media are about connections. Students tend to think that your classroom is like Las Vegas: what happens here stays here. You (probably) want your students to connect what they are learning with the outside world, and Twitter or Facebook are designed to do just that. Much Internet content (every news article or video, for example) now comes with an embedded way to share on common social media platforms. Try asking your students to share or post one article, story, or photo related to your course every day or once week. They will have to try and make connections (higher-order Bloom's!), and you will learn how they think.

Learn About Your Students

Social media allow you lots of opportunities to peer into student interests and processing. Asking students to share connections will reveal current trends, which you can use to design later lessons and entry points. Students will also share things about your class. A student in a women's studies class posted: "I am disappointed in myself. I have to write a paper for my women's studies class, but I don't have any stances on women's rights issues. I frankly don't think I am aware enough of women's rights issues. What are some? Include articles if you can." When another student suggested, "How about the glass ceiling?" the original poster asked, "What is that?" If you discover this in the last week of your class, you might want to reevaluate how engaged your students really are in your class. All of this will provide better ways to connect with your students.

Build Community

We know that study groups are an important support mechanism for students, and social media do make students feel more connected. They can also provide a place to go with questions or thoughts. Working in groups or even just knowing that others are struggling can be encouraging.

Demonstrate Slow Thinking

Texts and e-mail are fast, but they nevertheless provide an opportunity for you to model thoughtfulness in class. Students often confuse being smart with being the first to answer or having lots of information in their head. When you answer all of the questions in class off the top of your head, you reinforce that notion. E-communication provides the chance to say, "That is a great question, but I need to think about it" or "I need to do some research, and I will e-mail or post to the entire class later." It is even a chance to demonstrate that smart people change their mind: "Today's discussion in class has altered my opinion."

Step 7: Find Ways to Talk Face-to-Face!

EDUCAUSE performs a yearly study of undergraduate students' information technology preferences and experiences. The survey changes from year to year, but until the 2014 report, students were asked to rate various approaches and tools that faculty might choose to use to communicate with them. Sixty-six percent of respondents said they wished faculty used e-mail more often to interact with them, and 60% said the same about the LMS. These were also trending upward from the 2012 and 2013 reports. While e-mail and the LMS were, respectively, second and third on the list of preferences, students' number one preferred form of communication with faculty in 2013 was face-to-face interaction (EDUCAUSE Center for Analysis and Research, 2013). With approximately 113,000 student respondents, this reaffirms our commitment to face-to-face interaction.

For all of the reasons explored in this section (students' desire convenience and many will feel more comfortable testing the waters with you first online) and because you can't be everywhere all the time, technology enables us to develop a portfolio of communication strategies for our students. Having regular office hours is important, but look for other ways to be available too. Try to arrive early for class and also be available afterward. If you can have lunch in the dining hall or will attend a student concert, you can announce this on your social media site. Remember that while students desire face-to-face contact, their lifetime of devices has also given them less practice with this form of interaction, so your additional encouragement is essential.

Examples

Start with E-Mail

Jason Kaufman, Minnesota State University, Mankato

Certainly e-mail is the lowest-hanging fruit we have to connect with students outside class. Jason teaches educational leadership and uses e-mail to motivate student engagement even before the semester begins. One week before the first day of class every semester, he sends his students a welcome e-mail. He keeps the message intentionally brief and covers four main topics: (1) a welcome to the course, (2) information regarding the course location and start date and time, (3) an attached syllabus, and (4) assurance to students that he's accessible, including a description of his open door policy. He has found that this approach creates a back channel of e-mail communication regarding concerns students have that would otherwise go unvoiced. As a result, it serves to establish a tone for the course that encourages interaction and communication even before day one.

Matching Social Media to Learning Goals

Alice Miller, Goucher College

It is important to consider the attributes of social media as they relate to your course's learning goals, and if you're lucky, you will be able to highlight specific disciplinary concepts as well as benefit from the ways the tools function. Alice teaches instructional design, and her courses include an examination of social media for instruction. Because instructional designers often work to build online courses, notions of social presence are key outcomes for the course. Her students use Instagram and Twitter to make explicit strategies for constructing their own social media presence, and they examine how to leverage that process in online course settings. Developing rapport, inserting humor, and fostering ongoing communication are modeled for her students as she teaches them best practices with social media for their own professional context. Because social media are pervasive in many disciplines and professions, many of us enjoy the dual benefits that result from including social media in our courses.

Facebook

Joe Reinsel, University of Michigan-Flint,

One oft-voiced reason to use social media is to bring content to where the students are when they are not in class. Joe teaches a games and virtual art course and has structured his students' out-of-class interactions using two communication channels: one in the LMS (Blackboard) and one via Facebook groups. He finds that multiple paths for discussions lead to more open conversations as the semester progresses. Both tools have their strengths, but in Facebook, the comments area provides a threaded discussion of sorts that is coupled with the "liking" system. Because his art course is very visual, Facebook makes it easy for everyone to share course-related visual content and discuss it online. As a result, his choice of social media also supports the pursuit of specific learning goals. This matching is key, and he chooses which discussion tool to use based on the needs of the goal. His preference is often for Facebook because he finds that medium easy and quick for observing and participating in student conversations.

Google Plus

Hu Womack and Sarah McCorkle, Wake Forest University

While Google tools are available for anyone to use, some campuses have a formal relationship with Google that makes using the tools even easier and integrated with other systems on campus. Hu and Sarah work at a campus that has such a relationship. They often select to use Google Plus, one of the Google Apps for Education, as their social media platform of choice in the social science research courses taught by Hu. With it, students can submit reflective assignments, which their classmates can view and comment on. With Google Plus, students can also record themselves using webcam and submit a video status update. Incorporating such media assignments doesn't require any additional software for the students. Responses and commentary to these videos can take place outside class, leading to a conversation that is already in progress once face-to-face class time arrives.

Pinterest

Shelby Newport, University of Michigan–Flint

Social media tools certainly encourage sharing, but some also enable new or easier forms of collaboration. Shelby teaches a course on clothing in Western culture, and she has her students use Pinterest. In Pinterest, she has created a class board where students can post their online findings; it's a location where her entire class can see what is shared. Topics in her course, such as shoes of the Gothic time period, have visual elements, so having a range of "specimens" to consider fosters rich, in-class discussions. Students arrive to class as "mini-experts," having performed preclass research that leads to the selection and posting of relevant examples. The conversation is already under way when class begins around a shared set of resources that the students themselves have collected and curated.

Asynchronous Debates

Debra Ferdinand, University of the West Indies

Sometimes our e-communication strategies exist to deliver content to students, but often we hope to foster discussion that involves significant interaction among students before and after class. Debra teaches courses on workforce occupational analysis and has developed an assignment intended to foster such significant conversation. She describes her activity as an asynchronous team debate, which strives to develop critical thinking skills. For these debates, she divides the class into two teams that debate a topical issue related to readings, personal experiences, or societal concerns. Her debates consist of three rounds, and both teams are given the same instructions, the assignment's grading rubric, and time to determine their debate strategy. Debra moderates the asynchronous debate as it progresses to ensure that the "for" and "against" groups have equitable time for preparing responses. The rubric plays a significant role in determining the winner of the debate. Such high engagement through social media ensures her students are well prepared for her face-to-face activities with them.

Key Concepts

- Consider extending your classroom by creating an e-communication strategy that leverages technologies, websites, and devices.

- Increasing your social presence in all course settings can benefit student learning.

- A social media presence can be a particularly good way to let students know you care and encourage them to come to office hours.

- Students are neither multitaskers nor rapid switchers.

- Closely examine how student use of technology in your classroom may extend or inhibit student learning. Then create a strategy in advance based on what you learn.

- Multitasking is automatically diminished in active learning classrooms.

- Your LMS and e-mail can be coupled with Facebook, Twitter, Pinterest, Instagram, and other social media platforms to provide a rich, supportive presence for your course.

- Use your social media presence for brief but important content delivery, such as announcements, encouragement, hints, tips, summaries, introductions, and questions and answers.

- Specifically articulate your e-communication policies and strategies in your syllabus.

Further Resources

Tools

Google+, plus.google.com

This is Google's social networking platform. It has a range of features that enable you to organize your friends and students into circles. It also has excellent features associated with photography and video.

■ ■ ■

Hootsuite, hootsuite.com

This tool provides a social media dashboard that makes managing multiple accounts and multiple social media presences more, well, manageable.

Additional Readings

Knowlton, D. S., & Nygard, S. (2016). Twitter in the higher education classroom: Known fragmentations and needed frameworks. *Journal on Excellence in College Teaching, 27*(1), 117–151.

A historical overview of Twitter use in higher education for learning is provided. This article concludes with a discussion of theoretical frameworks that could be used to support Twitter-based assignments.

■ ■ ■

Malhotra, N. (2013). Experimenting with Facebook in the college classroom. *Faculty focus: Higher ed teaching strategies from Magna Publications.* Retrieved from http://www.facultyfocus.com/articles/teaching-with-technology-articles/experimenting-with-facebook-in-the-college-classroom/

The author shares her experiences using Facebook for instructional purposes in her class. She concludes by sharing what she has learned, which many readers of this book may find of interest.

■ ■ ■

McArthur, J. A., & Bostedo-Conway, K. (2012). Exploring the relationship between student-instructor interaction on Twitter and student perceptions of teacher behaviors. *International Journal of Teaching and Learning in Higher Education, 24*(3), 286–292. Retrieved from http://www.isetl.org/ijtlhe/pdf/IJTLHE1223.pdf

This article relates student perceptions of Twitter use across five colleges in a single institution ($n = 144$). Teacher credibility and immediacy are among the areas this study explored.

■ ■ ■

Straumsheim, C. (2016, May 13). Leave it in the bag: Study by faculty members at West Point finds students perform better academically when laptops and tablets are banned from the classroom. *Inside Higher Ed*. Retrieved from https://www.insidehighered.com/news/2016/05/13/allowing-devices-classroom-hurts-academic-performance-study-finds

A study at West Point revealed that students learn better when devices and laptops are banned from class.

■ ■ ■

Tananuraksakul, N. (2015). An investigation into the impact of Facebook group usage on students' affect in language learning in a Thai context. *International Journal of Teaching and Learning in Higher Education, 27*(2), 235-246. Retrieved from http://www.isetl.org/ijtlhe/pdf/IJTLHE1974.pdf

Sharing an international perspective on the use of Facebook groups in language learning course settings, some benefits were reported in that context in this small, qualitative study.

References

Aratani, L. (2007, February 26). Teens can multitask, but what are the costs? *Washington Post*. Retrieved from http://www.washingtonpost.com/wpdyn/content/article/2007/02/25/AR2007022501600.html

Carlson, S. (2005, October 7). The net generation goes to college. *Chronicle of Higher Education*. Retrieved from http://chronicle.com/article/The-Net-Generation-Goesto/12307

Chronicle of Higher Education. (2014). *2014 almanac of higher education*. Retrieved from http://chronicle.com/section/Almanac-of-Higher-Education/801

Duggan, M. (2015). *The demographics of social media users*. Washington, DC: Pew Research Center. Retrieved from http://www.pewinternet.org/2015/08/19/the-demographics-of-social-media-users/

Dunlap, J. C., & Lowenthal, P. R. (2014). The power of presence: Our quest for the right mix of social presence in online courses. In A. P. Mizell & A. A. Piña (Eds.), *Real life distance education: Case studies in practice* (pp. 41–66). Greenwich, CT: Information Age Publishing.

EDUCAUSE Center for Analysis and Research. (2013). *ECAR study of undergraduate students and information technology, 2013*. Retrieved from https://net.educause.edu/ir/library/pdf/ERS1302/ERS1302.pdf

Kosoff, M. (2016, February 9). Lulu, the app that lets women secretly rate men, just got bought by the biggest dating company in the world. *Business Insider*. Retrieved from http://www.businessinsider.com/badoo-acquires-lulu-2016-2

Lowenthal, P. R. (2009). Social presence. In P. Rogers, G. Berg, J. Boettcher, C. Howard, L. Justice, & K. Schenk (Eds.), *Encyclopedia of distance and online learning* (2nd ed., pp. 1900–1906). Hershey, PA: IGI Global.

Oser, K. (2005). Kids cram more hours into media day. *Advertising Age, 76*(46), 31.

Richardson, J. C., & Swan, K. (2003). Examining social presence in online courses in relation to students' perceived learning and satisfaction. *Journal of Asynchronous Learning Networks, 7*(1), 66–88.

Sana, F., Weston, T., & Cepeda N. J. (2013). Laptop multitasking hinders classroom learning for both users and nearby peers. *Computers and Education, 62*, 24–31.

Seemiller, C., & Grace, M. (2016). *Generation Z goes to college*. San Francisco: Jossey-Bass

Seidensticker, B. (2006). *Futurehype: The myths of technology change*. San Francisco, CA: Berrett-Koehler.

Strayer, D. L., Cooper, J. M., Turrill, J., Coleman, J. R., & Hopman, R. J. (2015). *The smartphone and the driver's cognitive workload: A comparison of Apple, Google, and Microsoft's intelligent personal assistants*. Washington, DC: AAA Foundation for Traffic Safety.

Wallis, C. (2006, March 19). The multitasking generation. *Time, 167*(13), 48–55.

Watson, C. E., Terry, K., & Doolittle, P. E. (2012). Please read while texting and driving. In J. E. Groccia & L. Cruz (Eds.), *To improve the academy, vol. 31* (pp. 295–309). Hoboken, NJ: Wiley.

Chapter 11

Integrated Courses and Sequence

PEDAGOGY IS MOSTLY a design problem, and two large-scale elements of design are sequence and integration. When do things happen, and how do they connect to what happened previously? These two key questions are at the heart of the course design challenge.

We intuitively know these two things are linked and important; for most of us, syllabus design started out as a sequence of topics and assignments. This is the macrolevel of sequence design—the progression through the semester. There is also a microlevel of sequence: how students progress through each day, topic, or lesson. This has been the emphasis here, described as the Teaching Naked cycle. We need, of course, to consider both and how they integrate with each other.

Fink (2013) describes integrated course design as the relationships among three key components: (1) learning goals, (2) teaching and learning activities, and (3) feedback and assessment (see Figure 11.1). What do you want your students to learn? How will you know they have learned this? And what activities will you design to move them forward?

What Fink is really describing, of course, are ongoing, interrelated processes that work together to ensure you create a course that will enable your students to achieve the goals you have in mind for them. These larger goals consist of smaller units, each with its own objectives, activities, and assessments. Your course has big goals that collectively comprise the overall purpose of your course, and each of these larger goals comprises smaller goals, which are typically described as specific, measurable learning outcomes. In many ways, this structure resembles a honeycomb (see Figure 11.2). Each module is designed to integrate learning goals, activities, and assessment, and modules are designed to connect and build on previous modules.

FIGURE 11.1

Key Components of Integrated Course Design

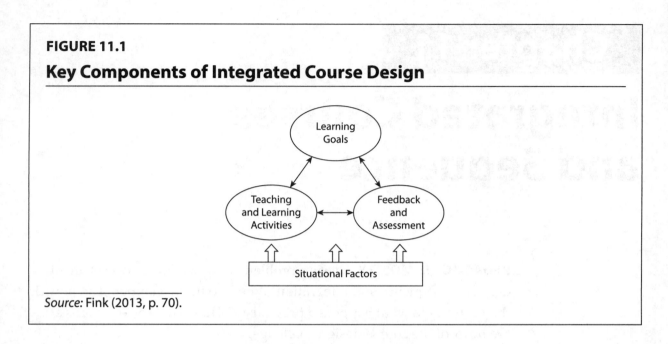

Source: Fink (2013, p. 70).

FIGURE 11.2

Honeycomb Diagram for Course Design

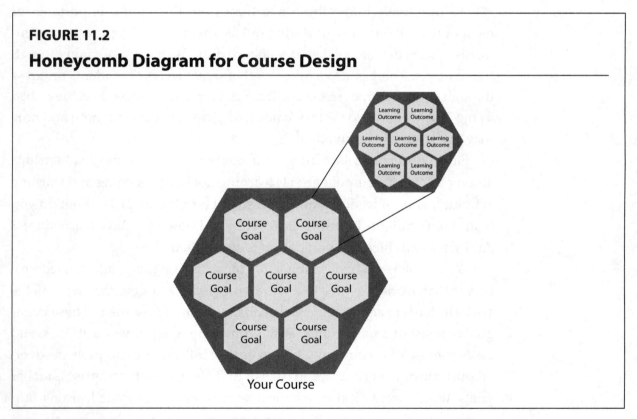

For each module, you will create activities and assessments that are designed to enable your students to achieve your learning outcomes. You do that design work for a learning outcome, and then you repeat it until you have designed the entirety of your course. Course design, however, is not simply creating learning for a series of discrete topics. Quality design work takes into account prior knowledge, how topics fit together, and what we know about how students learn while incorporating strategies that ensure synthesis, transfer, and integrative learning take place. It's complex work; however, there are processes and practices you can employ to ensure course design serves to maximize your students' academic success.

Course-Level Design Process

Start with the macro. What is the overarching purpose of your course, and what are your big goals? Start at the end and be ambitious, especially on the cognitive side. It is far better to have high standards you don't reach or complex goals that are hard to assess than to design a course around only things you can measure easily. This is the policy problem that is often characterized as teaching to the test. Teaching to the test is a good thing (look at Figure 11.1 again): if your activities don't line up with your assessments, you have a poorly designed course. But when the test has been designed primarily for ease of comparison or with someone else's learning goals, then you are forced to adopt teaching activities that will teach to someone else's goals. We know too that it is the combination of high standards and nurturing your students that is most effective in teaching. It is far better to have important learning goals rather than trivial ones that are easy to measure.

Most of us can create content goals with little effort, but for all of our rhetoric about the importance of critical thinking in higher education, we are often much less specific about cognitive outcomes. It is easy to assume that "the magic will happen" (as it did for many of us; again, we faculty are the exceptions, not the rule) or that the real cognitive benefits will manifest themselves only decades later. Even if we can't always measure the specific improvement in critical thinking and openness to new ideas, transparency and reflection will increase the chances for success: the "magic" is more likely to happen if we clearly identify cognitive goals for our students (Chapter 1) and allow time for self-reflection (Chapter 8). It is easier to hit the target when we know where it is and especially when it is a big target. Most faculty carry these cognitive goals in their head. We know what we think students should be able to do. We just don't always do a good job of making this clear to students and then designing courses that constantly direct students toward those goals.

What would change if we started with clearly defined thinking skills as the end point and then added the content around that? For many of us, that is implicit in our series of topics: we have built in increasing complexity, and our sequence is certainly intentional (even if it is chronological). But if we designed our courses as a related pattern of cognitive improvements, the content might play a different role, and we might design different assessments.

Once we have broken down our eventual goal into smaller goals, we can assign appropriate activities and assessment for each unit. Lots of low-stakes recall and practice improves learning, and it provides a way to connect the unit with related assessment and feedback. Is there going to be one big key project or type of activity, or will these vary with the type of mental work being done? If you have one big project, how will it be broken into smaller parts? Do the key big projects relate to the key cognitive goals?

A central problem of the midterm and final model is that they require integration when we have not (often) provided feedback on each individual area. For students who are struggling, our feedback at this stage is often too late and too complex. Think of something difficult that you have learned in an area outside your expertise. How easy would it be to learn tennis if you started with multiple concepts (grip, footwork, forehand, backhand, and strategy) and you were asked to integrate these skills without having practiced each separately first and then to perform opposite another person? A good teacher will provide one learning goal, one activity, and one assessment at a time. If the midterm is the first opportunity for feedback, you are almost certainly assessing too much at once.

Isolation and Integration

Integration, or helping students make connections between class sessions, assignments, and even courses, is the central problem of learning (Huber & Hutchings, 2004). Many of us are able to master individual levels of basic new skills or concepts. In isolation, our forehand grip and swing might be great, but once the stakes increase and we are asked to integrate this skill into a match, we start to make mistakes. Again, a good teacher will provide an opportunity to practice integration after each new concept: How does the new thing change what we knew before? If we have mastered our tennis forehand, then perhaps the next drill is to return to our neutral grip between every stroke, and then next to drop the racquet on the ground and pick it back up between each stroke.

Drills and isolation are a key component of learning anything, physical or mental. If pedagogy is mostly about design, then much of that design is about reducing complex problems to individual levels and steps. Recall that game designers require that each phase of mastery be broken down into "pleasantly frustrating" levels (Gee, 2005). Each level needs to have both enough challenge and opportunity for success that we keep playing. That means that each level is only incrementally more difficult, but also that there should be different paths to mastery.

Sequence and integration are essential to creating pleasantly frustrating classrooms. The order of goals and activities should increase in complexity so that we are constantly challenged, but we also need to be constantly engaged and motivated. This is hard. When experts begin to teach, they almost always start with too complex a stage and then simplify. This is also why teaching is itself a skill: if this were not hard, then anyone with content knowledge could be a good teacher. It is also why many good teachers tend to shed content over time and focus more on fundamentals.

Fink (2005) begins his twelve-step course design process by identifying the (1) situational factors (the bottom part of Figure 11.1) and (2) learning goals, formulating (3) appropriate assessments and (4) learning activities (the three ovals in Figure 11.1), and then (5) making sure these components are integrated (This is similar to our step 3 below). Fink then describes an intermediate design phase that begins with a "thematic structure" for the course (his step 6), which is again similar to the process we describe in this chapter: What is the sequence of topics, and how will new material be integrated with previous content (See Figure 11.3)? For each new topic, students need an introduction to the topic (white boxes) and then opportunities to apply and use the concepts and ideas in assignments (the shaded parts of the columns).

FIGURE 11.3

Organizing Topics into a Thematic Structure

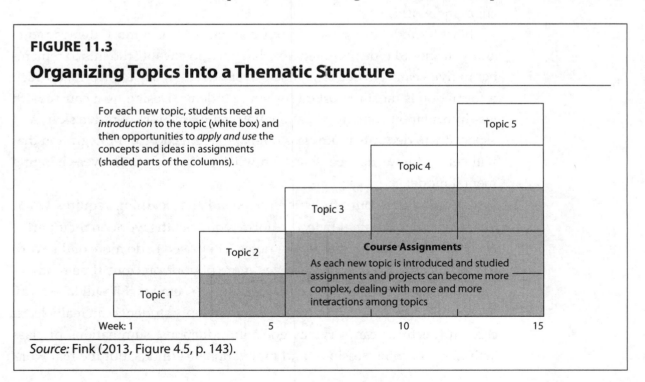

For each new topic, students need an *introduction* to the topic (white box) and then opportunities to *apply and use* the concepts and ideas in assignments (shaded parts of the columns).

Topic 5

Topic 4

Topic 3

Topic 2

Course Assignments

As each new topic is introduced and studied assignments and projects can become more complex, dealing with more and more interactions among topics

Topic 1

Week: 1   5   10   15

Source: Fink (2013, Figure 4.5, p. 143).

Fink then suggests that we select a teaching strategy that he describes as a "particular combination of learning activities, arranged in a particular sequence" (p. 144). He makes it clear that strategy (what we call design) is different from technique, which is a specific activity, like lecturing or discussion. The design problem is knowing both which activities connect with individual units and how techniques and topics fit together (see Figure 11.5 below).

In the end, there is certainly a trade-off between deep learning and content. Integration is partly a question of sequence (it is hard to integrate what you have not yet learned); it is also about reflection (Chapter 8), feedback (Chapter 9), and connections (Chapter 10). All of these take time, but the payoff is learning that is more likely to stick. Covering more content almost never results in more real learning. Students can cram more information in for a short period of time to pass exams or boards, but if we want graduates who can integrate on their own, we need to show them a path and allow them time to learn how to integrate.

All of this surely cannot be accomplished in the limited class hours we have. We have to make compromises, which is also the essence of good design. What is the best use of class time? Furthermore, if you can teach students how to prioritize their own time and how to use new knowledge to revise old thinking and reintegrate their mental model, then they will be able to continue learning once they leave your class—a skill that we constantly claim to teach and something they will certainly need in our rapidly changing world.

Start by reducing some of your content. Less is almost always more, and you should reduce content to what you most want students to remember in five years. No one remembers every detail, so try to prioritize which information is most important for your students. Designing a course with less information content will allow you more time for cognitive skills and especially to dedicate more class time to the reflection and integration that will connect your new content with what we hope is their ever-changing mental model.

Second, help your students understand that learning requires work. Your delivery of content in lecture form requires little work on their part—even if they are taking spectacular notes. They need to do more of the work to really learn. While spending even more of your precious time motivating students to learn on their own (Chapter 4) seems as if it will take away even more from your content, remember that only students can really learn content. Lectures can serve as good introductions, summations of class activities, coaching sessions, and motivational sermons, but the real work of learning is more difficult, and our goal should be to design classes and courses where students are the ones performing the cognitive heavy lifting.

Video games work because they are designed to motivate players to do the work. They stimulate users to spend hours and hours learning basic skills so they can advance to more complex skills. Video games are carefully designed to appeal to a wide range of learners. The sequence of skills is carefully crafted, and there is plenty of time for practicing individual skills in isolation and then integrating them before moving on to restart the process. Players who integrate and learn more quickly progress more quickly and stay engaged. Like a video game designer, your job is to create the drill, experiences, and conditions that will lead your students to follow through and both learn and change.

Teaching Naked Design Process: Microcycle

This book has largely described the design sequence or microcycle that happens for each unit: the motivation, exposure, recall, elaboration, complication, and reflection that is a part of each individual day or topic (see Figure 11.4). For each learning goal or unit of content, Teaching Naked offers a way to distinguish the individual parts of the pedagogical design process.

Technology now offers new possibilities for sequence. Before broad adoption of the World Wide Web, there were fewer options for where to put the entry point or first exposure. Students largely came to class unprepared

FIGURE 11.4

The Teaching Naked Micro-Cycle

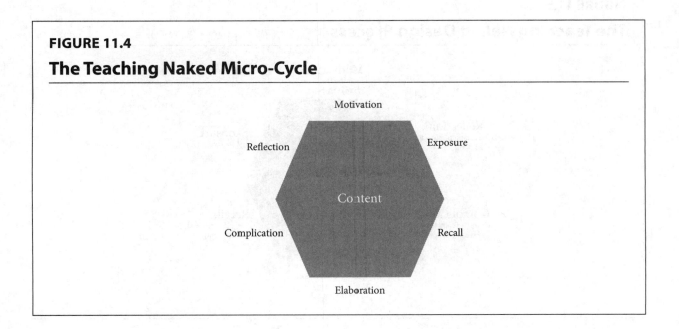

(except for the future faculty, who probably sat in the front), and the professor introduced the material, usually in class lectures. If you wanted to motivate the next topic and encourage students to do the reading, you might spend the last few minutes of class introducing the next subject (see Chapter 4 and the top of Figure 11.5).

Technology offers the chance to rethink the sequence of your entry point and other interventions (Figure 11.5, upper right corner). This is where students start. If you have a dramatic or fun group activity that serves as a captivating entry point, then it may be best to do this at the end of the previous class as a motivation for students to go home and prepare to solve the intriguing mystery in the next class session. Sadly, the power of your masterful demonstration of relevance will probably fade over time, and with alternative forms of stimulation constantly arriving on various mobile devices, it may be important to add perhaps another motivational prompt at the point where students need it most—usually the night before something is due. Think carefully about when key motivating information needs to arrive. Your inspirational text will have the most impact if it arrives just as students are deciding if they want to be doing the homework at all.

Think too about what students are really capable of learning on their own. We often use lectures as first exposure, assuming that students are capable of doing the "real work" on their own—even if they skipped the reading before the lecture. But perhaps some class time needs to be used to teach the skill of how to unpack a difficult reading or summarize a new

FIGURE 11.5

The Teaching Naked Design Process

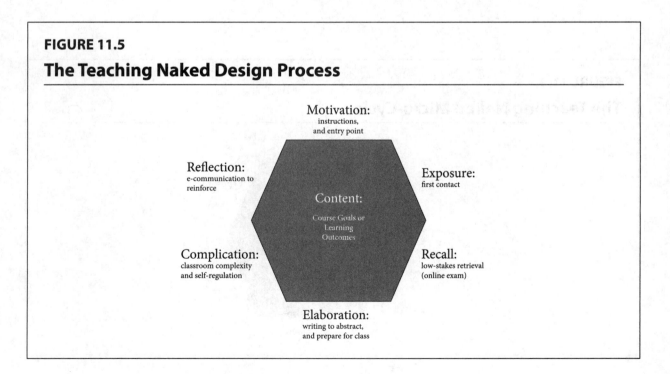

concept. Is it better for students to be reading and doing problem sets on their own, or is that activity important enough that you should dedicate some class time to practicing it? Is there an activity that will work in class only once they have specific preparation? Are there drills that require a live partner that might best be practiced in class?

You now also have new choices for timing writing, activities, and exams (Figure 11.5, lower right, bottom and lower left). Low-stakes recall (like online exams or index card summaries) is critically important for students and much less likely to encourage cheating. Do you need class time for testing at all? If you are worried about cheating and need some guaranteed Internet-free testing, then consider an exam in a testing center. Every campus has supervised computer labs and a place for students who need extra time on exams. Consider how you might leverage these resources to reclaim even more class time for important opportunities for learning.

For centuries, the arts have used a studio model that requires very long hours in a group setting, but often students worked individually on their own work (modern accreditors often have to make exceptions for the extraordinary number of class hours required for a single credit hour in the arts). You can, of course, learn to paint on your own, but the problem is that you do not usually know when you have gone astray and need a second eye. There are lots of nudges in an art classroom: little suggestions and trial balloons. It is also useful to know others are struggling and that everyone has both the same hill to climb and different paths to take. Both writing labs and study halls mirror some of these practices. Perhaps some of your class time needs to be studio time.

Technology now gives you design control over the exact moment when you want students to encounter a new concept or complication. Think about when you want the complication to arrive. Maybe you can save the hardest problem for class instead of the homework. Perhaps you want students to do a first draft without having to address a counterexample. You now have massively more choice in when you present individual pieces of guidance.

Step-by-Step Guide

Step 1: Create Course Learning Outcomes

Start with ambitious goals that include cognitive outcomes and specific improvement in mental complexity, and then move to the smallest cells of the honeycomb—the learning outcomes that collectively make up those larger goals (see Figure 11.2). As noted in Chapter 1, Bloom's taxonomy can provide a structure and vocabulary for crafting well-constructed outcomes.

Step 2: Break Down Your Learning Outcomes

The process of designing learning goals, rubrics, activities, and assignments is very much like a honeycomb. You have a larger structure of macrocourse goals and then, within each individual course goal, multiple intermediate goals that have varying complexities. These might be seen as cells that comprise the larger honeycomb (see Figure 11.2). You may find that some of these goals are of sufficient complexity that they need to be broken down further with layers within layers. You may find it valuable to break them into stages of increasing complexity. Think like a video game designer: What are the intermediate stages on the way to more complex skills and thinking? A first start can be made by simply replacing the verb with a lower-level Bloom verb. Consider this example:

> **Business Course Example (Honeycomb)**
>
> *Ambitious goal 1*: Students will create a business plan for a new venture.
>
> *Learning outcomes for ambitious goal 1* [to be attached to activities and assessments]: Students will:
>
> - Identify the components of a business plan.
> - Summarize the value of each stage of a business plan.
> - Categorize the most vulnerable stages of their venture.
> - Apply a model plan to their venture.
> - Discover evidence to support each stage of their plan.
> - Gather feedback about their business plan.
> - Assess the viability of their business plan.
> - Synthesize their feedback into a revised plan.

There are similar stages for each ambitious goal.

Step 3: Make Honey

What activities and assessments are connected to each learning outcome? Consider creating a chart like the one in Exhibit 11.1 (available as a template on TeachingNaked.com, or use Finks, 2013, Exhibit 4.4, p. 139) to ensure you address each outcome in a meaningful way. The chart can be customized to meet your individual approach (later in this chapter are examples of modifications). It is a best practice to first determine the outcomes and then the assessments (with rubrics, if appropriate). After those have been determined, you can turn to the instructional activities that will bring students to the outcomes you've defined.

Exhibit 11.1

Teaching Naked Macro-Course Design Template

Ambitious Course Goal 1

Learning Outcomes	Assessment or Feedback	Learning Activity
1a		
1b		
1c		

Ambitious Course Goal 2

Learning Outcomes	Assessment or Feedback	Learning Activity
2a		
2b		
2c		

Ambitious Course Goal 3

Learning Outcomes	Assessment or Feedback	Learning Activity
3a		
3b		
3c		

Ambitious Course Goal 4

Learning Outcomes	Assessment or Feedback	Learning Activity
4a		
4b		
4c		
4d		
4e		
4f		

Step 4: Harmonize Cognitive and Content Goals

Some basic content will be required before you get to more advanced content, but it is easy to assume that *all* of your content sequence is determined by its internal complexity. Including a breakdown of the cognitive stages in your alignment activities will allow you to rethink the sequence of content. Are there examples, activities, and content that require less or more advanced cognitive work that might occur out of the normal sequence? Remember that integration is more important than the volume of content (See Figure 11.3).

Step 5: Look for Connections

What are the connections between goals or activities in one area and then the next? Is it possible to break down one activity into two or connect one

FIGURE 11.6

One Honeycomb Cell

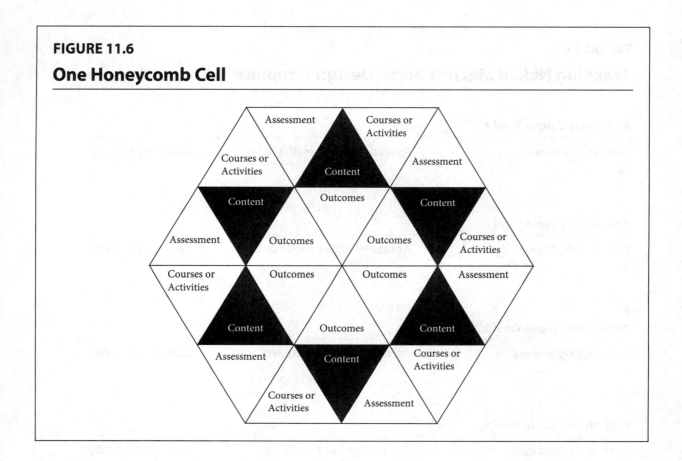

content area with another? Figure 11.6 shows how each outcome, which comes with its own integrated activities, assessment, and content, might be integrated with other individual units or cells. If you require integration of ideas on the midterm or final, can you provide earlier practice and feedback on each individual area first?

Step 6: Design the Sequence and Activities for Individual Units of Learning Modules

Technology expands the possibilities for what happens where. Class time is expensive and precious, so start by putting the most difficult learning or important integration there. Then consider the entry point and the when and where for first contact (see Figure 11.5). Are there new opportunities to deepen learning or provide feedback? Exhibit charts below (see Exhibits 11.2 and 11.3) offer different ways to plan how you might build integration and sequence. Template 1 is recommended (Exhibit 11.2) because it will encourage you to consider all of the steps that students will encounter. Items can be moved in class to out of class and vice versa, and other material could equally be assessed, but here are the most typical defaults.

Exhibit 11.2

Teaching Naked Micro-Cycle Design Template 1

Content Area	In Class?	Out of Class?	Activity	Assessment
Entry point				No
First exposure		Yes		
Retrieval		Yes		Yes
Elaborate		Yes		
Complication and failure	Yes			
Cognitive wrapper	Yes			No
Reinforce: e-communication		Yes		

Exhibit 11.3

Teaching Naked Micro-Cycle Design Template 2

Before Class	In-Between		In-Between	
	In Class		In Class		In Class

Template 2 is simpler (Exhibit 11.3). The point here is just to consider what activities will be most effective in or between classes. It is a useful starting place, but eventually we suggest moving to Template 1 (Exhibit 11.2) since your hopes for what students will do between classes need to be matched by a design that considers the additional components in Template 1. If you use Template 2, take the time to consider the entire cycle of motivation, exposure, recall, elaboration, complication, and reflection.

Examples

Building the "Beehive"

C. Edward Watson, University of Georgia

When first presented with the opportunity to teach College Teaching at UGA, I knew I wanted my students to leave my course with the ability to teach their first college course confidently and effectively. That was certainly the overarching course goal; however, many goals emerged as I examined that larger course goal. For instance, future teachers need preparation for course design and lesson planning, which are related subjects. Teaching effectiveness has even greater fine granularity as one considers the range of teaching strategies a new college teacher might employ, and then there are notions of grading and assessment. Students also need to understand and apply a variety of university policies and procedures. These larger goals were still quite broad, so I defined more specific learning outcomes within each larger goal. This is the honeycomb in practice (see Figure 11.2). As an example, for the domain of teaching practices, some of the outcomes were "students will be able to effectively lead class discussions," "foster a safe and welcoming classroom environment," and "employ a range of appropriate active learning strategies." Once this level of detail was reached, it was easier to imagine activities and assessments that might lead students to achieve these specific, measurable learning outcomes.

As you articulate and examine the outcomes that comprise your larger course goals, you will find that you are increasingly intentional in your choice of assessments, activities, and content, all of which will work to bring your students closer to achieving your course goals.

Designing the Sequence

José Antonio Bowen, Goucher College

Asked to do a week on blues and rumba for an Introduction to World Music course, I started with the assumption that I would do a day on the blues and then a day on the rumba so there would be plenty of time to cover each topic in depth. We have to start with content, but it is easy to fall into the content trap where we don't also consider the larger goals.

What I really wanted was for students to leave class understanding the differences in how these two musics sound and also to theorize why. Thinking about those learning goals led the design process in a better direction and eventually to a better distribution of material and an entirely different sequence. The preclass assignment for day one became: "Listen to examples of both blues and rumba, and then write a half- to one-page analysis comparing what you hear in each. What sorts of sounds, instruments, and voices do you hear? How many people are playing? How is each polyrhythmic?"

On the first day of the class, students shared what they had heard, and with a bit of guidance, they ended with a playlist of more recent examples of music from each tradition. Now that students could identify the different elements, they were ready to ask the "why?" question: If both musics are combinations of European and African musical traditions, *why* might they sound so different?

The preclass assignment for the second day was to make a long list of all of the possible things that might account for this: "Investigate both the European immigrants and the African slaves to both the United States and Cuba. Where did they come from, and when? What are the differences in climate, religion, and culture, and how might they matter? Then take one item from your list and (1) do a bit of research about it and (2) postulate a theory for how it might have influenced these musics. Bring your list (on the top half of the page) and your additional research and theory (on the bottom half of the page) to class, ready to hand in and discuss."

Learning Goal Example for Honeycomb #1

Identify the Components of a Business Plan

Learning Outcome #1 for Ambitious Goal #1: Identify Parts

Content Area: Business Plan

Teaching Naked Cycle	In Class?	Out of Class?	Activity	Assessment
Entry point		Yes	Plan for making dinner: parts?	No
First exposure		Yes	Read chapter x and a sample venture	No
Retrieval		Yes	Online exam	Yes
Elaborate		Yes	Summarize parts and diagram example on index card	Yes
Complication and failure	Yes		Create a plan for this new sample venture and compare answers	Yes: peer review
Cognitive wrapper	Yes		What mistake did you make today?	No
Reinforce: e-communication		Yes	What extra step would you add to your dinner plan?	No—or offer extra credit

Learning Goal Example for Honeycomb #2

Demonstrate an Application of Functions

Learning Outcome #2 for Ambitious Goal #1: Apply Math Concepts

Content Area: Functions

Teaching Naked Cycle	In Class?	Out of Class?	Activity	Assessment
Entry point	Yes		Examples of social multipliers	No
First exposure		Yes	Read chapter X	No
Retrieval		Yes	Short problem set	Yes
Elaborate		Yes	Make a 2-minute video explanation	Yes
Complication and failure	Yes		Harder problem set	No
Cognitive wrapper	Yes		What mistake did you make today?	No
Reinforce: e-communication		Yes	Share the best video	No

Key Concepts

- The two large-scale elements of classroom design are sequence and integration.

- Integration is the central problem of learning, and good teachers ensure that students understand how the current lesson connects and builds on other content in the course and the curriculum.

- Use sequence and integration to create pleasantly frustrating activities that balance enough challenge with opportunities for success.

- Start with cognitive goals, and then integrate with content.

- After defining course goals, identify the intermediate goals along the way.

- Assign appropriate activities and assessment to each of the smaller goals.

- Technology offers many opportunities to rethink when students do things.

- Low-stakes recall opportunities are critically important for students and are much less likely to encourage cheating.

Further Resources

Angelo, T. A., & Cross, K. P. (1993). *Classroom assessment techniques: A handbook for college teachers*. San Francisco, CA: Jossey-Bass.

A timeless volume, this book provides a range of assessment strategies that employ writing and other strategies in the service of assessing a range of such learning outcomes as critical thinking, problem solving, and integration.

■ ■ ■

Johnson-Laird, P. N. (2013). Mental models and cognitive change. *Journal of Cognitive Psychology, 25*(2), 131–138.

Those with a keen interest in mental models will enjoy the historical overview of theory and research regarding mental models provided by this article.

■ ■ ■

Reynolds, C., & Patton, J. (2014). *Leveraging the eportfolio for integrative learning: A faculty guide to classroom practices for transforming student learning.* Sterling, VA: Stylus.

One of the most efficacious strategies for fostering integrative learning is to employ strategies that leverage the capabilities of e-portfolios. Those interested in learning more about how this can be done effectively should explore this book.

■ ■ ■

Roediger, H. L. III, Putnam, A. L., & Smith, M. A. (2011). Ten benefits of testing and their applications to educational practice. *Psychology of Learning and Motivation, 55,* 1–36.

We have argued throughout this book that frequent testing offers many benefits. Much of the research of Henry Roediger and colleagues has focused on the direct and indirect effects of testing. This article provides a clear summary of the research along with ways to incorporate these practices within your courses.

■ ■ ■

Zaromb, F. M., & Roediger, H. L. III. (2010). The testing effect in free recall is associated with enhanced organizational processes. *Memory and Cognition, 38*(8), 995–1008.

This article provides the results of a compelling study that focuses on the testing effect. We see that there is a powerful effect of repeated testing that is easily applicable to instructional settings.

References

Fink, L. D. (2005). *A self-directed guide to designing course for significant learning.* Retrieved from https://www.deefinkandassociates.com/GuidetoCourseDesignAug05.pdf

Fink, L. D. (2013). *Creating significant learning experiences: An integrated approach to designing college courses* (2nd ed.). San Francisco, CA: Jossey-Bass.

Gee, J. P. (2005). Learning by design: Good video games as learning machines. *E-Learning, 2*(1), 5–16.

Huber, M. T., & Hutchings, P. (2004). *Integrative learning: Mapping the terrain.* Washington, DC: Association of American Colleges and Universities.

Chapter 12

Integrative Learning and Integrated Experiences

THIS BOOK BEGAN with a survey of the latest research on the brain and what conditions help us learn (see the Introduction). The techniques described in this book are all derived from this research, and indeed, the Teaching Naked cycle is largely a practical design checklist drawn from the key ideas in research and summarized in *Make It Stick: The Science of Successful Learning* (Brown, Roediger, & McDaniel, 2014).

Chapter 11 described how all of these pieces are connected at the course level: if students are better prepared, then class time can be spent deepening and applying knowledge. If you can motivate students in advance of first exposure and convince them that this content will help them achieve their goals, then students will be more likely to complete assignments. If you want students to do the readings, you can't spend the first two weeks giving lectures when they are not prepared.

That is hard, but there is an even harder part. If you flip your class while there is a similar lecture-based alternative, students may indeed choose what they correctly perceive as the easier option. One of the most difficult barriers to improving teaching is that we get the most impact when we challenge students to do more of the work and change the integration across courses, but there are many disincentives for making changes in isolation. For all of our emphasis on discovery and ideals, colleges can be very tradition-bound places, and changing one class can feel like pulling a long thread on a thick sweater that has kept us all warm for a very long time.

Most of our structures and systems are traditional and come from a time when we did not know a fraction of what we now know about learning. Are courses, semesters, grades, credit hours, majors, four-year degrees, general education, departments, classrooms, and office hours essential or merely traditional? What are the structures that will most support our fundamental goals of opening minds and helping students integrate new knowledge? Change then, really needs to be led at the institutional level and across departments.

For example, what might institutions do with the information that diet, water, sleep, and exercise are essential for learning (see Doyle & Zakrajsek, 2013)? Our wellness programs might suddenly look more important and worth more time and institutional support than we usually give them. Still, wellness programs by themselves (or indeed most other courses) are unlikely to alter student behavior. Astin (1993), Bowen (1977), Feldman and Newcomb (1969), and Pascarella and Terenzini (2005) all found that peer groups had the largest effect on student change. Astin (1993), for example, wrote, "Students' values, beliefs, and aspirations tend to change in the direction of the dominant values, beliefs, and aspirations of the peer group" (p. 398). We know that the teenage brain is different from the adult brain in many ways. For starters, students crave connection with each other, and the risk/reward structure is radically different (Jensen & Nutt, 2015; Siegel, 2014). Parents often wonder how anyone could spend that much time on Facebook (often forgetting how much time we spent on the phone when we were teenagers). If we really want to open minds and change students, we need to look at all of their experiences on campus, not just in the classroom, and especially at how students interact among themselves.

"Checking in" and accumulating points have become a part of our culture. Perhaps our wellness programs need to be an app that allows students to gain credit or recognition for eating well, exercising, or sleeping. Students now live in mortal fear of their devices running out of power. How can we convince them that they need to be just as attentive to their own "battery life"? Wearable health devices that provide biofeedback are a growth industry, and soon students may be able to read on their wrist that their current state of exhaustion means they have only 20% capacity for test taking. Just as electricity and charging stations have become a currency on campuses and at airports, helping students know when and how they can recharge will improve their learning.

We often treat our students as customers, as if we were in a retail business (and indeed revenue and margins are part of our business model). But as William Massy (2016) has pointed out, colleges operate in both a competitive market-driven economy and with a greater mission to do good. Doctors and hospitals also operate in a competitive and asymmetrical market (like colleges, the relationship is asymmetrical because patients and students both know much less about the procedure than doctors and faculty, and you are unlikely to purchase the same product more than once).

Schools do a pretty good job of controlling the academic environment, but we treat the rest of the campus experience like a spa. We offer great choices about where students live, how much they exercise or sleep, and what they eat. Hospitals have learned that if they will be assessed on the percentage of patients who get better (and not just patient satisfaction), then they need to control much more of the experience. Patients who go home are much less likely to take their medicine, so if the medicine is essential, it is sometimes more efficient to keep patients in the hospital and ensure they take it.

Might we improve learning if we integrated everything on campus and controlled a few more of the choices students make? We've invested money in residential education because we think it contributes. Suppose we used our beds and rooms more like a hospital does and monitored the things that science tells us are essential for learning. Bringing college in line with current brain and medical research might lead us to close the library earlier (midnight or 2:00 a.m., perhaps), schedule fewer early morning classes, serve water rather than coffee in the morning, and even cut off the Internet before a prescribed bedtime.

That is clearly too much to ask, but economists have recently explored how "nudges" or "choice architecture" can provide incentives for altered behavior (Thaler & Sunstein, 2009). It may be that there are other systems that we might implement that would improve learning.

We are, for example, more likely to accept the default settings for things, and indeed, technology companies have long understood that most of us do not want a blank canvas with all of the millions of options that are available. Most musicians ultimately never learned how to use the Yamaha DX7 synthesizer that allowed the user to create almost any sound imaginable. Instead, musicians wanted a simpler box with a few buttons of preset sounds (and perhaps the options to customize later), which is how virtually all synthesizers and electronic keyboards are packaged today. We want to use before we abuse. For all its irritations, this is the philosophy that made Apple one of the largest companies in the world: simplicity and ease of use over too much choice. While customers, economic theory, and market research all predict that more choice and more features are desirable, research demonstrates that "consumers tend to choose overly complex products that do not maximize their satisfaction, which results in 'feature fatigue'" (Debora, Hamilton, & Rust, 2005).

Why, then, are first-year students faced with staggering lists of choices and an empty calendar when they start college? Would it not be better to preload a standard set of courses as a default and then allow customization? A few preliminary questions (Do you want to be premed or an engineer?) might be enough to create presets for most students. This grates against a fundamental principal of the university—that we are a marketplace of ideas and passion—but it might lead to less anxiety and better preliminary choices.

Government food labels and calorie counts on menus seem to encourage some better choices. Would labels on cafeteria food, activities, clubs, or courses nudge students in the right direction? Should we perhaps be doing more to prepare students for courses they might enjoy or find challenging based on their past performance? Most colleges now have a unified student identification card that monitors where they go and when. Perhaps students could get points for going to the gym or drinking water before class. Perhaps, like a video game, we need to design an environment where students accumulate points and prizes (badges and certificates?) for behaviors that support learning.

The schedule is one of the biggest nudges a college has: students are far more likely to prioritize a class that fits in some way—for example, keeps Friday free, avoids the early morning, or allows them to have lunch with friends (Chambliss & Takacs, 2014). Are we scheduling classes for the right length and frequency? Is the semester too long or too short? Should all classes be the same length for all four years, or do some classes require more (or less) time? Certainly not every course topic throughout the curriculum requires exactly the same amount of time. Individuals have no control over the campus schedule, but the department schedule of courses, especially the timing of introductory and gateway courses, is a variable worth analyzing.

In the same way that we analyzed our individual courses for sequence and integration (in Chapter 11), we now need to look at the sequences of courses and the integration of everything on campus. Everything we do should be reexamined through the lens of how and where students learn. While individual faculty have limited ability to make these large structural changes, departments and groups of faculty can effect change in a number of areas that will enhance student learning.

None of us, of course, has the ability to even initiate change on that scale by ourselves. Where, then, to start?

Common Rubrics

If you have ever participated in a norming exercise, you know that even faculty in the same discipline can have radically different ideas about what constitutes good work or clear writing. Students with a history of good grades have often figured out that school is largely about anticipating what a teacher wants. They pick up on the clues you provide. When you tell them that providing a bibliography or showing their work is critical, they write that down and try to deliver what you value. These students will use your preferences ("I love this painting/formula/poem/trick") as a study guide for the final, and their good grades demonstrate that this strategy often works. At worst, students believe that grades are simply a reflection of how well students can read your mind, and at best, of their ability to translate your preferences into work you will like. At the very least, excellence becomes a moving target.

It does not have to be this way. If we want student writing, ability to solve problems, or cultural sensitivity to improve over four years, then we should fix the bar and help students make steady and continuous progress toward achieving the standard we have set. This involves compromise, but it is possible to create more uniform standards. AP tests, for example, are graded by hundreds of faculty who spend considerable effort comparing and norming their grading to ensure that student papers are scored in a similar way across the country. This is a difficult task; it is even more important for departments and colleges.

A common department or campus rubric will be hard, but it will improve student learning and level the playing field for everyone. A rubric consists of both criteria and standards. If you have departmental learning goals, then these are your criteria and you have finished one axis. The other axis of a rubric comprises the standards: how many levels you have and how each is defined (see Chapter 1). Just rearticulating that the department (or general education) outcomes are criteria for assignments in different classes will clarify expectations for students—even if the standards vary.

The definition of a "good" or "excellent" thesis may be different in different classes or disciplines (and if you are using your rubric directly for grading and you need to curve every class—not recommended—then your standard definitions will have to change as students advance), but it is enormously helpful for students to know that your department or college defines good writing, speaking, or thinking as always having consistent parts.

The emphasis or weighting of those parts may change. While more consistency is better, if Professor Jones wants to make grammar worth more and Professor Smith thinks argument is even more valuable, then just flag the differences for students. Sequencing these changes can even support student progress.

Once your department or college has decided its learning outcomes, the components of each goal become the criteria for a rubric. In the example, the weighting of grammar and argument can change as students progress through their years: perhaps grammar is weighted and taught more heavily in the first year, and then argument becomes a priority in year 2. These are choices for faculty. Students, however, will benefit greatly when faculty have these arguments in private and in advance and then articulate both the goals and the progression for majors or degrees. This transparency will improve student understanding of how concepts and courses are integrated, but it will also encourage faculty, especially in different fields, to help make these connections for students.

The Structure of Majors

Most majors are progressive for content—we have thought intentionally that students need organic chemistry before biology (or vice versa). We've often spent weeks, months, or years determining what math or survey requirement is needed before acceptance into the major, but we rarely scaffold the thinking as carefully as we do the content. The same honeycomb model of design that we suggested in Chapter 11 needs to be applied to curriculum over four years (see Figure 11.2) where courses are cells within an even larger honeycomb (the curriculum).

Clear departmental learning goals and rubrics will help. It is critical that these include cognitive goals and not just content. We all assume that students become more complex thinkers as they progress through our majors, but we have often prioritized content electives and choice over progression. Capstones are high-impact practices that require students to integrate, but like a final exam, they work best when students have been prepared gradually for them. Again, we assume that students will be able to write longer papers with more complex arguments and more original research as they progress though their major, but could we break down the steps for this and articulate exactly when and how each new level will be achieved?

This is sometimes called curricular mapping: we articulate both the breakdown of skills and in which courses they will occur. This usually means that we need to articulate how the content and cognitive goals will overlap. Students may need to learn about sources in the second year and counterarguments in the third year. At the same time, we may have a goal that students take American history in one year and European history in another. The problem we have all encountered is that some students in our European history course will already have taken American history or will take a course that required them to gain sophistication in the use of sources but others will not. In general, American higher education (rather uniquely) has chosen to tolerate these sorts of sequential problems in order to give both faculty and students more choices. An easy solution would be to require that all students take American history in their second year and make sure that sources are covered there. That would allow the third-year course to both assume previous content knowledge and require a more complex cognitive approach. There are many solutions, some more complicated than others; the key is that it is exceptionally important to scaffold cognitive goals through your curriculum.

Introductory Courses

Introductory courses should be true introductions to the values, insights, and benefits of the discipline. These courses, the recruitment program for the major, instead often end up serving as gateways that can create hurdles and limit admissions. They also create pressure for some faculty to teach large and unappealing survey courses.

If you must have survey or repertory courses, moving them to the second or third year can create multiple opportunities. The first-year course can now be period agnostic, which means anyone can teach it with any topic or content. It is not necessary to label this as a "methods" course or to make it comprehensive in any way. First exposure courses should function as examples of how people in your discipline think.

If disciplines are indeed lenses or tools that provide different perspectives on common problems or topics, identify some really interesting or unusual insights that only your discipline might provide. Musicology is a way of talking about music and situating it relative to other musics and other cultural ideas. Although the details will vary by culture and period, the perspective can be demonstrated with a course on any single composer, genre, or musical culture. This has the substantial fringe benefit of allowing faculty to teach in their favorite content area rather than having to march through multiple centuries or content where they have less interest.

Another option is to design a first-level course that includes introductions to the various subdisciplines or to a common problem that matters to students. Rather than requiring students to choose between electrical, mechanical, civil, and environmental engineering, or computer science, why not provide an introduction to all of engineering? An opening class that requires students to solve problems together and take on the role of engineers might provide insight into how the individual majors differ. Even if you can't actually decrease water use on campus, control a robot on Mars, or design housing for one dollar per square foot in one semester, the attempt may provide an incentive to learn more in a particular area—and that is the point of an introductory course.

E-Portfolios and Student Retention Software

A number of technologies are proving successful at increasing the quality of instruction and improving student success rates across a number of metrics. As we think about better learning, one of our goals is to reduce the fragmentation of the curriculum. In other words, we seek to promote integrative learning. Across higher education, many general education curricula currently use check sheets where students note the courses they complete in the various required areas. This approach unfortunately promotes siloed rather than integrative thinking. As you begin to consider how to foster integrative learning across courses, in either general education or your program, you will likely discover that fragmentation is a hard hurdle to clear.

One strategy is to implement e-portfolios and associated pedagogies. By implementing e-portfolios, students can collect the work they complete as they progress through the curriculum. Then, at multiple points in their progression, integrative assignments are given to students that evoke elements of this earlier work. Philosophy majors could be asked to revisit the work in their science classes as free will is debated; here, a homework assignment could be, "Revisit the papers you wrote in biology, physics, and/or chemistry. What do they add to this conversation?" Students are far less likely to lose items if e-portfolios are used, and evoking ideas from previous courses not only enables integration but encourages retention of those earlier ideas.

Capstone courses take on an entirely new character when students have access to all of their academic accomplishments since entering college. Many e-portfolio systems provide rubric tools and can assist with course-level and programmatic assessment and the students' own career development and job searches. As a result, there is much excitement around e-portfolios for collecting, assessing, and presenting student achievement.

Learning analytics and student retention tools are another set of emerging technologies. Learning analytics is typically seen as a way to take many of the strategies companies employ around Web analytics and apply those in educational settings (New Media Consortium, 2016). The thought is that students leave a great deal of "evidence" regarding their academic progress in their online learning activities. A university's learning management system (LMS) is often at the heart of these efforts. Collecting and analyzing data that result from students' learning might, for example, reveal predictive patterns that will enable us to launch academic interventions for the most at risk of our students.

Student retention systems typically evoke students' online learning footprints but also seek to incorporate the full range of university systems that contain or produce student data. In addition to academic systems, students engage with a range of financial and administrative systems. Some institutions even know how often their students visit the gym. Might this collection of student data, achievement, and behavior patterns reveal insights regarding how to help students succeed? The answer is proving to be yes.

Classrooms and Learning Spaces

Another way higher education is working to improve teaching and learning is through the development of innovative classrooms and learning spaces. The research supporting active learning is more than well established, so a great deal of energy is being expended in exploring and designing flexible instructional spaces that work to facilitate a range of active learning strategies. Probably the most recognized type of active learning spaces is known as the SCALE-UP (Student-Centered Active Learning Environments with Upside-Down Pedagogies) classroom. Pioneered in the sciences, these are rooms designed to foster collaboration and interaction through hands-on approaches to scientific problems (Beichner, 2011). These rooms also leverage computers in the classroom in meaningful ways. The best number seems to be nine students per round table (see Figure 12.1). This enables extensive opportunities for cognitive processing and solution comparison, which lead to multiple revisions of answers and result in increasing quality. Essentially, SCALE-UP enables an extended version of think-pair-share. Students might first work alone on a problem. Then, in groups of three, they can discuss solutions and revise toward a collective shared perspective. At the table, the three groups of three (now nine) might then discuss, compare, and revise further. As this work occurs, the instructor can monitor progress, provide guidance as needed, and then share the best of the table solutions with the entire class.

The computers enable students to use modeling and simulation software to explore scientific concepts using the tools of the trade, and the audiovisual systems within SCALE-UP rooms typically allow faculty to project an individual student computer on the various screens in the room. In Figure 12.1, you'll note that each table has a single television screen associated with it on the wall. This enables the students at each table to project the work on their screens, making it easier for the entire table to see and discuss. There are also two larger projectors for the entire class to see. This provides a variety of options for demonstrations and sharing. The placement of the instructor's station actually discourages lecturing.

While the technology in the room makes SCALE-UP an expensive solution, a great deal can also be accomplished in a room that simply lets you

FIGURE 12.1

A SCALE-UP Classroom for 72 Students[1]

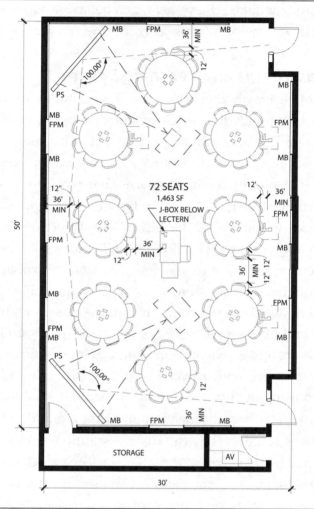

[1] MB = marker board; FPM = flat panel monitor; J-Box = Junction Box (for power, Internet, etc.)
Source: The University of Georgia Office of University Architects for Facilities Planning (2016, p.134)

move the tables and chairs around a bit. There's now even a classroom rating system that will let you determine how well a room supports active learning (Brown, 2015). If you're thinking about remodeling a classroom, this resource will enable you to make sure you are considering your redesign from multiple perspectives.

General Education and Change

Current general education programs are designed to provide breadth and a common set of skills, but most are expensive failures at both. Students who can interpret numerical data and do quantitative analysis are in huge demand, but instead we offer calculus and do nothing to combat math anxiety. We know the mind is resistant to change and that developing the ability to think about knowledge in new ways requires the integration of feelings and thoughts, and yet we mostly offer an assortment of unrelated courses. A more integrated curriculum, with common goals and rubrics across the campus, could lower costs and increase graduation rates by reducing complexity and improve learning. It could also reinforce a set of common skills. The Internet already offers more content or knowledge than any college does, and as the technology makes long-distance interaction more realistic, we will need even newer and better reasons to gather on a residential campus for four years. The total can be more than the sum of the parts if we better integrate experiences.

A general education is also the core of a liberal arts education, and its core purpose should be clear: to change students. However you define *critical thinking, discernment,* and *analysis*, they have long been at the core of a liberal arts education. The change from a world of limited but relatively reliable sources (encyclopedias and books) to one with many more sources of less reliable information (web pages, postings, tweets, and memes) has fundamentally changed our relationship with knowledge and learning (Bowen, 2012). While our phones all have access to more information than any classroom, calling this device a "smart" phone has confused quantity of information with the quality of knowledge. Smart people are not the ones who know the most; they are the people who know how to change their minds.

The jobs of the future belong to those who are more than just critical thinkers. We cannot teach students most of the information they will need in the future because it has not yet been discovered. More than ever before, students will need to continue learning after graduation. So while content remains critical (for its own sake and as a basis for learning and thinking), our real mission is to create voracious, self-regulated learners. This is but one more reason to decrease the volume of content in your courses.

Being self-regulated means you can manage your own assumptions and cognitive processes. It is related to metacognition, which is the conscious control over your own thinking, including what inputs you value; how you interrogate information; and your own resistance to new inputs, or your "immunity to change" (Kegan & Lahey, 2009). Context and integration are keys to change. Employers often ask for flexible and creative problem solvers, but this is really more a way of being than a set of skills. At its core, creative thinking is about an openness to new possibilities, the ability to attend to our own intellectual accent, the integration of conflicting ideas, and the willingness to have new knowledge change how we think about the world. A growth mind-set is the ultimate job skill.

Today we have two broad types of general education: the distribution model and the core model. Most colleges use the distribution model, where students get breadth by taking a mandated variety of courses within different departments. This gives both faculty and students great flexibility. A core system (like Columbia's) works differently: here, all students take a set of extradepartmental courses specially designed for this purpose. Many colleges have a mix of the two.

These two models represent two very different conceptions of general education. The distribution model says the liberal arts can't be reduced to any specific body of knowledge. Basically, every course in general education will provide students with a way of thinking that is more important than specific content. The core model is the reverse: specific ideas, values, and texts matter—not just any literature course will do.

The roots of general education began in the 19th century, when a bachelor's degree consisted of only required courses. Before this, there weren't any general education courses or majors. In the 1860s, college enrollments were declining, in part because students were given the choice between a bachelor's degree or an easier professional degree in law, medicine, or science.

When Charles Eliot arrived as the president of Harvard in 1869, half of the law students and almost three-quarters of the medical students had not previously been to college and did not hold undergraduate degrees. At the time, Harvard Law School had no admissions requirements beyond evidence of "good character" and the ability to pay the hundred-dollar tuition.

Eliot had the brilliant idea that the bachelor's degree could be a prerequisite for professional or graduate school (instead of being a separate equal path). This raised standards and made the professional schools more selective. Eliot had returned from Europe influenced by the German model, where universities of greater disciplinary specificity had become a national economic engine through research, and he introduced both research and departments to U.S. higher education. This also led him to create separate professional (graduate) doctoral programs in 1872.

One final Eliot innovation was the introduction of the elective system. If students were going to get professional training later, then the undergraduate degree could be, as he wrote in the *Atlantic Monthly*, "the enthusiastic study of subjects for the love of them without any ulterior objects" (1869, p. 214). Eliot's critics also pointed out that electives brought a loss of coherence, depth, and breadth (i.e., fragmentation).

All of these innovations—the bachelor's degree as preparation for graduate school, the creation of autonomous departmental fields of study, the elective system, and an emphasis on research—were all widely imitated. They were all expensive, but Harvard could afford it. Eliot understood this, but he bargained that faculty would support it because they could teach what they wanted. By allowing students to choose professors—Eliot also created the modern course with a name, number, and professor listed—he also hoped teaching would improve. Most of the schools that copied this Harvard model did not have the same resources, but this collection of ideas has defined U.S. higher education ever since.

This kind of curricular freedom radically changed U.S. higher education. The absolute separation of undergraduate education from the vocational professional schools, and the separation of knowledge into individual disciplines, triumphed; it created the U.S. liberal arts ideal and opened the door for a massive expansion of bachelor's degrees. However, it also created a stubborn resistance to connecting undergraduate learning across disciplines and with the "real world." General education was invented to try to bridge the gap between both disciplines inside the academy and the world beyond its walls.

We can see early examples of this in the core courses universities introduced during World War I. Columbia's famous contemporary civilization course was initially called War Aims. Stanford and Dartmouth followed suit with Problems of Citizenship courses. Williams called its version American National Problems. Eventually these became the common "Western civilization" requirements.

These core courses had a social motive: to give students a common understanding of society, shared value judgments, universal traits and outlooks, and a collective experience that would bind society together. Columbia's other famous core course, Literature Humanities, was organized initially by English professor John Erskine, who was worried that new immigrants, and especially Jewish students, would not share in the common culture of the "great Anglo-Saxon writers." In 1934, Jacques Barzun and Lionel Trilling (a student of Erskine) revived this as The Colloquium in Important Books.

Harvard's core originated in a 1945 report, *General Education in a Free Society*, which became known as the Redbook (because of its crimson binding). Harvard president James Bryant Conant (who served from 1933 to 1953) discovered that the elective system had indeed created more courses, but he also hoped to create a meritocracy and began using the new SAT for admissions. Conant thought the elective system was too easy to game and not integrated enough. But the Redbook also had a clear social motive: to give students "a common . . . understanding of the society which they will possess in common" as Americans at the beginning of the Cold War (Conant, 1945, p. 8). General education was, in other words, driven by fears of increasing social mobility and declining moral authority in a time of national crisis.

As both the canon and society were opened up in the 1960s, curricular cores had to change; they became more about method and learning how to learn. Brown introduced Modes of Thought courses in 1969, and Harvard created a core in 1970 requiring students to take courses in 7 or 11 areas (still extradepartmental). In 1974, Michigan introduced Approaches to Knowledge.

Some of this also represents a crisis of confidence in what the core knowledge or context might be for all students, which was also part of the 1960s revolution. In the same way that Barzun and Trilling at Columbia taught books that were "important" (and not because of great truths they contained), the renamed "Western Civ" programs justified their core texts simply as a common heritage. As the college population and the faculty began to diversify, scholars began to study new and more diverse traditions. Faculty and students specifically rejected many of the common value judgments of the old core. The same books assigned to bind us together could also alienate.

Now what? Suppose the point of general education (and perhaps even the graduation standard) was the ability to hold two opposing ideas in your mind at once? Previous editions of general education tried to bridge the gap between the liberal arts and the real world and prepare students to live in that same real world. Imagine the real-world implications for our democracy and our nation if opening minds became the outcome of general education.

Most colleges still have some general education requirements, but what are we actually trying to accomplish, and how might we rethink general education in a liberal arts context? Louis Menand suggests that the liberal arts have their roots in knowledge we pursue with "disinterest." He writes, "Garbage is garbage, but the *history* of garbage is scholarship" (2010, p. 55). Academic freedom and the move to distinguish scholarship as "value neutral" were also a way of balancing the religious roots of most U.S. universities. John Dewey and Arthur Lovejoy founded the American Association of University Professors in 1915 partly to make sure religious or political views were not the basis for hiring, but it was also part of the professionalization of faculty. Is scholarship really disinterested and devoid of personal values? Should it be?

One side of the coin is the benefit to analyzing all sides of an issue from the relative safety of the blackboard (or the Ivory Tower). Americans tend to use *academic* as a pejorative synonym for *theoretical*, *abstract*, or even *useless*, but *theory* and *disinterest* are useful precisely because they provide an abstract space to play with alternatives without having to make up our minds. Planning for contingencies that have not and might not happen is the essence of practical strategy—for games, business, and life.

The ability to always see the other side of a debate or issue can, of course, also be debilitating (and incredibly irritating to your children). While we mistakenly draw a clear bright line between theory and practice, we do, in fact, often need action, which requires a decision. Art works the same way; there may be lots of equally good or interesting ways to play Hamlet or paint a tree, but picking one at a time and doing it with conviction is essential for any good performance.

"Disinterest" is also seen as a pillar of science. We tend to privilege the scientific method as being separate from politics or bias, but even science is guided by the interests and priorities of scientists, society, and the government. We can't ever be entirely disinterested or rational, but disciplinary training provides a framework.

This is sometimes used as a justification for the humanities. Science may be peering intently at the real world, but it is using a lens, and the humanities is the study of that lens. Similarly, the "academic disinterest" of majors like classics or art history is defended precisely because it is abstract and removed from the practical.

Economist Tyler Cowan (2013) argues that we should emphasize the economic power of the humanities in business. He has a point: creativity and an understanding of the human condition are surely useful in any enterprise, and these skills easily and often translate into employment. Still, most of us would hesitate to make the value of general or liberal education purely economic.

Academics call the units or departments of our world "disciplines." These are internally consistent and self-governing systems of value. As the word *disciplines* implies, they provide discipline—a structure for organizing and verifying knowledge. They can also be confining.

Another common function of general education, therefore, is to introduce students to the different disciplines (or systems of thought). Some general education programs are trying to create a space for a renewed desire for interdisciplinarity. (Remember that the question of whether to teach general education inside or outside the disciplines was an important difference between the distribution and core systems of general education.)

For all of this history and suspicion of the practical, the liberal arts are not truly disinterested. Many disciplines and institutions are also deeply invested in the world, real problems, the character of our students, and our local communities. Many liberal arts skills are also manifestly practical. Writing skills, for example, are at once a prime vehicle for thinking through abstract complex problems and the world's most basic job skill.

General education has then been conceived as a way

- To stimulate learning for its own sake
- To connect students to the real world
- To give students a common cultural or intellectual vocabulary
- To introduce students to a variety of ways of thinking

Some of these seem mutually exclusive, and clarifying which of these matters for each program is an important first step in helping students understand how the pieces of a breadth or distribution system come together.

Content was never the primary goal of a liberal arts education, but with the increased pace of new knowledge and our easy access to more content on every device, thinking and analysis have become even more important. As noted earlier, new employer surveys articulate a desire for graduates who are able to solve complex problems with people who think in different ways (Association of American Colleges and Universities, 2015). Ethics, writing, and intercultural skills are also increasingly desired.

None of this is a prescription for your new general education curriculum, but it is an argument for more integration and for more careful thinking about the systems on our campuses that work together. The Internet is fundamentally disaggregated. There is more and more information on our phones every day, but Siri is not getting any smarter because she remains disaggregated: More and more pieces of information just mean more bits and bytes. Ultimately, new content becomes knowledge only when it is connected to what we already know. Content has to be integrated within people and thinking minds, and this happens best in a community. College and our general education curriculum have to be about more than content. Our real products are integrated and happy people who are voracious, self-regulated, lifelong learners.

This makes integration ever more important in the design of our new general education systems. The whole now truly has to be more than the sum of the pieces.

Step-by-Step Guide

Institutions should institute mandatory naps without devices between every class (if we could figure out how to do that), but individuals surely can't do that. So what sorts of small changes can we make to conform to best practices in brain science?

Step 1: Talk About the Brain

Tell students often about how their brain works and how their choices can affect the performance of their brain. Remind them that lack of sleep can be masked with coffee, drugs, or short-term adrenaline, but that cognitive function and student performance seriously decline with a lack of sleep (Walker, Stickgold, Alsop, Gaab, & Schlaug, 2005). Sleep is also an important processing time for your brain, which prioritizes the last thing you do before falling asleep. Facebook before bed tells your brain that it should focus on remembering Facebook. Instead, advise students to go through their flash cards one more time just before they fall asleep.

Step 2: Incorporate Emotion into Your Design

Developing the ability to think about knowledge in new ways requires the integration of feelings and thoughts. We know that "positive emotions influence learning by affecting students' attention, motivation, use of learning strategies, and self-regulation of learning" (Pekrun, 2014, p. 12). This suggests we need to rethink the importance of classroom climate and how we might instill passion in our classroom presence (Cavanagh, 2016). In truth, numerous pieces of the university educational experience might be modified. Everything on campus needs to be integrated to foster the desired change.

Step 3: Emphasize Diet, Water, and Exercise

Students often lose sight of the close connection between our brain and the system where it lives. In fact, some researchers argue that the most important thing we can do to improve learning is to engage in moderate aerobic exercise (Ratey, 2008). Given that research shows that diet and exercise improve focus, attention, motivation, and patience, colleges and universities have important evidence on which to base a range of practices and interventions. As an example, since our brain is mildly dehydrated each morning, we need to encourage students to drink water (and not coffee) before morning classes. A jug of water on your desk might be the best new pedagogy you have tried.

Step 4: Consider Classroom Design and Environment

Sometimes when you enter a classroom, the arrangement of the furniture and its lack of flexibility can seem to dictate your pedagogical approach. You are probably stuck with the chairs and desks you have for now, but you may wish to develop some short- and long-term goals in this area. Short term, consider how you might adjust certain elements of your classroom environment. Can you make your classroom more welcoming? Can you move the chairs? Can you find inventive ways to overcome the seating to support effective group activities? As an example, consider having students make groups with those sitting behind them instead of collaborating in the same row.

Long term, learn about your university's classroom technology refresh cycle and how it is funded. You may find that your institution's facilities team works with classroom support units on campus as well as the architect's office to schedule renovations that touch almost every aspect of the classroom. Get out ahead of that cycle by learning when your room is slated for an update. The typical classroom refresh cycle on most campuses is between four and seven years. Find out when the rooms you typically teach in are due for an upgrade and advocate for the types of furniture and other room attributes that foster, rather than inhibit, learning.

Step 5: Make Time for Reflection

While you can't force your students to nap after class, you can provide them with time for reflection in class. Cognitive wrappers (Chapter 8) are one example, but routinely asking students to pause and reflect (without devices) will improve the quality of both their discussion and thinking. This will also help them remember. In addition, it turns out that reflection and pausing are essential for developing deeper and more complex states of empathy (Immordino-Yang, McColl, Damasio, & Damasio, 2009). Give your students the opportunity to develop as better human beings.

Step 6: Provide Common Rubrics

Here again you probably can't act alone, but finding any subset of classes or a shared learning goal in your department is an opportunity to create greater transparency for students. An opportunity for such change comes around at most universities on a scheduled basis. Take advantage of program review season in your department or an accreditation cycle to suggest common rubrics as a way to improve consistency and learning.

Step 7: Collaborate on Integrative Curriculum

Can your department agree to sequence a group of skills across multiple courses? Can you consider a capstone project or course? What needs to happen in earlier courses to make the capstone viable? Curriculum mapping activities can make this process easier, and having the location of your learning goals documented will make it easier to integrate newly hired professors into your new integrated approach.

Step 8: Use E-Portfolios

Determine if your college or university already has an e-portfolio system that it has adopted and is supporting. If one hasn't been selected, there are a few free web creation platforms, such as Wix and Weebly, though such systems don't typically have features, such as rubrics, that are commonly found in systems designed to support e-portfolio pedagogies. Tools such as Digication, which have built systems specifically for e-portfolios in educational settings, also have a variety of billing options. Either students can pay for a yearly account or the institution can purchase licenses for students.

What is the scope of impact you are envisioning for your e-portfolio adoption? Maybe you hope to foster integrative learning across the assignments and topics within your own course. You could be thinking bigger and hoping to help students synthesize content from various courses in your program. The latter typically requires leadership that fosters faculty engagement with the new processes. Integrative approaches across courses require faculty to talk to one another and agree on a common goal and purpose; however, the benefits of e-portfolios have been shown not only to foster integrative learning but also have a positive impact on key student success metrics (Eynon, Gambino, & Török, 2014).

Examples

Critical and Integrative Thinking

Washington State University

Once WSU decided that critical thinking was important, a committee needed to define it and identify the components. They ended up with seven learning outcomes:

1. Identifies, summarizes (and appropriately reformulates) the *problem, question, or issue.*

2. Identifies and considers the influence of *context* and *assumptions.*

3. Develops, presents, and communicates OWN *perspective, hypothesis, or position.*

4. Presents, assesses, and analyzes appropriate *supporting data/evidence.*

5. Integrates issue using OTHER (disciplinary) *perspectives and positions.*

6. Identifies and assesses *conclusions, implications, and consequences.*

7. *Communicates effectively.*

These became the criteria for the rubric they entitled *Guide to Rating Critical and Integrative Thinking* (Washington State University, 2006). WSU chose six levels of standards: two levels each of emerging, developing, and mastery, with a score of 4 representing competency (or the pass level) for students graduating from WSU.

The Art History Major

Southern Methodist University

The design of art history majors often puts a survey of European art, heavily emphasizing the memorization of a basic canon of artworks, at the beginning. This has three severe consequences. First, these courses make art appear to be an exclusively European endeavor, which can discourage students from other backgrounds from being interested (and result in a less diverse population of students). Second, students can come away thinking that the discipline of art history is largely about memorizing slides in the dark. Third, the content and format end up disguising the usefulness of observation, discernment, and cultural context as important life and job skills. Would the population of majors look different if the introductory course was Women and Art or African American Artists?

In the end, the department settled on two 3-credit foundation courses (Introduction to Art History and Research, and Methods in Art History) that were about how art historians think and work, not about which repertoire or canon was covered. Students would then take four 3-credit courses in periods ("Temporalities"), still without requiring a chronological march through Western art. (Instead, 6 hours of pre-1500 and 6 hours of post-1500 are required, with some overlapping 6 hours also including a global perspective to ensure that students had substantial exposure to non-European material). Six hours of Methods and Theories (including one seminar) and 12 hours of electives (with no more than half at the introductory or basic level—what many schools designate by numbering them 100 or 1000) round out the major. This new curriculum made it easier to explain to students how the curriculum mirrored what the discipline was actually about and created a path for more complex thinking.

A Scaffolded General Education Curriculum

Goucher College

The faculty at Goucher College recently revised the liberal education requirements for all students, with the goal of student-centered education that incorporates students' own curiosity and desire to learn as the starting point for learning that is sequenced and integrative. First-year students begin with a seminar focused on understanding inquiry; the topics are put forward by the faculty, but the learning goals are the same for all seminars.

From this starting point, students choose an additional three common courses sponsored by groups of faculty representing different but related disciplines, and set up so that students are introduced to the different methodological practices embodied by the liberal arts. These courses allow students to follow the interests generated from their study during the first-semester seminar and, importantly, conclude by the end of their junior year. Senior year includes a capstone experience that allows students to pull the different aspects of their learning together, including their major(s) and minor(s).

Other aspects of the liberal education requirements are also sequenced. The writing requirement includes a first-year course, a writing-enriched course taken in the second or third year, and a writing-in-the-discipline course typically completed in the junior or senior year. When students are ready, they submit a portfolio to demonstrate writing proficiency. The former mathematics requirement has shifted to a requirement in data analytics, and the introductory course is followed by a data analytics course focused on the student's major or in some other way on applied work. Furthermore, the key college values of racial and cultural literacy and environmentally sustainable practice are scaffolded through both academics and student life. Learning goals are made clear to students, additional experiences and courses are required, and this learning, as with other aspects of student learning, becomes part of the student learning portfolio, where reflection is also required. In this way, curricular and cocurricular learning happen in intertwined ways appropriate to a residential college experience.

E-Portfolios for Integrative Learning

University of Michigan

In 2005–2006, research at the University of Michigan (UM) revealed that student leaders thought very highly of their UM learning experiences; however, most could not describe what they learned, why it was important, or how they would apply that knowledge in the future (Pathways Report, 2006). The MPortfolio Project was established in 2008 to provide reflective opportunities for students to integrate and describe what they had learned. A pedagogical approach, the integrative knowledge portfolio process, was developed to guide students as they developed a better understanding of the connections between their varied learning experiences. Students were found to have significant gains across six dimensions targeted by the pedagogy, and these gains were found to be significant regardless of discipline, ethnicity, gender, or year of school (Peet et al., 2011).

Key Concepts

- Sleep, water, eating, exercise and time (SWEET) are integral to effective learning, and we should consider strategies that might help students know when and how they can recharge their biological batteries.

- Peer groups have a large impact on student choice and student change.

- Most university structures and systems are inherited. What might we change now that we know so much more about student learning?

- Might we improve learning if we integrate everything on campus and control a few more of the choices students make?

- If we want student writing, problem solving, or cultural sensitivity to improve over four years, we should fix the target with shared rubrics and help students make steady and continuous progress toward achieving the standard we have set.

- Introductory courses should be inspirational introductions to the values, insights, and benefits of the discipline.

- Integration needs to be an essential attribute of our new general education systems.

- E-portfolios are a proven strategy that, when done well, can foster integrative learning.

- Capstones are a high-impact practice that require students to integrate. Like a final exam, they work best when students have been prepared gradually for them.

- While most of this integration must come from college or departmental leadership, there are a number of smaller changes that individual faculty can make.

Further Resources

DeFrancesco, V. (2014, October 6). Video: Interview with Dan Chambliss, an author of "how college works." *Chronicle of Higher Education*. Retrieved from http://chronicle.com/blogs/bookclub/2014/10/06/video-interview-with-dan-chambliss-an-author-of-how-college-works/

Hear Dan Chambliss chat about the value of faculty and administrator contact, and why we should be facilitating more relationships with our students. He shares several practical examples in this five-minute interview.

■ ■ ■

International Journal of ePortfolio. (2017). Retrieved from http://www.theijep.com/

This open access journal provides full text to all of the articles it has ever published. Those interested in learning more about the range of practices or the integrative learning possibilities of e-portfolios will be thrilled to find this free, open resource.

■ ■ ■

Jankowski, N. (2014). *Mapping learning outcomes: What you map is what you see*. Champaign, IL: National Institute for Learning Outcomes Assessment. Retrieved from http://www.learningoutcomesassessment.org/Presentations/Mapping.pdf

We've described curriculum mapping as a key practice for determining where in the curriculum various learning goals reside. This presentation provides examples of templates for performing curriculum mapping, as well as descriptions of the process and links to additional scholarship on the subject.

■ ■ ■

Watson, C. E., & Doolittle, P. E. (2011). E-portfolio pedagogy, technology, and scholarship: Now and in the future. *Educational Technology, 51*(5), 29–33.

This article presents a primer on e-portfolios—what they are and the range of ways they can be used in higher education. It also includes a discussion of some of the pitfalls and technological limitations of these tools.

■ ■ ■

Zull, J. E. (2011). *From brain to mind: Using neuroscience to guide change in education*. Sterling, VA: Stylus.

Those interested in more deeply exploring the connections between neuroscience and educational practice will welcome this book.

References

Association of American Colleges and Universities. (2015). *Step up and lead for equity: What higher education can do to reverse our deepening divides*. Washington, DC: AAC&U.

Astin, A. W. (1993). *What matters in college*. San Francisco, CA: Jossey-Bass.

Beichner, R. J. (2011). *SCALE-UP*. Raleigh, NC: Physics Education R&D Group, NC State. Retrieved from http://scaleup.ncsu.edu/

Bowen, J. A. (2012). *Teaching naked: How moving technology out of your college classroom will improve student learning*. San Francisco, CA: Jossey-Bass.

Bowen, H. (1977). *Investment in learning: The individual and social value of American higher education*. San Francisco, CA: Jossey-Bass.

Brown, M. (2015, February 22). *Seven principles for classroom design: The learning space rating system*. *EDUCAUSE Review*. Retrieved from http://er.educause.edu/articles/2015/2/seven-principles-for-classroom-design-the-learning-space-rating-system

Brown, P. C., Roediger, H. L. III, & McDaniel, M. A. (2014). *Make it stick: The science of successful learning*. Cambridge, MA: Belknap Press of Harvard University Press.

Cavanagh, S. R. (2016). *The spark of learning: Energizing the college classroom with the science of emotion*. Morgantown: West Virginia University Press.

Chambliss, D. F., & Takacs, C. G. (2014). *How college works*. Cambridge, MA: Harvard University Press.

Conant, J. B. (1945). *General education in a free society: Report of the Harvard Committee*. Cambridge, MA: Harvard University Press.

Cowen, T. (2013). *Average is over: Powering American beyond the age of the great stagnation*. Boston: Dutton.

Debora, V. T., Hamilton, R. W., & Rust, R. T. (2005). Feature fatigue: When product capabilities become too much of a good thing. *Journal of Marketing Research, 42*(4), 431–442.

Doyle, T., & Zakrajsek, T. (2013). *The new science of learning: How to learn in harmony with your brain*. Sterling, VA: Stylus.

Eliot, C. (1869). The new education: Its organization. *Atlantic Monthly, 23*, 203–220.

Eynon, B., Gambino, L. M., & Török, J. (2014). What difference can e-portfolio make? A field report from the Connect to Learning Project. *International Journal of ePortfolio, 4*(1), 95–114. Retrieved from http://www.theijep.com/pdf/IJEP127.pdf

Feldman, K. A., & Newcomb, T. M. (1969). The impact of college on students. *American Educational Research Journal, 7*(3), 455–458.

Immordino-Yang, M. H., McColl, A., Damasio, H., & Damasio, A. (2009). Neural correlates of admiration and compassion. *Proceedings of the National Academy of Sciences of the United States of America, 106*(19), 8021–8026.

Jensen, F. E., & Nutt, A. E. (2015). *The teenage brain: A neuroscientist's survival guide to raising adolescents and young adults*. New York, NY: HarperCollins.

Kegan, R., & Lahey, L. L. (2009). *Immunity to change: How to overcome it and unlock the potential in yourself and your organization*. Cambridge, MA: Harvard Business Review Press.

Massy, W. F. (2016). *Reengineering the university: How to be mission centered, market smart, and margin conscious*. Baltimore, MD: Johns Hopkins University Press.

Menand, L. (2010). *The marketplace of ideas: Reform and resistance in the American university*. New York, NY: Norton.

New Media Consortium. (2016). *NMC horizon report: 2016 higher education edition*. Retrieved from https://library.educause.edu/~/media/files/library/2016/2/hr2016.pdf

Pascarella, E. T., & Terenzini, P. T. (2005). *How college affects students. A third decade of research*. San Francisco, CA: Jossey-Bass.

Pathways Report. (2006). *How student leaders make sense of their learning at the University of Michigan*. Unpublished manuscript. Ann Arbor: University of Michigan.

Pekrun, R. (2014). *Emotions and learning*. Geneva, Switzerland: International Academy of Education.

Peet, M., Lonn, S., Gurin, P., Boyer, K. P., Matney, M., Marra, T., . . . Daley, A. (2011). Fostering integrative knowledge through e-portfolios. *International Journal of ePortfolio, 1*(1), 11–31. Retrieved from http://www.theijep.com/pdf/IJEP39.pdf

Ratey, J. J. (2013). *Spark: The revolutionary new science of exercise and the brain*. New York, NY: Little, Brown.

Siegel, D. J. (2014). *Brainstorm: The power and purpose of the teenage brain*. New York, NY: TarcherPerigee.

Southern Methodist University Meadows School of the Arts. (2017). B.A. in Art History. Retrieved from https://www.smu.edu/Meadows/AreasOfStudy/ArtHistory/UndergraduateStudies/ArtHistoryBA

Thaler, R. H., & Sunstein, C. R. (2009). *Nudge: Improving decisions about health, wealth, and happiness* (2nd ed.). New York, NY: Penguin Books.

The University of Georgia Office of University Architects for Facilities Planning. (2016). *The University of Georgia, design and construction supplemental general requirements and standards*. (p. 134) Retrieved from https://www.architects.uga.edu/sites/default/files/documents/standards/complete_uga_design_and_construction_standards_-_august_1_2016.pdf

Walker, M. P., Stickgold, R., Alsop, D., Gaab, N., & Schlaug, G. (2005). Sleep-dependent motor memory plasticity in the human brain. *Neuroscience, 133*(4), 911–917.

Washington State University. (2006). *Guide to rating critical and integrative thinking*. Pullman, WA: WSU Center for Teaching, Learning and Technology. Retrieved from http://www.cpcc.edu/learningcollege/learning-outcomes/rubrics/WST_Rubric.pdf

Chapter 13

Being a Superhero
Pedagogy as Human Relationships

WHEN YOU ASK students about good teaching, their responses typically fall into two general categories: human and design characteristics. This book has largely concentrated on the design component of teaching; it matters deeply to students that you are fair and organized. Students correctly perceive that they learn more when you have designed the activities and sequence carefully and that you have clearly marked the path for their success. If you are transparent and stimulating and communicate early and often about your course, you will have gone a long way to satisfying the design side of expectations.

Most of these traits, however, also overlap with students' perceptions of you as a human being. Designing motivating entry points and engaging assignments demonstrates a passion for your subject and your students. Equally, clear communication is also a sign that you care and are approachable. Student are sensitive to the perception that you have some emotional engagement with their success, but if you are not the type who wants to be friends on Facebook or eat in the dining hall with students every day, you can still design a supporting and welcoming structure.

In today's litigious and harassment-sensitive environment, it would be easy to retreat to a position where students see you only as a "professional." We all value people who are competent and skilled at what they do, and we would want the stern but professional surgeon to operate on us rather than the chatty slipshod one. Still, given the choice, most of us would also rather have pleasant interactions with our server or attendant. We would like to trust our car mechanic and believe that the police officer who has pulled us over is still able to see our humanity.

Difference and privilege are marked in many ways in our academies. Still, it is important that faculty also project humanity, even while wearing more formal clothes, speaking in a louder professional voice, or calmly commanding the room. There is also no single way to manage these issues. The balance of authority and humility is different for each person.

We know that students learn more when we care about their learning, so our belief in their abilities is an important pedagogical tool. This can be especially effective when people are interacting in physical classrooms, but this is expensive. For those of us who believe in the importance of face-to-face teaching and residential campuses, it is especially important that we maximize the return on this massive investment. Relationships are at the heart of great teaching, but we need to invest our personal emotions and resources if this is to work. Teaching Naked is about maximizing the value of authentic human interactions that are costly but also add such value.

Being Human

You do not have to be funny and you do not have to be everyone's friend, but you need to appear approachable and authentic. Students (correctly) assume that the vast majority of college professors (regardless of your actual title) have training and knowledge that far exceeds their own. They assume that you know your subject. This matters, and students are indeed impressed with faculty who appear to have infinite knowledge, but this is not what distinguishes the great from the good. Students care more that you are genuinely supportive of their learning.

The Gallup-Purdue Index (2014) sought to find connections between well-being and work life and what happens in college. Over 30,000 graduates were surveyed for their workplace and adult life satisfaction and also asked to reflect on their college experiences. The result, that it was "not where you go but how you go," has spurred countless articles and books. While the public's focus and institutional interest has mostly been on choosing the right college or comparing the value of various college experiences for the price, the findings have deep implications for how faculty view their core responsibility.

The most important combination of factors in college turns out to be (1) a professor who cared about you as a person, (2) a professor who made you excited about learning, and (3) finding a mentor who encouraged you to pursue your dreams. A student who encountered all three of these was twice as likely to be engaged at work as students who did not. Only 14% of college graduates reported having all three of these experiences in college.

A single professor can make a massive difference in the life of a student. Gallup also measured life achievement and satisfaction in five ways: purpose, social, financial, community, and physical well-being (referred to as the Gallup-Healthways Well-Being 5). One professor who thinks a particular student might be a great writer or chemist or takes the time to ask what he or she plans to do with his or her gift for psychological or financial insights can change a life—across a range of metrics—forever.

Success and happiness in life turn out not to be tied as closely to your grades or how much you learned, but to your relationships with faculty. It is a sobering finding; as scholars, we are obligated to ponder this research carefully and ask how we might change how we interact with students. This is why approachability matters.

Especially in a large class, it will be impossible for faculty to get to know every student, and certainly mentoring hundreds of students at a time is unrealistic. But the Gallup data are emphatic: each student needs only to find one professor who cares, excites him or her about learning, and believes in his or her dreams. You will never know how many students admired you and wanted to ask you for advice but did not because they were afraid of or intimidated by you. The best we can hope for is to open our doors a bit wider and hope that a few more students wander in.

The most important way to communicate this is to be yourself. Again, this is in addition to appearing professional and organized, which is different for different people. There is no one correct way to do this, but focus on being authentic. Talk about yourself as a person and not just as a scholar. Articulate that you care about students and their learning. Be self-deprecating and tell stories about mistakes you made when you were young (or yesterday). Students will be surprised by your earlier self-doubt or lack of confidence—and indeed countless movies and books focus on the theme of the surprise when discovering the person who has everything you want has the same fragile emotions that you do.

Be authentic and personal in your examples. If you want to protect your family or your parents, then make the stories about your friends or someone you knew. People like stories, and listening to how you tell a story is one of the great ways that people connect.

Learning names is one of the most important ways you demonstrate you care. If your learning management system (LMS) can produce a role sheet with photos, you can surprise a few students each day by calling on them by name. Early in the semester, as you're learning their names, ask students to write their names on an index card and hold them up when they ask a question; then you can call on them by name. Very little communicates that you care more than taking the time to learn a student's name.

Ask students about campus events. Are they on a sports team or in a play? Is there an event you can attend to support them outside class? Have they written something for the school paper? Being visible on campus, in the community, or in the dining hall will increase the likelihood that students will talk to you.

Don't be afraid to encourage and even praise your students as they work and when they succeed. A key component of student motivation is their own self-efficacy in the topic at hand. Research shows that you and your words serve as a source of students' self-efficacy (Bandura, 1997). Of course, not all encouragement and praise has the intended effect. They will receive meaningless platitudes as disingenuous, and Dweck (2007) further discourages us from using words that suggest a student's success is hinged on his or her inherent intelligence. Those choices in how to praise further promote a fixed mind-set in students where they see their success as dependent on how smart they are rather than on how much effort they put into a task. Consider encouragement like, "You're really coming along; I bet if you give it one more try, you'll get it right," as does praise like, "Everyone really struggles with those concepts, and I know it takes a lot of time, but you really worked through and mastered it. Awesome!" Such language serves to foster greater self-efficacy in your students and contributes to the development of a growth mind-set.

If you appear open, authentic, encouraging, and trustworthy, students will be much more likely to visit you during office hours and ask you for advice or letters of recommendation. Letters of recommendation, of course, are a fabulous way to get to know your students. Instead of asking for a résumé and some information, take the time to have the student come talk to you about his or her dreams.

This, of course, creates another drain on your time, and you will not receive additional compensation for this extra effort. It is, however, immensely satisfying, and it does change lives. Virtually nothing else you could do with your time will have as much impact on the world and perhaps even the long-term financial health of your institution.

Another common fear is that you will appear inappropriate or students will then call you and ask for help solving their romantic problems. You need to set boundaries with some students, but for the vast majority, your attention will be transformative. Especially for traditional-aged college students, you can occupy a unique role in their lives.

Lowman and Aldrich (2016) offer a series of tips for your private discussions with students:

- *Listen more and talk less.* Being an attentive listener, staying calm, making eye contact, and nodding a bit can reassure students that you think their story is important. And even if it is not for you, their ability to tell it out loud to someone may be all they need.

- *Guide students to think more broadly about their problems and options.* Ask students for clarification, and perhaps try to fill in the gaps or broaden the context. Repeat back to them what you think you have heard, and let them ponder their own problems. Learning more about a student's life will also give you a broader perspective on their academic work.

- *Strive to understand and help students moderate their own level of distress.* Being a good listener and being able to show empathy by just saying "aw" has salvaged many intense or even hostile situations. Many times, just being heard makes a difference to students. Your goal is not to uncover deeper emotions—this is not therapy—just to affirm the existence of strong emotions.

- *Don't offer advice unless it is a resource.* This is nearly impossible for most of us, but it is the same mistake for which we often criticize parents. Students need to make their own decisions, and if we do it for them, we stunt their own learning and growth in self-sufficiency. You can point out options and other resources. If the concerns involve parents, relationships, or a violation of policy, you may have less choice: know what you need to report and what resources to recommend.

- *Keep it short, and recommend follow-up.* Adolescents can talk and process for hours. Express your concern by asking students to get back to you, but emphasize that they have to make the decision. Thank students for coming and talking to you.

If all of that is obvious, then you are in good shape. Few of us were trained as counselors, therapists, diplomats or customer service, and we may even have spent a long time avoiding this, but seeking out more and deeper relationships with students will pay dividends for both you and your students.

Avoiding Failure

If you are about to redesign any aspect of your courses after reading this book, then the trust of your students will become even more important. Students walk into your classroom believing that you know things they want to know: if you talk, they will write it down. But if you ask them to operate in different ways than they have in previous classrooms, they will want to know why.

If students in a traditional classroom care that you are fair, organized, and approachable, those perceptions will matter even more when you ask them to try a new type of learning. You need to earn their trust.

Students understand the rules of traditional classrooms. They know that paying attention, taking notes, and reviewing "the material" is a path to success on tests. They may not understand how discussion, activities, or making a video will improve their ability to do math problems. They know that if they don't do the reading, you will cover the "important" content and tell them exactly what will be on the exam. They correctly perceive that this is easier than your new proposal to motivate them to do more of the learning on their own.

Moving away from the comfortable and familiar is like any other change: it adds a level of anxiety and energy to what is already a difficult process for many students. More responsibility for work done outside class and a more active and noisy classroom will be something new for most students. There will be resistance from some because they know how to operate in the traditional classroom and fear they might not do as well in your naked classroom. Others may fear that this is all some sort of educational experiment. As with any other change management process, start with transparency and communication. Explain to students why you are doing this and how this sort of learning will help them reach their goals. Reassure them that while traditional lecture classes are familiar and appear easier, all of the literature supports the conclusion that students will learn more in this new classroom. Cite the copious studies and recent science about learning and the brain often. Articles by Freeman et al. (2014) and Hake (1998) contain compelling graphs that can help you make your case with your students and highlight that the impact of active learning is stable regardless of generation. Be explicit and transparent that you are trying something new that you believe will improve their learning.

There is, of course, a literature on how to do this, and you might start with Felder and Brent's "Sermon for Grumpy Campers" (Interlude before Chapter 11 in 2016; see also Felder, 2011). Both resources provide a list of six mistakes to avoid (see Table 13.1).

TABLE 13.1
Six Common Active Learning Mistakes

Mistake	How to Avoid the Mistake
1. Plunge into active learning with no explanation.	First explain what you're going to do and why it is in the students' best interests.
2. Expect all students to eagerly get into groups the first time you ask them to.	Be proactive with reluctant students in the first few group activities you conduct.
3. Make activities trivial.	Make active learning tasks challenging enough to justify the time it takes to do them.
4. Make activities too long, such as assigning an entire problem in a single activity.	Keep activities short and focused (5 seconds to 3 minutes). Break large problems into small chunks.
5. Call for volunteers after every activity.	After some activities, call randomly on individuals or groups to report their results.
6. Fall into a predictable routine.	Vary the formats and lengths of activities and the intervals between them.

Source: Felder and Brent (2016).

Be proactive about the first two. We've discussed transparency at length, and when starting a group activity, some students will simply ignore you and start to work on their own.

We discussed items 3 and 4 in Chapters 7 and 9: this is the analogue of designing activities that are pleasantly frustrating for the widest number of people. Starting with shorter and chunked activities will help. Provide lots of feedback since students will not be as certain of how this is all supposed to work. It is equally important, however, that you also allow students time enough to complete the task. We professors are used to talking, and we are like air to a vacuum: we rush to fill the void. If students seem to be working or at least engaged, then find something to do to avoid interrupting their activities. Look at your watch and set a minimum time limit before you intervene. Remember: engagement before coverage. If students are engaged, they are learning. That is not generally the case when you are "covering" the material.

Items 5 and 6 recognize that there is a problem with how you get from small groups back to the larger group. Randomly calling on volunteers every time sets up a pattern, and most students will recognize that there is no accountability and simply wait for someone else to fill the silence. Of course, we've all sat through the dreaded reporting-out part of an activity where each table says the same things we have already heard. There are several ways to avoid these problems:

- *Call on individuals randomly after activities.* Cold calling is always a risk, but after a group activity, everyone should be able to report out on something that was said or heard. Knowing that this is a possibility will keep more students engaged.

- *Require all students to report in writing.* You don't need to grade these, but providing students with some time to write (and reflect) on what was accomplished will make sure every student participates. These can also be posted to social media for all to see.

- *Use whiteboards.* One way to avoid both the embarrassment of being underprepared and the monotony of reporting out while still engaging the maximum number of students is to design an activity that uses a flip chart or a whiteboard. Modern classrooms are increasingly being designed with more writable surfaces. If you have the ability to project from any device to the entire classroom, that can work as well. Ask groups to list or draw something. You can then observe which ones might be most worth sharing.

- *Try the same activity again with new material.* This is probably new for you, so expect there to be a learning curve on your part. If you try the same exercise with new material, you can tweak your approach and determine if you had the wrong content, the wrong activity, or simply the wrong framework. It might just be *you* who needs the practice.

- *Vary the activity.* There are many approaches and books full of new ideas for your classroom. You won't know until you try them if they work with your content, your students, and your personal style. Varying the activity, the size, the scope, where you place it, and the amount of time you devote to it will keep you and your students on their toes.

On the first day of class, you should do more than just explain: students need to discover for themselves both the what and the why of how your course will operate. Fink (2013) suggests starting right away with a little bit of whatever students will be doing for the first time in your class. If your class will use groups or reflective writing, have them try a bit of this on the first day and then talk immediately about the payoff. Gary Smith (2008) asks students two questions on the first day of class:

1. What is the value of different types of learning?
2. What can you learn outside class, and what should we focus on in class?

Smith has found that students generally come to the conclusion themselves that they can discover content on their own by reading at home and that *they* would be better off if class time was used for applying what they had already learned in active and more complex situations. Importantly, Smith also found that this first-day intervention led to significantly higher course evaluations.

In a sense, you also need an entry point for your new pedagogy. How will students first encounter this new learning environment, and how can you use their own motivation to build engagement? Building trust, stress-testing your new approach for potential pitfalls, and preparing students for your new classroom activities are important steps to consider before you launch new pedagogies.

Accepting Failure

Most of us learned (at least something) with traditional teaching methods and probably even thrived with them. Most of us did the readings, took good notes, studied, and eventually were successful. By the time we get to be faculty, we have a lot of experience with this and are pretty good at traditional teaching. If you made it this far in this book, you have certainly already added enough innovation to get rewarded by students and our peers.

Still, the first time we try something completely new and different, we are likely to be less good at it. These pedagogies are new for virtually all of us, and while we have practiced and polished our lectures, our first game or active learning session is surely not going to be our best execution. It is important to give the new pedagogy a chance to improve. Our first lectures were not that good either, but gradually we learned how to improve our teaching in the traditional model.

We learned over time to judge the quality of our teaching. We learned how to recognize the slump of sleeping students and when to insert a video to break up the monotony. We also know (sort of) how it works. We know that if we cover the content in certain ways and assign these problem sets, students will be able to solve certain types of problems on the midterm. Even our course evaluations tend to relate to traditional lectures, with questions asking about the clarity of the presentation. Suppose you don't give presentations?

You need to prepare to fail. This is okay; failure is a part of any learning process, and you are learning how to teach in a very different way. Use this failure to model for students how failure is integral to learning. Not everyone is an early adopter of new technology, but consumers, and especially Generation Z students, have become used to making choices about new products that might fail. We now often face the choice of a device that is proven but limited (think of your landline phone), or a new device that does things we did not even imagine we needed (think of your current cell phone). We have all been aggravated by the lack of cell service just when we need to use our cellular map, but few of us are willing to go back to paper maps. Not everyone will always choose the experimental product or procedure, but we have an obligation to try and convince students that these new pedagogies really work, even if they will sometimes fail because of our own lack of experience. If you give students clear learning outcomes, tell them what we know about learning and how you have designed activities that are informed by that research to get them to those goals, they will usually give this a try.

You will need to practice both the design and delivery of new modes of teachings. Starting with a module or unit that you use every semester, perhaps even in different courses, will give you a chance to practice and refine a specific project or learning activity. This is certainly the most efficient way to build your own confidence.

Embracing Failure and Modeling Change

There have been lots of calls for faculty to rethink their role. As the focus for higher education has shifted from teaching to learning, we have heard the call to move from a sage on the stage to the guide on the side many times.

While pithy, this formula also seems to trivialize what is incredibly hard and demanding work. Here is a different way to think about the changing role of faculty.

Now that we inhabit a world of increasing access and ever expanding knowledge, simply knowing more than students has less value than it once did. While we are called professors and students have high confidence in how much we know, more is not always better. Your phone now knows more than you do. It professes much, and that is a substantial part of its value. We use our computers and phones to find information quickly all the time, but that does not make our smartphones smart because the Internet is fundamentally disaggregated. It is a giant mass of pieces of useful information mixed in with even more massive amounts of junk. While Google and artificial intelligence will continue to leap forward and astound us, humans will always be valued for our integration and the interconnectedness of our relationships. The Internet is full of connections, but those connections are not organic.

More information does not make us smarter in the same way that more fitness equipment does not make us more fit. More and more fitness equipment in your home would just get in the way. So we rely on a "fitness coach" whose role is much more complicated than just telling us to "get on the bike." A coach knows the pathway, the equipment, and our bodies. A coach takes measurements and can assess progress and roadblocks. A coach understands context and motivation and recognizes that we are not the same person every day. If good teaching starts with what matters to your students (and ends with what matters to you), then coaching is surely the best metaphor for great teaching. The recognition that your motivation for coming to the gym is to wear a new outfit on your anniversary is not trivial, even if it only results in the suggestion to pedal faster.

A coach adds value by combining superior knowledge with an understanding of individual and group dynamics. It is not knowing more by itself that makes a coach great; it is relationships, caring, inspiration, and timing. As faculty, we should all aspire to be great cognitive coaches.

Students know you are smart, but they are confused about what this means. They know that when they need to find information, they can look it up on their smartphone, and most of the people they know and admire seem also simply to "know more" than others. Their parents, clergy, teachers, doctors, and politicians have all impressed them by knowing the answers (immediately and consistently) to difficult questions. In an age where faster is almost uniformly better, slow thinking, changing your mind, and, especially, learning from failure are increasingly rare. You can change all of that.

It is not what you know but who you are that matters most to students. You appear to students as a superhero (you even get to wear the cape at graduation!). You have powers that students covet; they just often don't know that it is your ability to change your mind that is truly special. All of this authenticity and experimentation is a chance to demonstrate that failure is an opportunity. Superheros are hardly infallible: the drama is in seeing how they will overcome their mistakes. Students want to be superheros, and they want to be like you: they want to be smart. If you embrace your own failure and actively demonstrate how you change with new information, you can be a new model for students of what it really means to be smart.

Step-by-Step Guide

Step 1: Design Your Own Humanity and Authenticity into Your Pedagogy

Recognizing the importance of relationships in teaching, what can you do to appear more approachable? It is different for each teacher, but you can learn names, have open hours in a coffee shop, or change your communication policy. Note that the transparency of learning goals and rubrics are both part of course design and a demonstration of your openness and humanity.

Step 2: Be Intentional About Encouragement and Praise

Words of encouragement and praise serve to let students know that you are not disinvested in their success and can also have a positive impact on their motivation and interest in your subject matter. If encouragement and praise aren't part of your usual teaching repertoire, add them to your lesson planning activities. Consider when encouragement and praise might be warranted in the upcoming class, and then craft a sentence or two of meaningful encouragement or praise that promotes a growth mind-set. Be ready to use them in the upcoming class at the appropriate time.

Step 3: Be Transparent and Build Trust

Let students know you care and what you are trying to do with both your policies about student meetings and trying new elements of course design. Connect new activities to learning goals and research on learning. Create entry points, and set clear expectations for new activities.

Step 4: Prepare to Fail

Be easy on yourself, and recognize that you have had a long time to practice traditional teaching. New pedagogies will also take time to practice and improve.

Step 5: Acknowledge Failure

Knowing that you want students to learn more will build trust with students. Acknowledge what could be improved, and ask for their help in figuring out how to become a better teacher.

Step 6: Model Change

Be aware that students want to be like you and that they will emulate their perception of the way you think. The way that you answer questions and deal with uncertainty are models for them of what it means to be smart.

Examples

Developing Student Self-Efficacy

C. Edward Watson, University of Georgia

I was at Virginia Tech the first time I taught the two-course graduate sequence Quantitative Research Methods. A required course for many education graduate students and meeting for three hours each class period, this course sequence offered the entirety of the process associated with performing quantitative educational research. As you might imagine, statistics, measurement, and designing research studies were among the topics covered in these courses.

On the first day of class, as the course was discussed and an introductory activity was provided, one student in particular grew visibly more anxious. During the break in the middle of class, I asked to speak with her and discovered she had a high degree of anxiety regarding the class. It wasn't that she didn't think she was smart enough to pass the class; she simply felt she was too far removed from being a student and from taking math to have any hope of being successful in the course. It was really a question of preparedness and self-efficacy rather than mind-set.

I met with her later that week during office hours, and the student was thinking of dropping the class and out of graduate school. I encouraged her to wait a couple of weeks to see if the preparedness hurdle was too much to overcome. Applying the research on self-efficacy, I provided early opportunities for success in class (mastery experiences) and deliberately gave words of encouragement, reassurance, and praise.

At the conclusion of the third class, we again chatted about her progress. She still felt she would struggle in the course, but she no longer felt that completing the course was impossible. As the semester progressed, this student often attended office hours to receive assistance, and the in-class self-efficacy strategies became an ongoing part of classroom practice. Fostering self-efficacy and providing approachable avenues to speak with the instructor were among the pedagogical keys contributing to her success in these courses.

Becoming Approachable

José Antonio Bowen, Goucher College

I have always tried to be an approachable teacher. While learning names has always been a struggle, showing up early to class and being visible in the dining hall and on social media seemed to have encouraged students to ask questions and start important conversations. But then, without realizing it, I got old. To make matters worse, apparently students identified me as "the dean" and then "the president" before I walked into class. Being labeled as "intimidating" was both a shock and a sadness for me. I had to realize that my administrative position was going to change the way students viewed me and that gray hair and a suit had changed first impressions. Scheduling and coming to an appointment with the president is different than it is for another faculty member. The question was how to balance being open and honest with students with the other responsibilities of being an administrator. (As we discussed in Chapter 10 on e-communication, anything you say to one student "confidentially" can immediately be posted on social media. Information is a currency, and I was constantly being pumped for it.)

My response was to be direct and honest about the advantages and limitations of having an administrator as your teacher. I am very clear about the best ways to communicate with me, and I'm very responsive to e-mail from students. I establish that all students have access to the president, but students in class have additional access to me as *the professor*. I had to work even harder to listen actively and try to separate the roles and, as a professor, not simply try to fix student problems.

Relationships still matter, and they still take time and care to develop. Ultimately though, "president" is just another role model and another opportunity to model that smart people need to be evidence-based, good listeners, open to failure, and willing to change their minds.

Key Concepts

- A single professor can make a massive difference in a student's life.

- The most important lifelong impact of college for students turns out to be (1) a professor who cared about you as a person, (2) a professor who made you excited about learning, and (3) finding a mentor who encouraged you to pursue your dreams.

- We know that students learn more when we care about their learning, so making transparent our belief in their abilities is a pedagogical tool.

- You do not have to be funny and you do not have to be everyone's friend, but you do need to appear approachable and authentic. Be authentic and personal in your examples.

- Don't be afraid to encourage and even praise your students as they work and when they succeed.

- Take the time to anticipate mistakes and prepare students for a new learning environment.

- It's okay if your first attempt isn't a stellar success; you'll have opportunities to revise and improve next semester.

- Model change. Make your ability to think and change visible to students.

Further Resources

Dweck, C. (2014). The power of believing that you can improve. *TED: Ideas worth spreading*. Retrieved from https://www.ted.com/talks/carol_dweck_the_power_of_believing_that_you_can_improve

Listen to Carol describe some of her key mind-set concepts in this TED Talk. She provides some practical guidance to promote growth mind-sets.

■ ■ ■

Gallup-Purdue. (2014). *Great jobs great lives: The 2014 Gallup-Purdue Index report: A study of more than 30,000 college graduates across the U.S.* Washington, DC: Gallup. Retrieved from https://www.luminafoundation.org/files/resources/galluppurdueindex-report-2014.pdf

This is a brief but powerful report on the importance of faculty as role models. The combination of massive research and succinct analysis will change the way you approach your teaching.

■ ■ ■

Intrator, S. M., & Scribner, M. (Eds.). (2014). *Teaching with heart: Poetry that speaks to the courage to teach*. San Francisco, CA: Jossey-Bass.

Offering a range of human experiences associated with the act and art of teaching, this book can provide points of reflection as you design your own humanity and authenticity into your pedagogy.

■ ■ ■

Kolowich, S. (2015, January). Could video feedback replace the red pen? *Chronicle of Higher Education—Wired Campus*. Retrieved from http://chronicle.com/blogs/wiredcampus/could-video-feedback-replace-the-red-pen/55587

This story provides an interesting narrative from faculty who give video rather than written feedback to students. They report that their students find it clearer and "seemingly more sincere" than written comments.

■ ■ ■

Palmer, P. (1999). *The courage to teach: Exploring the inner landscape of a teacher's life.* San Francisco, CA: Jossey-Bass.

An excellent book to reinspire you in the classroom. It frames the importance of teacher integrity, identity, and related concepts in the development of good teaching.

■ ■ ■

Zimmerman, B. J. (2000). Self-efficacy: An essential motive to learn. *Contemporary Educational Psychology, 25,* 82–91.

This article provides a clear narrative regarding the relationship of self-efficacy to learning. It's quite nuanced and deserving of attention in our teaching practice.

References

Bandura, A. (1997). *Self-efficacy: The exercise of control.* New York: Freeman.

Dweck, C. S. (2007). The perils and promises of praise. *Educational Leadership, 65*(2), 34–39.

Felder, R. M. (2011). Hang in there: Dealing with student resistance to learner-centered teaching. *Chemical Engineering Education, 45*(2), 131–132.

Felder, R. M., & Brent, R. (2016), *Teaching and learning STEM: A practical guide.* San Francisco, CA: Jossey-Bass.

Fink, L. D. (2013). *Creating significant learning experiences: An integrated approach to designing college courses.* San Francisco, CA: Jossey-Bass.

Freeman, S., Eddy, S. L., McDonough, M., Smith, M. K., Okoroafor, N., Jordt, H., & Wenderoth, M. P. (2014). Active learning increases student performance in science, engineering, and mathematics. *Proceedings of the National Academy of Sciences, 111*(23), 8410–8415.

Gallup-Purdue. (2014). *Great jobs great lives: The 2014 Gallup-Purdue index report: A study of more than 30,000 college graduates across the U.S.* Washington, DC: Gallup.

Hake, R. R. (1998). Interactive-engagement versus traditional methods: A six-thousand-student survey of mechanics test data for introductory physics courses. *American Journal of Physics, 66*(1), 64–74.

Lowman, J., & Aldrich, H. (2016). Just listen. *National Teaching and Learning Forum, 25*(2), 1–3. doi:10.1002/ntlf.30054

Smith, G. (2008). First day questions for the learner-center classroom. *National Teaching and Learning Forum, 17*(5), 1–4.

Index